SISTER OF WISDOM

Frontispiece.   *Caritas as "supreme and fiery force."* Divine Love, holding the Lamb of God, tramples upon discord and the devil. Below, Hildegard receives fire from heaven and transcribes her visions on wax tablets; one of her nuns assists her and the monk Volmar copies the text into a book. *De operatione Dei* I.1, Lucca, Biblioteca Statale, Cod. lat. 1942. Courtesy of Biblioteca Statale di Lucca.

SISTER OF WISDOM

ST. HILDEGARD'S THEOLOGY
OF THE FEMININE

BARBARA NEWMAN

University of California Press
Berkeley · Los Angeles

University of California Press
Berkeley and Los Angeles, California

First Paperback Printing 1989

Library of Congress Cataloging-in-Publication Data

Newman, Barbara, 1953–
  Sister of wisdom.

  Discography:p.
  Bibliography:p.
  1. Hildegard, Saint, 1098–1179. 2. Woman
(Christian theology)—History of doctrines—Middle
Ages, 600–1500.   I. Title.
BX4700.H5N48   1987   230'.2'0924   86–16094
ISBN 0-520-06615-4

Printed in the United States of America

   2   3   4   5   6   7   8   9

The Northwestern University Research Grants Committee
has provided partial support for the publication of this book.
The University of California Press gratefully acknowledges
this assistance.

Say to Wisdom, "You are my sister,"
and call insight your intimate friend.

Proverbs 7:4

O form of woman, sister of Wisdom,
how great is your glory!

Hildegard of Bingen
Epilogue, *Life of St. Rupert*

Contents

List of Illustrations

List of Illustrations

List of Abbreviations

AASS   Joannes Bollandus et al., *Acta sanctorum . . .
                        editio novissima* (Paris, 1863–).

Acta   *Acta inquisitionis de virtutibus et miraculis sanc-
                        tae Hildegardis*, ed. J.-P. Migne, *Patrologiae
                        cursus completus: series latina* [hereafter PL],
                        197 (Paris, 1855), cols. 131–40.

Causae et curae   Hildegard of Bingen, *Causae et curae*, ed. Paul
                        Kaiser (Leipzig, 1903).

CCCM   *Corpus christianorum: continuatio medievalis*
                        (Turnhout, 1966–).

CCSL   *Corpus christianorum: series latina* (Turnhout,
                        1953–).

Comment.   Commentarium or Commentariorum . . .
                        libri

CSEL   *Corpus scriptorum ecclesiasticorum latinorum*
                        (Vienna, 1866–).

DOD   Hildegard of Bingen, *De operatione Dei* (also
                        known as *Liber divinorum operum simplicis
                        hominis*), ed. J. D. Mansi, in *Stephanus Ballu-
                        zius: Miscellanea*, 2 (Lucca, 1761); rpt. Migne,
                        PL 197: 741–1038.

Echtheit   Marianna Schrader and Adelgundis Führ-
                        kötter, *Die Echtheit des Schrifttums der heiligen
                        Hildegard von Bingen* (Cologne and Graz,
                        1956).

Ep.   Epistola

Festschrift	Anton Brück, ed., *Hildegard von Bingen, 1179–1979. Festschrift zum 800. Todestag der Heiligen* (Mainz, 1979).
Fragment	Heinrich Schipperges, ed., "Ein unveröffentlichtes Hildegard-Fragment," *Sudhoffs Archiv für Geschichte der Medizin* 40 (1956): 41–77.
Lieder	*Hildegard von Bingen: Lieder [Symphonia armonie celestium revelationum]*, ed. Pudentiana Barth, M.-I. Ritscher, and Joseph Schmidt-Görg (Salzburg, 1969).
LSM	Hildegard of Bingen, *Liber simplicis medicinae* (also known as *Physica* and *Subtilitatum diversarum naturarum creaturarum libri novem*), ed. Charles Daremberg and F. A. Reuss in PL 197: 1125–1352.
LVM	Hildegard of Bingen, *Liber vitae meritorum, per simplicem hominem a vivente luce revelatorum*, ed. J.-B. Pitra, *Analecta Sanctae Hildegardis* (Monte Cassino, 1882): 7–244.
Maria	Hubert du Manoir, ed., *Maria: Études sur la sainte Vierge*, 7 vols. (Paris, 1949–1964).
MGH.SS.	*Monumenta Germaniae Historica: Scriptores* (Berlin, 1826–).
Ordo virtutum	Hildegard of Bingen, *Ordo virtutum*, ed. Peter Dronke, in *Poetic Individuality in the Middle Ages* (Oxford, 1970): 180–92.
PG	*Patrologiae cursus completus: series graeca*, ed. J.-P. Migne, 162 vols. (Paris, 1857–1866).
Pitra	J.-B. Pitra, ed., *Analecta Sanctae Hildegardis*, vol. 8 of *Analecta Sacra* (Monte Cassino, 1882).
PL	*Patrologiae cursus completus: series latina*, ed. J.-P. Migne, 221 vols. (Paris, 1841–1864).

Scivias

Hildegard of Bingen, *Scivias*, ed. Adelgundis Führkötter, CCCM vols. 43–43a, with continuous pagination (Turnhout, 1978).

Vita

Gottfried of St. Disibod and Dieter of Echternach, *Vita Sanctae Hildegardis*, ed. J.-P. Migne, PL 197: 91–130.

Preface

There was a time, not very long ago, when St. Hildegard's theological enterprise could be dismissed as a curiosity in church history, and she herself patronized as a token woman and thereby marginalized. But that day is past. Within the last decade, this exceptional woman of God has finally won some recognition in the English-speaking world. Nevertheless, Hildegard studies in this country remain at an embryonic stage. We still have few reliable editions and even fewer translations and useful studies of her work, aside from the brilliant essays of Peter Dronke. What is more, Hildegard confronts us too often as an anomalous figure—a woman fascinating in the sheer breadth of her accomplishment, yet strangely alienated from her context. Few medievalists today would deny her a place in the history of spirituality, of medicine, or of music. But if we try to glimpse the totality of her life and work, where are we to "place" Hildegard of Bingen? To what cultural traditions does she belong? What contexts will help us to discern the richest dimensions of her texts?

The background against which we are most often encouraged to see Hildegard is that of "female mysticism." There is no denying that she was female, and she can pass for a mystic if that dangerous term is held to cover her special gifts of vision and prophecy. I submit, however, that this category is less helpful than it seems. In the first place, it can be misleading to study female saints as if they formed a subculture unto themselves, isolated from the overwhelmingly male culture that surrounded them. Such a subculture may have existed among holy women of a later age, but it did not exist in twelfth-century Germany, and we learn little about Hildegard by studying her as part of a "female tradition" in which she herself is the first major figure. Second, to regard her primarily as a mystic is to create a false impression of her interests. Despite her visionary gift, she did not write about mystical prayer, nor did she influence the mystical theory and practice of later generations. Even her protégée, Elisabeth of Schönau, saw her more as a prophetic role model than as a teacher of contemplation. The texts in which Hildegard described her religious experience are justly famous, but they have little bearing on the actual content of her works, and they form only a minuscule fraction of her literary output.

If the category of women's mysticism or (a fortiori) "women's writing" is too broad to give us a suitable context for Hildegard, what are some of the alternatives? A church historian, looking at her activities rather than her gender, might see her as a leading proponent of the Gregorian reform and associated monastic reform movements. Staunchly papalist, unyielding in her defense of hierarchy, insistent on the purity as well as the dignity of priests, she opposed imperial encroachments on the Church and defended clerical privilege with all the intransigence of a Thomas Becket or an Anselm of Canterbury. The importance of her political stance has been obscured by concentration on her mysticism, although in this respect she anticipated later political visionaries like Catherine of Siena and Birgitta of Sweden. Her apocalyptic preaching—the only aspect of her work that remained widely influential in the next three centuries—was closely connected with her program for the reform of the Church.

From a different perspective, Hildegard might be placed among those highly prolific authors of the early twelfth century—Hugh of St. Victor, Rupert of Deutz, Honorius of Regensburg—who used to be classified as "prescholastics." All these authors wrote voluminously. And, like Hildegard, they all ran the gamut of Christian thought, offering a mélange of Biblical commentary, moral and spiritual teaching, and dogmatic instruction in forms that range from the libellus to the encyclopedia. Hildegard's works, despite their peculiarities of style, present a body of essentially conservative teaching that recalls these older contemporaries both in scope and in specific doctrines. The stunning originality of her formulations must not be allowed to obscure her fundamental orthodoxy or her classic Benedictine approach to the spiritual life.

In this book, however, I will consider Hildegard from another standpoint. I have tried to place her in a "vertical" tradition—one that will link her not only with contemporaries but also with kindred spirits of other times and places—by looking at some of her central themes in light of what I shall call the *sapiential tradition*. By this term I refer to the perennial school of Christian thought that centers on the discovery and adoration of divine Wisdom in the works of creation and redemption. Theologians of this school, whose history extends from the ancient Church into the twentieth century, share a predilection for certain themes: divine beauty, the feminine aspect of God, the absolute predestination of Christ and Mary, the moral and aesthetic ideal of virginity, and the hope of cosmic redemption. For a variety of reasons, both historical and philosophical, sapiential theologians often favor the use of feminine imagery for the Holy Spirit, the Church, and the cosmos. At its further reaches, and particularly in the last two centuries, this theological tradition has tended to merge with romantic philosophies of the eternal feminine. But the seeds of this merger lie deep in the soil of history. One aim of the present study is to explore, in some detail, the historical process by which certain ways of thinking about God have affected Christian ways of thinking about women and the feminine, and vice versa. St. Hildegard provides an ideal focus for such a study because she was not only an exponent of sapiential thought but also, I believe, a pivotal figure in its development.

Her gender is, of course, no accident. We may boldly claim Hildegard as the first Christian thinker to deal seriously and positively with the feminine as such, not merely with the challenges posed by and for women in a male-dominated world. But she formulated her thoughts within the traditional framework of Christian symbolics, through reflection on the great feminine paradigms of Eve, Mary, and Ecclesia, or Mother Church. And at the heart of her spiritual world there stands the numinous figure she called Sapientia or Caritas: holy Wisdom and Love divine, a visionary form who transcends allegory and attains the stature of theophany. These four figures, then, will provide the focal points of my analysis. Around them Hildegard developed a richly nuanced theology of the feminine that belongs wholly to the realm of the symbolic, both in the broadest sense of that term and in the narrower sense allied with medieval allegoresis. Of necessity, therefore, much of this study will be devoted to the interpretation of highly symbolic texts, together with the manuscript paintings that illustrate them.

Nevertheless, symbolic thinking does not exclude practical application. Hildegard was an abbess, a spiritual counselor, and a physician as well as a theologian. In the course of her pastoral and medical work, she had many occasions to observe the particular gifts and problems of women. Moreover, as she pursued her highly "unfeminine" career as writer, reformer, and preacher, she naturally encountered opposition, both from her enemies and from within her own psyche. As a result, she developed an unusual degree of self-awareness about her gender and its social and spiritual implications. In order to grasp the full depth and complexity of her views on the feminine, therefore, it is necessary to set her lofty symbolic theology alongside what we know of her dealings with the women around her, her self-perception as female, and, not least, her unique contributions to gynecology. Such juxtapositions shed light on the most significant tensions in Hildegard's thought; for example, she combined a holistic cosmology with a dualistic system of ethics, a strong scientific interest in sexuality with an aesthetic and moral disdain for it, and an exalted view of woman's cosmic significance with a practical view of femininity as a form of weakness. All these dichotomies elude easy schematization, however, for they are deeply rooted both in Hildegard's own culture and in the older traditions on which she drew. It is difficult to say how much she herself was aware of them.

In my last chapter I have looked beyond Hildegard and her era in order to sketch, albeit briefly, the subsequent evolution of her ideas as outlined in this volume. Sapiential theology, and theologies of the feminine, have pursued a curious course over the centuries—sometimes widely acclaimed, sometimes mired in a bog of esoterica, sometimes dormant and all but forgotten. In recent decades the tradition has come under fierce attack, chiefly by feminists; but certain elements of it are experiencing a miniature revival, also among feminists. I believe that the current wave of excitement over St. Hildegard has much to do with the rediscovery of this age-old tradition and the ambivalent reactions it has aroused in contemporary culture, and I present this book as a contribution to that process of rediscovery.

A word about usage may be in order here. All Biblical passages have been translated directly from the Vulgate, although when possible I have remained close to the language of the Revised Standard Version. The numbering of Psalms also follows the Vulgate. Hildegard's poetry has been newly edited for this volume; the reader will find the Latin texts of twelve poems in Appendix B. In original translations throughout the book, I have tried to distinguish between inclusive and noninclusive usage of the Latin *homo*. In the singular I have used *man* for *male* and *person* or *human being* if the usage is not gender-specific. In the plural, *men* refers solely to males, while *mankind* and *humanity* are to be taken as inclusive. However, I have retained the singular collective *man* for a very frequent medieval usage in which *homo* simultaneously designates the human race and the unique individual Adam, in whom the whole race is seminally present. This usage is especially frequent in the contexts of creation, the fall, and the Incarnation. As I will argue in the following chapters, Hildegard preferred the collective personification of humanity as female in the figure of Ecclesia, but she could also conceive this corporate person as male in the figure of Adam.

I would like to express special thanks to Peter Dronke and to Caroline Bynum, whose studies of St. Hildegard and of gender in twelfth-century religious life have laid the foundations of my work. I am grateful to both for allowing me at various times to consult their unpublished manuscripts. John

van Engen, Bernard McGinn, and Robert Lerner offered many
useful suggestions. My husband, Richard Kieckhefer, has
scoured these pages almost as many times as I have, providing good cheer, bracing criticism, and much-needed encouragement at every stage. In a different realm, it gives me joy
to thank Harriet Gilliam, Kelsey Cheshire, and Susanne Sklar
for sharing what they know of the living Light. To them and
to all the sisters of wisdom who have brightened my path—
including Adrienne, Marcia, Susan, Susanna, Cathy, Maria
Eva, Sandy, and Starr—I dedicate my work.

1

"A poor little female"

Some years ago, wrote the monk Guibert to his friend Radul-
fus, strange and incredible rumors had reached his ears at the
Belgian monastery of Gembloux.[1] They concerned an old
woman, abbess of the recent Benedictine foundation at Bin-
gen-am-Rhein, who had gained such fame that multitudes
flocked to her convent, from curiosity or devotion, to seek her
prophecies and prayers. All who returned thence astonished
their hearers, but none could give a plausible account of the
woman, save only that her soul was "said to be illumined by
an invisible splendor known to her alone."[2] Finally Guibert,
impatient with rumor and zealous for the truth, resolved to
find out for himself. In the year 1175 he wrote to this famed
seer, Hildegard, with mingled curiosity and awe. Surely she
had received "rare gifts, till now practically unheard of
throughout all ages"; in prophecy she excelled Miriam, Deborah, and Judith; but let her recall that great trees are up-
rooted sooner than reeds and keep herself humble.[3] Meanwhile, perhaps she would deign to answer a few questions
about her visions. Did she dictate them in Latin or in German?
Was it true that, once she had spoken, she could no longer
recall them? Had she learned the alphabet and the Scriptures
as a child, or had she been taught by the Holy Spirit alone?
As the abbess sent no reply, Guibert tried again some time
later, having thought of more questions in the meantime. Did

1. Portions of this chapter have previously appeared in my article "Hildegard of Bingen: Visions and Validation," *Church History* 54 (1985): 163–75.
2. Ep. 164, Pitra 576. All translations in this book are mine unless otherwise noted.
3. Ep. 1, Pitra 328–31.

Hildegard receive her visions in ecstasy or in dreams? What did she mean by the title of her book, *Scivias*? Had she written any other books? And so forth.[4]

In the end the seer favored Guibert with a reply—a detailed account of the mode of her visions—which so overwhelmed him that he declared that no woman since the Virgin Mary had received so great a gift from God. Hildegard, he continued, "has transcended female subjection by a lofty height and is equal to the eminence not of just any men but of the very highest."[5] The white monks of Villers, with whom he shared her letter, saluted the abbess in even more exalted terms.

> Hail, after Mary full of grace: the Lord is with you! Blessed are you among women, and blessed is the word of your mouth, which brings the secrets of the invisible world to men, unites heavenly things with earthly, and joins the divine to the human.[6]

In contrast, Hildegard herself had composed her reply to Guibert with characteristic modesty, stressing her own frailty and insecurity. Like any monastic writer, she adopted formulas of humility that had long been de rigueur; but, like Guibert and the monks of Villers, she also realized that her gender had no small bearing on her vocation. When she identified herself as *ego paupercula feminea forma*—"a poor little figure of a woman"[7]—she was appealing inversely to the same complex of ideas that led the Cistercians to compare her to the Virgin. Mary, the handmaid of God, "humble and exalted above every creature," typified for them a central paradox of Christianity: all who humble themselves will be exalted. But something other than Mary's personal humility and glory inspired the comparison. Lowliness, if not grace, could be generic; and, according to some of the most reputable theolo-

---

4. Ep. 14, Pitra 378–79.
5. Ep. 16, Pitra 386.
6. Ep. 21, Pitra 395. This letter bears the name of Guibert, but the monk later advised Hildegard's nuns that his brothers at Villers had written and sent it without his knowledge (Ep. 22, Pitra 396).
7. Ep. 2, Pitra 332.

gians and scientists of the Middle Ages, it pertained generically to the bodies, minds, and mores of women.[8] It followed that, if only the humble could be exalted, women had a paradoxical advantage—at least in theory. In practice, of course, this advantage was seldom apparent. To her admirers, therefore, Hildegard was a live epiphany of a truth that the social and even the religious establishment had done its best to suppress.

The dialectic cut both ways: a "poor little female" could be exalted to miraculous heights only on condition that her normal status remained inferior and subservient. Hildegard's activity as a prophet could seem divinely powerful only because it was humanly impossible. Thus, the very constraints that made her privilege so astonishing to her peers also gave it an added luster, which, in a more egalitarian Church, it could not have possessed. And Hildegard, no less than her contemporaries, accepted the paradox. Never did she suggest that, as a woman and a Christian, she had any "right" to teach or prophesy in the Church. Nor did she claim or demand equality with men. Rather, she insisted that God had chosen a poor, frail, untutored woman like herself to reveal his mysteries only because those to whom he had first entrusted them— the wise, learned, and masculine clergy—had failed to obey. She lived in a "womanish age" (*muliebre tempus*) in which men had become so lax, weak, and sensual—in a word, effeminate—that God had to confound them by making women virile.[9] Choosing an instrument by nature frail and despicable, he proved again that he could work wonders despite all human order and disorder. "God chose what is foolish in the

8. Philippe Delhaye, "Le dossier antimatrimonial de l'*Adversus Iovinianum* et son influence sur quelques écrits latins du XIIᵉ siècle," *Mediaeval Studies* 13 (1951): 65–86; Vern Bullough, "Medieval Medical and Scientific Views of Women," *Viator* 4 (1973): 485–501; Julia O'Faolain and Lauro Martines, eds., *Not in God's Image* (New York, 1973); Marie-Thérèse d'Alverny, "Comment les théologiens et les philosophes voient la femme," *Cahiers de civilisation médiévale* 20 (1977): 105–29.

9. Fragment IV.28, p. 71. For the *muliebre tempus* see Ep. 13 (PL 197: 167b), Ep. 26 (185c), Ep. 49 (254cd).

world to shame the wise; God chose what is weak in the world to shame the strong; God chose what is low and despised in the world, even things that are not, to bring to nothing things that are, so that no flesh might boast in the presence of God" (I Cor. 1:27–29).

It is this conviction that underlies Hildegard's prophetic call, announced at the beginning of the *Scivias*:

> O frail human form from the dust of the earth, ashes from ashes: cry out and proclaim the beginning of undefiled salvation! Let those who see the inner meaning of Scripture, yet do not wish to proclaim or preach it, take instruction, for they are lukewarm and sluggish in observing the justice of God. Unlock for them the treasury of mysteries, which they, the timid ones, bury in a hidden field without fruit. Therefore pour out a fountain of abundance, overflow with mysterious learning, so that those who want you to be despicable on account of Eve's transgression may be overwhelmed by the flood of your profusion.[10]

Such was Hildegard's mission: to unlock the mysteries of Scripture, to proclaim the way of salvation, to admonish priests and prelates, to instruct the people of God. And all this was entrusted by God to a woman, despite the transgression of Eve, because "the wise and the strong" had fallen even lower than women.

At the close of this introductory chapter, I shall return to the question of female authority and the strategies that a twelfth-century visionary could use to reinforce it. First, however, an account of Hildegard's career and of her prolific writings will serve to reveal the degree and types of authority that she actually claimed.

BIOGRAPHICAL SKETCH

Our information about Hildegard's life is unusually thorough, for we possess several hundred letters written to or by the saint. Many of these contain biographical data. Hildegard's

---

10. *Scivias* I.1, p. 8.

Vita, composed between 1177 and 1181 by the monks Gott-fried of St. Disibod and Dieter of Echternach, incorporates memoirs dictated by the saint in the first person. A fragmen-tary *Vita* by Guibert of Gembloux provides further details. Other sources include chronicles, documents pertaining to the two monasteries founded by Hildegard, and the *Acta* com-piled in 1233–1237 for her canonization.[11] These last deal chiefly with miracles of healing and exorcism ascribed to Hil-degard, so their main historical value lies in the evidence they furnish about her cult.

Born in 1098 at Bermersheim bei Alzey, Hildegard was the tenth child of noble parents, who dedicated her to God as a tithe.[12] Three of her siblings also devoted their lives to the Church: one brother was a cantor at the Mainz Cathedral, another became a canon in Tholey, and a sister took the veil at Hildegard's convent. In 1106 the eight-year-old girl entered a hermitage near the flourishing monastery of St. Disibod to be raised by the highborn anchoress Jutta of Sponheim. From Jutta she "learned the Psalter," in other words, she was taught to read Latin.[13] Her further education was entrusted to the monk Volmar of St. Disibod, who would become her lifelong friend, confidant, and secretary. During her teens (c. 1112–1115) Hildegard made her profession of virginity and received the veil from Otto, bishop of Bamberg. In the meantime, the hermitage had grown into a full-fledged monastery observing the Benedictine Rule, and, when the mistress Jutta died in

---

11. For the *Vita* and *Acta* see PL 197: 91–140. Guibert's *Vita* appears in Pitra 407–14. Other documents pertaining to Hildegard can be found in AASS September, vol. 5, 629–701; *Mainzer Urkundenbuch*, ed. P. Acht, vol. 2, pt. 1 (Darmstadt, 1968); *Annales Zwifaltenses maiores* ad 1142 (MGH.SS. 10, p. 56); *Vita S. Gerlaci* 8, AASS January 5; *Chronicon Alberici* ad 1141, 1153 (MGH.SS. 23, p. 842); *Gesta Senoniensis Ecclesiae* IV.15 (MGH.SS. 25, p. 306); Vincent of Beauvais, *Speculum historiale* 27.83 ad 1146 (Douai, 1624; rpt. 1965). The fif-teenth-century humanist Trithemius of Sponheim referred to Hildegard in many of his writings. See his *Chronicon Hirsaugiense* ad 1149, 1150, 1160, 1180; *Chronicon Sponheimense* ad 1136, 1148–1150, 1179, 1498; *Catalogus illustrium virorum Germaniae*, p. 138; *De scriptoribus ecclesiasticis*, p. 281, all in *Opera his-torica*, ed. Marquand Freher (Frankfurt, 1601; rpt. 1966).

12. *Vita*, auctore Guiberto 1, Pitra 408.

13. *Vita* 1.2, PL 197: 93ab.

1136, the nuns elected Hildegard as her successor. Five years later the abbess[14] received her prophetic call and began to compose the *Scivias*, with the help and encouragement of Volmar and her favorite nun, Richardis von Stade. A thirteenth-century miniature shows the seer in action: illumined by fire from on high, she transcribes the heavenly dictation on wax tablets, while Volmar copies the corrected text into a book, and a nun stands by to assist her mistress (frontispiece).

From early childhood, long before she undertook her public mission or even her monastic vows, Hildegard's spiritual awareness was founded in what she called the *umbra viventis lucis*, the reflection of the living Light.[15] Her letter to Guibert of Gembloux, written at the age of seventy-seven (1175), describes her experience of this light with admirable precision.

> From my early childhood, before my bones, nerves, and veins were fully strengthened, I have always seen this vision in my soul, even to the present time, when I am more than seventy years old. In this vision my soul, as God would have it, rises up high into the vault of heaven and into the changing sky and spreads itself out among different peoples, although they are far away from me in distant lands and places. And because I see them this way in my soul, I observe them in accord with the shifting of clouds and other created things. I do not hear them with my outward ears, nor do I perceive them by the thoughts of my own heart or by any combination of my five senses, but in my soul alone, while my outward eyes are open. So I have never fallen prey to ecstasy in the visions, but I see them wide awake, day and night. And I am constantly fettered by sickness, and often in the grip of pain so intense that it threatens to kill me; but God has sustained me until now.
>
> The light that I see thus is not spatial, but it is far, far brighter than a cloud that carries the sun. I can measure neither height, nor length, nor breadth in it; and I call it "the

14. Hildegard's title is normally given as *magistra* or *preposita*, with such honorifics as *mater*, *domina*, and *sponsa Christi*. The title *abbatissa* appears only in a document addressed to her by Frederick Barbarossa in 1163.

15. Hildegard used the word *umbra* to denote images reflected in the *fons vitae*, which is literally a shining pool or fountain. The *umbra viventis lucis* is a "shadow" with respect to the *lux vivens* itself, but the shadow is nonetheless brighter than the light of common day.

reflection of the living Light." And as the sun, the moon, and the stars appear in water, so writings, sermons, virtues, and certain human actions take form for me and gleam within it.

Now whatever I have seen or learned in this vision remains in my memory for a long time, so that, when I have seen and heard it, I remember; and I see, hear, and know all at once, and as if in an instant I learn what I know. But what I do not see, I do not know, for I am not educated, but I have simply been taught how to read. And what I write is what I see and hear in the vision. I compose no other words than those I hear, and I set them forth in unpolished Latin just as I hear them in the vision, for I am not taught in this vision to write as philosophers do. And the words in this vision are not like words uttered by the mouth of man, but like a shimmering flame, or a cloud floating in a clear sky.

Moreover, I can no more recognize the form of this light than I can gaze directly on the sphere of the sun. Sometimes— but not often—I see within this light another light, which I call "the living Light." And I cannot describe when and how I see it, but while I see it all sorrow and anguish leave me, so that then I feel like a simple girl instead of an old woman.

But because of the constant sickness that I suffer, I sometimes get tired of writing the words and visions that are there revealed to me. Yet when my soul tastes and sees them, I am so transformed that, as I say, I forget all pain and trouble. And when I see and hear things in this vision, my soul drinks them in as from a fountain, which yet remains full and unexhausted. At no time is my soul deprived of that light which I call the reflection of the living Light, and I see it as if I were gazing at a starless sky in a shining cloud. In it I see the things of which I frequently speak, and I answer my correspondents from the radiance of this living Light.[16]

A revealing passage in the saint's *Vita* suggests that, although Hildegard perceived this extraordinary light from her infancy, decades were to pass before she understood the light and the figures she saw in it as a gift from God. At the age of three, Hildegard told her biographer, she shuddered at the vision of a dazzling light that she was still too young to describe.[17] When she was five she startled her nurse by looking

16. Ep. 2, Pitra 332–33.
17. *Vita* 2.16, PL 197: 103ab.

at a pregnant cow and accurately predicting the color of the unborn calf.[18] Often she foretold the future. In her teens, however, the naive and fragile girl finally realized that no one else could see what she saw. Embarrassed, she ceased to recount her strange experiences, although the visions continued. The girl confided only in her mistress, Jutta, who reported the visions to Volmar.

With the exception of this discerning monk, those around Hildegard do not seem to have understood her predilection for visions as a charism. It is impossible to say whether the child's peculiarity inspired or merely confirmed her parents in their pious wish to present her as an oblate, for they might have feared that her frailty and eccentricity would disqualify her for a normal married life. Monasticism in this period frequently served as a refuge for weak and handicapped children of the nobility.[19] Even after Jutta's death, when Hildegard became abbess of her convent, she did not at once take advantage of her authority to disclose her visions. It is significant that, after she had responded to the call of 1141 and begun to write, she never described any of the visions she had seen prior to that year. Only in retrospect, it appears, did Hildegard recognize these early experiences as a stage of preparation for her calling.

Despite her assurance of divine revelation, the seer sought further confirmation from the Church. In 1147 she wrote to St. Bernard, whom she greatly admired, to request his prayers and counsel. In this letter, the first of more than three hundred ascribed to her, Hildegard called herself "wretched and more than wretched in the name of woman," and bewailed her sickness, insecurity, and fear; but she went on to describe her visions as "great marvels" revealed by the Spirit of God.[20]

---

18. *Acta* 7, PL 197: 136b.
19. Pierre Riché, "L'Enfant dans la société monastique au XIIᵉ siècle," in *Pierre Abélard—Pierre le Vénérable: Les courants philosophiques, littéraires et artistiques en Occident au milieu du XIIᵉ siècle.* Colloque international de Cluny, 1972 (Paris, 1975): 692–93.
20. Ep. 29, PL 197: 189–90. For a corrected edition of this letter see *Echtheit* 105–8.

The abbot of Clairvaux endorsed Hildegard's gift, though with some reserve. Meanwhile, Volmar had told Kuno, abbot of St. Disibod, of his protégée's visions, and Kuno in turn informed Heinrich, archbishop of Mainz. When Pope Eugenius III, a Cistercian and disciple of Bernard, presided over a synod at Trier in 1147–48, Heinrich broached the matter of Hildegard's visions.[21] Intrigued by his report, the pope sent two legates to the nearby St. Disibod to visit the seer and secure a copy of her writings. They returned with the still incomplete *Scivias*, from which Eugenius himself read publicly before the assembled prelates. The council was suitably impressed, especially as Bernard chose this moment to intercede for the visionary who had besought his aid. At his suggestion, Eugenius sent Hildegard a letter of greeting, giving her apostolic license to continue writing.[22] From this point on, her fame and her circle of correspondents grew steadily until her death.

Once Hildegard had become a celebrity, her convent at St. Disibod began to attract so many postulants that the monastery could not house them. For this reason she decided to move, founding a new community at the Rupertsberg opposite Bingen—a site revealed to her in a vision.[23] The monks of St. Disibod, reluctant to lose their new source of prestige and revenue, opposed this plan. However, Hildegard used her family connections to secure the support of Heinrich of Mainz. At the same time, she fought the monks with passive resistance, taking to her bed with a paralyzing sickness that she ascribed to her delay in fulfilling God's will. This visitation finally won the skeptical Kuno's assent, upon which the seer immediately rose from her sickbed. The property was acquired, the convent built, and in 1150 Hildegard and eighteen of her nuns moved to the new foundation. She now began to struggle for independence from the monks, finally securing

21. *Vita* 1.5, PL 197: 94–95.
22. Ep. 1, PL 197: 143ab. On Bernard's role see Jean Leclercq, *La femme et les femmes dans l'oeuvre de saint Bernard* (Paris, 1982): 52–56.
23. *Vita* 1.6, PL 197: 95cd.

exclusive rights to the Rupertsberg property from Kuno and his successor in 1155. Three years later Heinrich's successor, Arnold of Mainz, granted the convent his protection and regulated the temporal and spiritual relations between St. Disibod and the Rupertsberg nuns. Throughout these negotiations, the seer's health continued to fluctuate in accord with the success or setbacks met by her plans. By 1165 the Rupertsberg had become so prosperous that Hildegard was able to found a daughter house at nearby Eibingen. This convent, now the Abbey of St. Hildegard, is still in existence, although the original Rupertsberg was destroyed during the Thirty Years' War.[24]

In the meantime, the abbess continued her literary activities and gradually became a public figure. Her celebrated first book, *Scivias*, takes its short title from the exhortation *Scito vias Domini*, or *Know the Ways of the Lord*. After completing the *Scivias* in 1151, she began work on a major scientific and medical encyclopedia: *Nine Books on the Subtleties of Different Kinds of Creatures*. This work, also known as the *Book of Simple Medicine*, or *Physica*, includes a comprehensive herbal, a bestiary, and a lapidary. Hildegard supplemented the encyclopedia with her *Book of Compound Medicine*, or *Causes and Cures*, a handbook of diseases and their remedies.[25] During the same period she continued to compose liturgical poetry and music, for which she was already well known by 1148.[26] Her songs would eventually be arranged in a cycle under the title *Sym-*

24. For a history of these communities see Maria Brede, "Die Klöster der heiligen Hildegard Rupertsberg und Eibingen," in *Festschrift* 77–94.

25. *Subtilitatum diversarum naturarum creaturarum libri novem*, ed. Charles Daremberg and F. A. Reuss in PL 197: 1117–1352; *Causae et curae*, ed. Paul Kaiser (Leipzig, 1903). Closely related to these works is the fragment from Berlin Cod. lat. 674, edited by Heinrich Schipperges. This text consists of medical and theological notes or *sententiae* arranged in haphazard order, but often parallel to material in the *Causae et curae*. Although the manuscript tradition for Hildegard's medical works is weak, their authenticity is attested in three contemporary lists of her works: LVM Preface, Pitra 7; Ep. 8, Pitra 346; *Vita* 2.4, PL 197: 101a.

26. Odo of Soissons to Hildegard, Ep. 127, PL 197: 352a: Dicitur quod elevata in coelestibus multa videas, et multa per scripturam proferas, atque modos novi carminis edas, cum nihil horum didiceris.

phony of the Harmony of Celestial Revelations.[27] In 1158 she began the second volume of her visionary trilogy, the *Book of Life's Merits,* completed in 1163.[28] The third and last volume, *On the Activity of God* (or *Book of Divine Works*), occupied her between 1163 and 1173.[29]

Hildegard's correspondence spans the three decades from 1147 to her death and ranges over all sectors of society, from popes, emperors, and prelates to abbots and abbesses, priests, monks, and laypeople.[30] By the mid-1150s her fame was such that Frederick Barbarossa invited her to meet with him at his palace in Ingelheim, although the content of their interview is not known.[31] Between 1158 and 1161, despite a prolonged illness, Hildegard undertook the first of four extended preaching journeys. Traveling east along the river Main, she preached at communities in Mainz, Wertheim, Würzburg, Kitzingen, Ebrach, and Bamberg, furthering the cause of monastic and clerical reform. The letters she sent to these communities after her visits indicate the tenor of her preaching. In 1160 she made another trip, this time south to Lorraine, stopping in Metz and Krauftal; on Pentecost she

27. *Hildegard von Bingen: Lieder,* ed. Pudentiana Barth, M.-I. Ritscher, and Joseph Schmidt-Görg (Salzburg, 1969). I am currently preparing a new critical edition with English translations of the *Symphonia.* For a discography of the music see Appendix A.

28. *Liber vitae meritorum, per simplicem hominem a vivente luce revelatorum,* Pitra 7–244. All citations from this work refer to Pitra's edition.

29. This work is usually cited as *Liber divinorum operum,* its title in the Mansi edition reprinted in PL 197: 741–1038. But the earliest manuscript, prepared at the Rupertsberg c. 1170–1174 (Ghent, Universiteitsbibliotheek Cod. 241), gives the title *De operatione Dei.* This manuscript, which records authorial revisions and corrections, is the basis for Albert Derolez's critical edition now in progress. My translations in this book are based on the ms readings, but I have supplied references to the printed text for convenience.

30. Migne printed 145 of Hildegard's letters in PL 197, together with epistles addressed to the saint, and Pitra added another 145. Eleven more have been edited by Francis Haug in *Revue bénédictine* 43 (1931): 59–71. The Berlin MS. Cod. lat. 674 contains 44 letters, of which 12 have been recently edited by Peter Dronke in *Women Writers of the Middle Ages* (Cambridge, 1984): 256–64.

31. Frederick to Hildegard, Ep. 27, PL 197: 186bc: Notum facimus sanctitati tuae, quoniam ea quae praedixisti nobis, cum Ingelheim manentes, te ad praesentiam nostram venire rogavimus, jam in manibus tenemus.

preached publicly in the cathedral city of Trier. Her third journey, between 1161 and 1163, carried her down the Rhine to Boppard, Andernach, Siegburg, and Werden. In Cologne she addressed clergy and people together.[32] After another serious illness in 1167–1170, the seer, now in her seventies, undertook a fourth and final preaching tour in Swabia, visiting Rodenkirchen, Maulbronn, Hirsau, Kirchheim, and Zwiefalten.

While writing six major books, founding two monasteries, and preaching throughout Germany, Hildegard also found time for various occasional and controversial works. Among her opuscula are expositions of the Benedictine Rule and the Athanasian Creed, lives of her patron saints Rupert and Disibod, and solutions to thirty-eight theological questions propounded by Guibert and the monks of Villers.[33] A series of Gospel homilies, probably transcribed by her nuns in chapter, displays a strong originality despite the sketchy transmission.[34] Perhaps the oddest of all her works is the so-called *Unknown Language*, a list of about nine hundred artificial nouns and other words with an accompanying German glossary. The purpose of this invented language is unclear, although it includes many names for plants and herbs and may have been related to Hildegard's medical work.[35] More urgently, she was always willing if need be to engage in polemic. During the 1160s the Cathars were making headway in the Rhineland, and, at the request of a religious community in Mainz, Hildegard wrote a tract against them.[36] At about the same time Eberhard, bishop of Bamberg, requested her opinion in his christological quarrel with Gerhoch of Reichersberg.

32. For the text of her sermon see Ep. 48, PL 197: 244–53.

33. For these works see PL 197: 1037–1116. Pitra edited the *Prooemium to the Life of St. Disibod*, 352–57, and the *Epilogue to the Life of St. Rupert*, 358–68. The latter composition, which includes several songs and a homily, was apparently intended for liturgical performance by the nuns on their patronal feast.

34. *Expositiones quorumdam evangeliorum*, Pitra 245–327.

35. Fragments in Pitra 496–502.

36. "De Catharis," Pitra 348–51.

The saint's answer is an exposition of her own Trinitarian theology.[37]

In political affairs Hildegard could take advantage of her aristocratic standing and her celebrity to obtain privileges from the great; but she could equally well oppose them, qua prophet, in the name of God. The most outstanding case is her double-edged relationship with Barbarossa. In 1163, several years after the meeting at Ingelheim, Frederick granted the Rupertsberg an edict of imperial protection in perpetuity.[38] Ever since 1159 this emperor had been technically schismatic in backing a papal candidate of his own, Victor IV, against Pope Alexander III. Hildegard had taken no stance in the schism. But when Victor died in 1164 and Frederick named a successor, Paschal III, the abbess sent him a sharp rebuke, comparing him to an infant and a madman.[39] He remained obdurate, however, and on Paschal's death in 1168 appointed yet another antipope, Calixtus III. This time Hildegard thundered forth the wrath of God: "He Who Is says: I destroy contumacy, and by myself I crush the resistance of those who despise me. Woe, woe to the malice of wicked men who defy me! Hear this, king, if you wish to live; otherwise my sword shall smite you."[40] Even so the emperor did not relent, and the schism dragged on until 1177. Nevertheless, despite Hildegard's savage outbursts against Frederick, his letter of protection kept the Rupertsberg safe from all harm during the factional warfare.

The last years of Hildegard's life were marred by two further controversies. The first began in 1173 when her secretary,

37. Ep. 14, PL 197: 167–71.
38. *Mittelrheinisches Urkundenbuch* I, no. 636, p. 694: Ipsum itaque locum cum sanctimonialibus et possessionibus sub nostram imperialem protectionem suscipientes, statuimus et imperiali edicto sancimus, ne aliquis advocatiam eiusdem loci sibi usurpet, verum ab omnibus infestationibus et iniuriis imperiali dextera et Maguntini archiepiscopi auxilio liber semper et securus existat.
39. Ep. 37, Pitra 523–24; *Echtheit* 128.
40. Ep. 127, Pitra 561.

Volmar, who was also provost of the convent, died and the monks of St. Disibod refused to replace him. In this emergency Hildegard turned to Alexander III, whose rights she had so vehemently defended.[41] By the pope's intervention she finally attained a new provost, Gottfried, who took advantage of his office to begin composing the saint's *Vita*. Gottfried himself died in 1176, but by this time Hildegard had found a new patron in Guibert of Gembloux. The ardent Walloon monk, inspired by his correspondence with the seer, eventually came to visit her in Bingen and became her secretary in 1177, remaining at the convent until after her death.

In 1178 the eighty-year-old abbess faced the gravest trial of her life: an interdict laid upon her community.[42] The ostensible cause of this ban was the burial of an excommunicated nobleman in the Rupertsberg churchyard, although the deceased had been reconciled with the Church before his death. The canons of Mainz Cathedral demanded that his bones be exhumed, but Hildegard refused and instead solemnly blessed the grave with her abbatial staff. Philip, archbishop of Cologne, intervened for the abbess and found reliable witnesses to prove that the dead man had been absolved and deserved sacred burial. On their testimony the canons, in the absence of the usurping Archbishop Christian, then lifted the interdict. However, Hildegard's enemies managed to persuade Christian, who was attending the Third Lateran Council in Rome, that the canons' action infringed on his rights. Christian thereupon renewed the ban temporarily, in spite of the abbess's unrelenting protests. This interdict occasioned a lengthy epistle from Hildegard to the prelates of Mainz, including a passionate defense of the liturgical music that was forbidden to her nuns under the ban.[43] The sentence was not lifted until March of 1179, six months before the seer's death on September 17.

41. Ep. 4, PL 197: 154–56.
42. See correspondence between Hildegard and Christian, archbishop of Mainz, Epp. 8 and 9, PL 197: 159–61; cf. *Acta* 6, PL 197: 135b.
43. Ep. 47, PL 197: 218–21.

Veneration of Hildegard as a saint began at once, and Pope Gregory IX opened proceedings for canonization in 1233. For technical reasons, this process was never concluded: the inquisitors did their work shoddily and failed to record names, dates, and places in their account of Hildegard's miracles.[44] According to Trithemius of Sponheim, further abortive inquiries were mounted in 1243 and 1317, but no records corroborate his testimony. Legend has it that the saint's miracles had ceased in the meantime because a steady stream of pilgrims had been disturbing the nuns, who asked the bishop if he might order their deceased founder, under obedience, to work no more wonders.[45] Nevertheless, her local cult remained strong. Since 1940 her commemoration on September 17 has been observed as a double feast, by permission of the Sacred Congregation, in all Catholic dioceses of Germany.[46]

SURVEY OF HILDEGARD'S WORKS

Hildegard's visionary oeuvre—rich, opaque, and unwieldy—is a phenomenon unique in twelfth-century letters; yet at the same time her books provide a compendium of contemporary thought. In the *Scivias* her emphasis is doctrinal; in the *Book of Life's Merits*, ethical; in the *Activity of God*, scientific. But despite their differences in content, the three volumes of the trilogy bear one unmistakable impress. Hildegard's is a world in which neither the distinctions of the schoolmen, nor the negations of the apophatic doctors, nor the raptures of the nuptial mystics have any place; yet no less than theirs, it is a world instinct with order, mystery, and flaming love. Her uni-

44. Odoricus Raynaldus, *Annales ecclesiastici* ad 1237, no. 50 (PL 197: 88a): cum enim habeatur in depositionibus testium ad nostram praesentiam destinatis, quod eadem multos curaverat daemoniacos et infirmos, nec personae, nec loca, nec tempora designantur; neque reperitur in eis quid vel quae magistra dixerit.

45. *Acta* 10, PL 197: 138c.

46. Helmut Hinkel, "St. Hildegards Verehrung im Bistum Mainz," in *Festschrift* 385–412; Hildebrand Fleischmann, *Hildegard-Eigenoffizium* (Freiburg and Regensburg, 1952).

verse rings with the most intricate and inviolate harmonies, yet seethes with the strife of relentlessly warring forces. Things above answer to things below: the eyes of cherubim mirror the faces of saints, and the children of Eve shine like stars in heaven. Soul, body, and cosmos interact in patterns as dynamic as they are eccentric. And the living Light irradiates all—yet even at the heart of the cosmic dance, the power of darkness has its place, if only to lie prostrate beneath the feet of Love. The fragile soul, graced with the fateful knowledge of good and evil, torn by celestial yearnings yet prey to infernal promptings, makes its precarious way through the world under the guidance of Church and Empire, free at every moment to rebel or to obey.

In the *Scivias*, Hildegard's most famous work, the play of "visionary forms dramatic" shapes a comprehensive guide to Christian doctrine. Despite its outlandish imagery, in substance the book is not far removed from Hugh of St. Victor's summa, *On the Sacraments of the Christian Faith*, written only a decade or two earlier (c. 1134). Like Hugh, though less systematically, Hildegard ranged over the themes of divine majesty, the Trinity, creation, the fall of Lucifer and of Adam, the stages of salvation history, the Church and its sacraments, the Last Judgment and the world to come. She lingered long over the subjects of priesthood, the Eucharist, and marriage—all doctrines openly rejected by the Cathars; and she returned time and again to two of her favorite themes, the centrality of the Incarnation and the necessity of spiritual combat. In the third and longest portion, she described a vast architectonic structure that represents the "edifice of salvation"—the City of God, or the Church in the fullness of its divine and human reality.

Within the walls of this allegorical city dwell a host of women, the *Virtutes*, whose dress, attributes, speeches, and gestures express meaning down to the least detail. Although these Virtues may appear to be conventional figures in the tradition of Prudentius's *Psychomachia*,[47] they actually have a

---

47. See Adolf Katzenellenbogen, *Allegories of the Virtues and Vices in Mediaeval Art*, trans. A. J. Crick (London, 1939).

far deeper significance. For every virtue, Hildegard wrote, is in truth "a luminous sphere from God gleaming in the work of man"[48]—not a personified moral quality, but a numinous force that appears in human form only because it empowers human action. The seer's German translators correctly render *Virtutes* as *Kräfte*, not *Tugenden*, for the Virtues' moral significance is secondary to their divine, ontological power. Like Christ and the Church, the Virtues have a dual nature; they indicate, first, divine grace and, second, human cooperation. Through them Hildegard conveyed her profound conception of synergy—salvation as the joint effort of God and humanity. (As we shall see, their feminine form is no mere accident of grammar.) The *Scivias* ends with an apocalyptic section, a cycle of hymns in honor of the blessed, and a morality play— by far the oldest example of this genre—in which the Virtues help a penitent soul to resist diabolic wiles and find salvation.[49]

For students of medieval art, the *Scivias* is of particular interest because of the striking illuminated manuscript prepared at Hildegard's own scriptorium, most likely under her supervision, around 1165 (Wiesbaden, Hessische Landesbibliothek, Hs. 1).[50] This manuscript was ill-advisedly taken to Dresden for safekeeping during World War II and has been missing since 1945. Fortunately, however, the nuns of Eibingen had prepared a handwritten and hand-painted facsimile during the late 1920s, and it is from this copy (Eibingen, Abtei St. Hildegard, Cod. 1) that most of the illustrations in this

48. *Scivias* III.3.3, p. 375.

49. A fuller version of this play, the *Ordo virtutum*, exists independently of the *Scivias* and may be related to Hildegard's *Symphonia*. See "The Text of the *Ordo Virtutum*," ed. Peter Dronke, in *Poetic Individuality in the Middle Ages* (Oxford, 1970): 180–92. There is a performance edition with music edited by Audrey Davidson, *The* Ordo Virtutum *of Hildegard of Bingen* (Kalamazoo, 1985).

50. On this manuscript see Louis Baillet, *Les Miniatures du* Scivias *de Sainte Hildegarde* (Paris, 1911); Hans Fegers, "Die Bilder im *Scivias* der Hildegard von Bingen," *Das Werk des Künstlers* 1 (1939): 109–45; and Christel Meier, "Zum Verhältnis von Text und Illustration im überlieferten Werk Hildegards von Bingen," *Festschrift* 159–69. The paintings are reproduced in color in the CCCM edition of the *Scivias* and in Matthew Fox, *Illuminations of Hildegard of Bingen* (Santa Fe, 1985).

volume are taken. The Rupertsberg *Scivias* paintings are unique, stylistically remote from the work of contemporary manuscript painters. Some in fact are reminiscent of early woodcuts. They have all the freshness of naïf art, and, like Hildegard's prose, they atone for a certain lack of finesse by their startling energy and originality. Although standard iconographic motifs can be recognized in them, they occur in unusual combinations, and many of the images are so eccentric that it is reasonable to posit a close working relationship between the visionary and the unknown artist—possibly one of Hildegard's nuns.

The *Book of Life's Merits*, the second volume of her trilogy, is organized around a single visionary figure. Hildegard here envisioned God in the form of a winged man (*vir*), whose head and shoulders rise into the pure ether. From his shoulders to his thighs, he is wrapped in a shining cloud; from thighs to knees, enveloped in the air of this world; from knees to calves, immersed in the earth; and his feet rest in the waters of the abyss. From the breath of his mouth issue three clouds—one flaming, one stormy, and one luminous—representing three orders of blessed spirits. This colossal figure surveys and sustains the cosmos, which unfolds around him, filling it with a boundless vitality. He is called *vir*, the seer explained, because from him proceed all strength (*vis*) and all things that live (*vivunt*). The eternity of God, which he embodies, "is a fire . . . not a hidden fire, or a silent fire, but an active fire" that animates the world.[51] This divine immanence will be the major theme of the *Activity of God*. But in the present book, Hildegard was content to let the grandeur of God highlight the sins of men and women, which form her principal subject.

The book is carefully structured. In each of the first five parts, a brief vision of the Cosmic Man introduces a dialogue in which a group of Vices advertise their wickedness, only to be confounded by the corresponding Virtues. Unlike the Vir-

---

51. LVM I.32 and I.39, Pitra 17 and 19.

tues, the Vices do not present their traditional feminine forms; rather, they are grotesques whose elements—part male, part female, and part bestial—reveal their moral deformity. Hardness of Heart, for example, is a dense cloud of smoke with no human features but a pair of great, black eyes, fixed on the darkness; Witchcraft has the head of a wolf, the body of a dog, and the tail of a lion; Self-Pity is a leper who wears nothing but leaves and beats his breast as he speaks.[52] After each set of dialogues, Hildegard gave an exegesis of her vision, interspersed with Biblical glosses and theological commentary; explained the appearance of each Vice allegorically; and concluded by presenting the pains that Vice would merit in purgatory, together with penances the sinner might do here and now to avoid them. In the sixth and last part of the book, she added brief descriptions of heaven and hell to complement this long *Purgatorio*.

On the Activity of God, at once the most systematic and the most digressive of Hildegard's books, presents a teeming moralized cosmos in which anything may symbolize anything else. After an overpowering vision of divine Love as the author and vital force of creation (see frontispiece), Hildegard recounted nine cosmological visions, which convey a mathematically precise yet intensely dynamic model of the world, superimposed on the human form divine and on the City of God envisioned in the *Scivias*. Once again, a versatile technique of allegoresis supplies links between the most disparate phenomena. Some of her interpretations are fairly conventional, as when she compared the sixteen principal stars to the doctors of the Church. Their number represents the ten commandments plus the six ages of the world, or the four corners of the earth times the four holy fears, or the eight beatitudes multiplied by the two forms of charity.[53] Other readings are more abstruse. In one section Hildegard worked out an elaborate set of correlations between months of the

---

52. LVM I.16, p. 12 (Obduratio); V.8, p. 186 (Maleficium); II.17, p. 68 (Infelicitas).

53. DOD I.2.42, PL 197: 786d–87b.

year, parts of the body, ages of life, and passions of the soul. Some of these, quaint though they seem, display a lively feeling for the depths of experience hidden in everyday life. The month of November, for example, is correlated with the knees, the age of senility or second childhood, and the pangs of remorse.

> An old man, for fear of the chill, folds his limbs to warm himself by the fire, because he is naturally cold. Even so this month, which is cold every day and lacks the jollity of summer, is like the knees that a man bends in sorrow, remembering his beginnings—when with folded knees he sat like a captive in his mother's womb.[54]

What sustains this phantasmagoria of symbols? Although its wealth of detail can seem turgid, its ordering principles are few and cohesive. First, Hildegard, in typical twelfth-century fashion, saw the world as a divine milieu in which every being is both a sign of the Creator's plenitude and a potential instrument for his action. Her outlook was profoundly theocentric. Second, within this divine milieu, the human being holds the place of honor as the image of God. And in the third place, because the most important activity in life is the salvation of the soul, the cosmos is to be read as one vast and complicated moral lesson. So at the heart of her book Hildegard set two long Biblical commentaries, one on the prologue of St. John's Gospel and one on the first chapter of Genesis. The Gospel text rightly precedes, for only the Word-made-flesh can interpret the creative Word uttered by God in the beginning. That same Word now addresses the believing soul from every nook and cranny of creation, as in the celebrated verse of Alan of Lille:

> Omnis mundi creatura
> Quasi liber et pictura
> Nobis est et speculum.[55]

---

54. DOD I.4.98, PL 197: 883cd.
55. The whole created world is like a book, a picture, and a mirror for us. Alan of Lille, *Rhythmus alter*, PL 210: 579a.

For Hildegard, therefore, the moral interpretation of the east wind, the eyebrows, or the creation of fish was no decorative fancy, but mattered as much as the phenomena themselves; for all creatures were fabricated for man (*homo*), the body for the soul, and the soul for the glory of God.

Even the angels exult in the good works of the saints, because man is the consummate work of God, fashioned from the four elements to receive the splendor that was Lucifer's before he fell. While the angels were created as spiritual beings alone—pure instruments of praise—the human being is destined for both praise and work, possessing an earthen body as well as a fiery spirit. What is more, he is the very garment of the incarnate Word, the creature in whom God vested himself to display his royal majesty.[56] Yet this exalted view of human dignity is balanced—or undercut—by a dualism that goes so far as to claim that the sinful body can defile the pure soul even against its will. In a passage dealing with infants, Hildegard maintained that the newborn soul is pure as Adam in Paradise until the age of weaning, when the child's body and bones grow stronger. Then the teething baby wails in pain over the loss of its primal joy, because the soul, "oppressed against its nature, has been overcome by the body living in sin."[57] Thus, Hildegard oscillated between a joyful affirmation of the world and the body, and a melancholy horror of the flesh—and its master, the devil. This anthropological tension is deeply rooted and ubiquitous in her works. Often, as we shall see, it takes the form of a dichotomy between a bold and affirmative use of sexual symbolism and a largely negative view of sexual practice.

In the last visions of the *Activity of God*, Hildegard turned from cosmology to history, ranging with equal assurance over past, present, and future. A panegyric on the Apostles leads to a critique of the contemporary Church, which in turn ushers in a passage of apocalyptic prophecy. Her views on the Antichrist are beside my purpose, but it is worth noting that,

---

56. DOD I.4.105, PL 197: 889bc.
57. DOD I.4.42, PL 197: 836c–37a.

although her trilogy as a whole found few readers in her own age or any other, her prophecies held the interest of many generations.[58] John of Salisbury, in the seer's lifetime, asked Girardus Pucelle to scour her books for revelations about the papal schism and the unhappy fate of Rome.[59] In 1220, forty years after Hildegard's death, the Cistercian prior Gebeno of Eberbach compiled an anthology of her prophetic and apocalyptic writings. This influential text, entitled *Pentachronon* or *Mirror of Future Times*, survives in well over a hundred manuscripts—as compared with eleven for the *Scivias* and four for *On the Activity of God*.[60]

The reason for this lack of readership is not obscure. Gebeno himself, one of Hildegard's admirers, had to admit in his preface that "most people dislike and shrink from reading St. Hildegard's books, because she speaks obscurely and in an unusual style—not understanding that this is a proof of true prophecy."[61] The saint's Renaissance eulogist, Trithemius of Sponheim, echoed Gebeno's opinion and ascribed the obscurity of Hildegard's style to her inspiration; "no mortal can understand" her works, he maintained, "unless his soul has in truth been inwardly reformed to God's likeness."[62] But even a devout reader must face difficulties other than those inherent in the matter. For Hildegard, despite her encyclopedic knowledge, never mastered Latin grammar well enough to

---

58. Charles Czarski, *The Prophecies of St. Hildegard of Bingen* (Ph.D. Diss., University of Kentucky, 1983); H. D. Rauh, "Hildegard von Bingen," in *Das Bild des Antichrist im Mittelalter: Von Tyconius zum deutschen Symbolismus* (Munich, 1973): 474–527.

59. Visiones et oracula beatae illius et celeberrimae Hildegardis, quae apud vos sunt [mittite]. Quae mihi ex eo commendata est et venerabilis, quod eam dominus Eugenius specialis charitatis affectu familiarius amplectebatur. Explorate etiam et rescribite, an ei sit de fine huius schismatis aliquid revelatum. Praedixit enim in diebus papae Eugenii, quod non esset, nisi extremis diebus, pacem et gratiam in Urbe habiturus. PL 199: 220c. On this subject Hildegard remarked, "De schismate Ecclesiae non jubet me Dominus loqui, sed gladium suum vibrat, et arcum suum tendit." Ep. 64, Pitra 534.

60. Fragments of Gebeno's work appear in Pitra 483–88, under the title *Speculum futurorum temporum*. The complete text has never been edited.

61. Gebeno of Ebernach, *Speculum* Prologus 3, Pitra 484–85.

62. Trithemius, *Chronicon Hirsaugiense* ad 1149, in *Opera historica* 132.

write without a secretary to correct her cases and tenses.[63] Even with such assistance, her style suffers from redundancies, awkward constructions, and baffling neologisms; and her ideas often stretched her limited vocabulary to the breaking point.

Yet although the seer was self-conscious about her "unpolished" style, she seems to have cherished it as a mark that her inspiration must be divine because she herself scarcely knew how to write. When Guibert of Gembloux, with his humanistic love of eloquence, succeeded Volmar and Gottfried as her secretary, he and the abbess had a heated argument over the question of style. Hildegard first commended the nuns who took her dictation, as well as her "only beloved son of pious memory, Volmar," for contenting themselves with her *ipsissima verba* in all simplicity. Guibert, however, proposed the classic Augustinian argument that even wisdom needs the seasoning of eloquence: "inept" and "inharmonious" writing repels readers, but a becoming style moves and inspires them. Whether St. Hildegard was genuinely persuaded or merely desperate, she finally conceded:

> When you correct [the *Life of St. Martin*] and the other works, in the emending of which your love kindly supports my deficiency, you should keep to this rule: that adding, subtracting, and changing nothing, you apply your skill only to make corrections where the order or the rules of correct Latin are violated. Or if you prefer—and this is something I have conceded in this letter beyond my normal practice—you need not hesitate to clothe the whole sequence of the vision in a more becoming garment of speech, preserving the true sense in every part. For even as foods nourishing in themselves do not appeal to the appetite unless they are seasoned somehow, so writings, although full of salutary advice, displease ears accustomed to an urbane style if they are not recommended by some color of eloquence.[64]

63. See Ildefons Herwegen, "Les collaborateurs de Ste. Hildegarde," *Revue bénédictine* 21 (1904): 192–203, 302–15, 381–403; *Echtheit* 143–53.
64. Guibert of Gembloux, Ep. 29.25–27, Pitra 431–33. For Guibert's argument cf. Augustine, *De doctrina christiana* IV.3 and IV.26 (CCSL 32, 117 and 134–35).

This letter was written by Guibert in Hildegard's persona, and we may suspect that the eager monk exaggerated his own victory. Nevertheless, the *Life of St. Martin* as "corrected" by his eloquence can scarcely be recognized as Hildegard's. Purists can at least rejoice that their collaboration began only after the seer's major works were completed.

Yet despite its obscurity, Hildegard's style has a fascination of its own. As Peter Dronke has observed, "it is a highly individual language, at times awkward and at times unclear; the adjectives can be repetitious and limited in range, the interjections excessive. It is the language not of a polished twelfth-century humanist but of someone whose unique powers of poetic vision confronted her more than once with the limits of poetic expression."[65] Although Dronke was writing of the seer's verse, his comments apply just as well to her prose works. For, despite her defective Latin, Hildegard could be a remarkably "poetic" stylist. It is not only that her writings are governed by symbolic rather than logical thought—a distinguishing feature of monastic vis-à-vis scholastic theology.[66] Even in the context of twelfth-century symbolics, Hildegard had no peer in her kaleidoscopic array of metaphors, her figures within figures, her synesthetic language. In the midst of a routine bit of exegesis, she would suddenly convey some new insight with an arresting turn of phrase, or use a familiar typological image in a wholly new sense. Expressive flashes of alliteration punctuate otherwise plodding texts. At times a passage will rise to a pitch of lyric intensity, almost to incantation, then as quickly return to bare expository prose.

One of the most distinctive features of her style is the contrast between her visions themselves—described in meticu-

---

65. Dronke, *Poetic Individuality* 178–79.
66. For this distinction see Jean Leclercq, *The Love of Learning and the Desire for God*, trans. Catherine Misrahi (New York, 1961): 233–86. Two good introductions to twelfth-century symbolics are M.-D. Chenu, *Nature, Man, and Society in the Twelfth Century*, trans. Jerome Taylor and L. K. Little (Chicago, 1968); and M.-M. Davy, *Initiation à la symbolique romane, XIIᵉ siècle* (Paris, 1964).

lous detail—and the far longer glosses furnished by a "voice from heaven." Christel Meier has noted that Hildegard's visions are sometimes incoherent on the literal plane because their component parts are related not to each other but directly to the thing signified.[67] Hence the images do not immediately evoke the desired interpretation, as in conventional iconography; they require glossing by the celestial voice and the visionary forms themselves. All that is elusive and tantalizing in the visions takes on a fixed, unalterable sense in the interpretations, as the evocative freedom of ambiguity hardens into the sharp precision of allegory.[68] Hildegard is one of the rare medieval authors who can be cited both as a textbook example of allegoresis and as a precursor of the Symbolist poets. And she is certainly the only twelfth-century writer to have composed hymns and sequences in free verse. Dronke has cited the liturgical cycle of Notker as a source of her inspiration,[69] but although Hildegard may have taken his cyclic form as a model, her own compositions bear little resemblance to the classic sequence. Her unrhymed, unmetrical songs, wholly unpredictable as to line division, length, and stanzaic pattern, follow the rhythms of thought alone. Their content belongs to the twelfth century, but their form anticipates the twentieth.

From a literary standpoint, the only authors who left an unmistakable mark on Hildegard's style are the Biblical prophets.[70] Like them she appealed to direct experience ("And I saw . . . and I heard"); like them she expressed her awe and terror before the Presence; like them she used metaphor and

67. Christel Meier, "Zwei Modelle von Allegorie im 12. Jahrhundert: Das allegorische Verfahren Hildegards von Bingen und Alans von Lille," in Walter Haug, ed., *Formen und Funktionen der Allegorie* (Stuttgart, 1979): 78.

68. Kent Kraft has compared the shifting imagery of the visions with the commentary, which "spans them out and freezes them, 'frame by frame,' as it were." *The Eye Sees More than the Heart Knows: The Visionary Cosmology of Hildegard of Bingen* (Ph.D. Diss., University of Wisconsin, 1977): 104.

69. Dronke, *Poetic Individuality* 157; Peter Dronke, "Problemata Hildegardiana," *Mittellateinisches Jahrbuch* 16 (1981): 116–17.

70. Cf. Adelgundis Führkötter, introduction to *Scivias* xviii.

parable, attempting when all else failed to express the inex-
pressible with qualifiers (*velut, quasi, forma, imago, similitudo*).
Like Ezekiel she gave the precise date of her calling.

> Now it came to pass in the thirtieth year, in the fourth month,
> on the fifth day of the month, when I was in the midst of the
> captives by the river Chobar, the heavens were opened, and I
> saw the visions of God.
>
> (Ezek. 1:1)

> It came to pass in the one thousand one hundred forty-first
> year of the Incarnation of God's Son Jesus Christ, when I was
> forty-two years and seven months old, that the heavens were
> opened.[71]

Like Jeremiah she did not trust herself to speak, but opened
her mouth only by the command and power of God.

> Then I said, "Ah, Lord God! Behold, I do not know how to
> speak, for I am only a youth." But the Lord said to me, "Do
> not say, 'I am only a youth'; for to all to whom I send you you
> shall go, and whatever I command you you shall speak."
>
> (Jer. 1:6–7)

> But because you are timid in speaking and simple in expound-
> ing and unlearned in writing these things, tell and write them
> not in accord with human speech, or the understanding of hu-
> man invention, or the will of human composition, but in ac-
> cord with what you see and hear in the heavens above, in the
> marvels of God. . . .
>   And again I heard a voice from heaven saying to me: "Cry
> out, therefore, and write thus."

Another aspect of Hildegard's prophetic style is her frequent, sometimes disconcerting change of grammatical persons. The voice from heaven often speaks in the divine first
person; locutions like "My Son, Jesus Christ" indicate that
God the Father is speaking through the seer. Without warning, however, the narration will suddenly shift from the first
person to the third, as prophecy subsides into exposition. But
even when Hildegard spoke in her own persona, she ascribed

71. This passage and the next are from *Scivias*, Protestificatio, 3–6.

her words to the celestial exegete, whose voice thus interprets and governs the entire visionary opus. It is significant that, apart from her lyrics, she scarcely ever addressed God in the second person; her writings are proclamation, not prayer.

Hildegard's style, then, clearly proclaims her prophetic self-awareness. Her correspondents, too, compared her to the Biblical prophets—from Deborah, Olda, Hannah, and Elizabeth to Balaam's ass.[72] And, like the great seers of the Old Testament, she sought by all possible means to bring the people of God to repentance. To that end she used both threats of catastrophe and promises of grace, conveyed in graphic and often startling imagery. Exempla from Scripture, symbols from the world of nature, and prophecies of things to come could serve her equally well as vehicles for the critique of abuses, coupled with the call to renewed moral and spiritual zeal.

Typical of Hildegard's prophetic style is the sermon she preached in Trier on the feast of Pentecost, 1160.[73] It begins with a typical protestation of modesty: "I, a poor little figure without health or strength or courage or learning, myself subject to masters, have heard these words addressed to the prelates and clergy of Trier, from the mystical light of the true vision." In the peroration that follows, Hildegard laments that because prelates neglect to "sound the trumpet of justice," the four quarters of the earth are darkened: in the east the dawn of good works is extinguished, in the south the ardor of virtue is chilled, and in the west the twilight of mercy yields to midnight blackness. But from the north, the figurative realm of Satan, comes a hissing wind of pride, infidelity, and neglect of God.

This grandiloquent imagery sounds vague enough; but, reading between the lines, one can find more specific complaints. In the first place, the prophet opposed excessive clerical wealth: prelates, she said, shall find that the breadth of their estates has forged constraints for their souls. Their easy

---

72. Epp. 75 (PL 197: 297c); 6 (157c); 92 (313a).
73. The quotations that follow are from Ep. 49, PL 197: 254–58.

living has turned virile courage into feminine weakness, which has no strength to fight because man is naturally the head; and this effeminate age began "with a certain tyrant," the source of all the Church's present woes. This "tyrant" is of course Barbarossa, whom Hildegard warily avoided naming; she had yet to declare open conflict with him. But her implicit message is clear: the German bishops, all too ready to accept imperial election and control, have become emasculated and lost the courage to oppose a now-schismatic emperor. After a long digression on the heroes of salvation history—meant to underscore the difference between obeying God and obeying men—Hildegard threatened a lax and worldly Church with the fate that it deserved.

> But now the law is neglected among the spiritual people, who scorn to do and teach what is good. And the masters and prelates sleep, while justice is abandoned. Hence I heard this voice from heaven saying: O daughter of Sion, the crown will tumble from your head, the far-flung pallium of your riches will be drawn in and confined to a narrow measure, and you will be banished from region to region. Many cities and monasteries shall be dispersed by the powerful. And princes will say: Let us take from them the iniquity that turns the whole world upside down among them.

The prophecy continues: because of their injustice and conspicuous wealth, priests will be persecuted and the Church purified. "Virile times" will return with warfare, by the judgment of God, and afterward there will be a renascence of prophecy, learning, and reverence. Even secular people will be converted by the example of their superiors to a holy way of life. Finally, the Antichrist will arise, but God will crush him as a craftsman smashes the useless works in his shop.

At the end of her sermon, Hildegard returned to her most pressing message. Once, in a vision, she saw the city of Trier aglow with Pentecostal fire so that its streets glistened like gold; but now it is so defiled that fiery vengeance from its enemies will fall upon it, unless the city repents like Nineveh in the days of the prophet Jonah. A medieval chronicler might easily see Hildegard's prophecy confirmed by the internecine warfare, the growing breach between Frederick and the German clergy, and the confiscation of church lands that resulted from the continuing papal schism. But even the political message, like the apocalyptic and the visionary language, remains subordinate to the overriding ethical demand. "Repentance" here entails, but is not limited to, restoration of the proper authority and autonomy of the German bishops. It also requires absolute fidelity to the Word of God as set forth in Scripture, tradition, and—not least—the seer's own prophetic writings. This breadth of intention may be one reason why Hildegard was often deliberately vague about names and events, although she did not hesitate to take sides in current affairs. Like the Biblical prophets, she preferred to veil her advice in symbolic language that could apply to a wide range of situations.

In addition to preaching and apocalyptic, Hildegard's prophetic activity extended to the private sphere. Of her many correspondents, the priests and monastics—by far the majority—wrote to ask her for prayers, counsel, and revelations concerning their personal and communal lives. Her answers, dictated "by the living Light," present a miscellany of visions and teachings, often of very general import. But sometimes the questions are more specific: Should I resign my abbacy or persevere? How can we monks correct our fraternal bickering? Are our relics genuine? How can we exorcise a woman obsessed by devils? Should we receive the erring brother who wants to return? And laypeople asked: Are my kinsmen suffering in purgatory? Will my husband recover from his illness? Should I take my inheritance case before the emperor? Hildegard did not always answer such questions: sometimes she explained that God had not shown her everything, or that it was better for the writer not to know. But in trying to reconstruct her daily life and work, we must not forget the constant stream of messengers and pilgrims who honored and sometimes plagued her with these requests. And while we cannot survey the whole of her correspondence, we can imagine her as a woman among women by looking at three letters to persons of widely differing rank: an abbess, an empress, and an afflicted matron.

Much of Hildegard's activity was directed toward monastic reform. We may take her letter to Sophia, abbess of Altwick, as typical both of contemporary monastic problems and of the seer's characteristic imagery in writing of women. Sophia, like so many twelfth-century superiors, yearned to lay down the burden of pastoral care, which weighed heavily upon her, in exchange for an eremitic life "in the solitude of some little cell."[74] But to the seer, this seemingly pious wish was a snare and a delusion.

> O daughter born of the side of man, and figure formed in the building of God: why do you languish so that your mind shifts like clouds in a storm, now shining like the light and now darkened? . . . You say, "I want to rest and seek a place where my heart can have a nest, so that my soul may rest there." Daughter, before God it is useless for you to cast off your burden and abandon the flock of God, while you have a light to illumine it so that you can lead it to pasture. Now restrain yourself, lest your mind blaze in that sweetness which would greatly harm you in the vicissitudes of the solitary life.

In the lure of the hermitage, Hildegard saw only a spurious and irresponsible pietism. Far better is the onerous but necessary care of souls in fidelity to a vow once taken. With but one exception, she gave the same counsel to all the abbots and abbesses who raised this question—although in each case she claimed to have a special revelation for her correspondent.[75] Collectively, then, the letters express an aspect of Hildegard's concern for effective and vigilant pastoral care at all levels, while her imagery varied with each correspondent's

---

74. Ep. 100, PL 197: 321–22. On twelfth-century ambivalence and antagonism toward the abbatial role see Pierre Salmon, *The Abbot in Monastic Tradition*, trans. Claire Lavoie (Washington, 1972): 95–99; and Caroline Bynum, *Jesus as Mother: Studies in the Spirituality of the High Middle Ages* (Berkeley, 1982): 154–59.

75. For similar advice cf. Epp. 32, 33, 37, 42, 44, 66, 70, 74, 77, 78, 86, 101, 108, and 112 in PL 197; and Epp. 39, 57, 61, 63, 76, 83, 89, 98, 118, 137, 138, 151, and 159 in Pitra.

personal need. In this letter to Sophia, she began by comparing the abbess to Eve, then figuratively to Ecclesia—the "new Eve" taken from the side of Christ, the new Adam, to be God's living temple. The greeting reinforces Hildegard's explicit message on the symbolic level: it is by fulfilling her appointed task of leadership in the Church that Abbess Sophia will also live out her feminine role as a figura of it.

In her dealings with the secular powers, Hildegard was not always as harsh as she was with Frederick. One of her letters, addressed to "Bertha, queen of the Greeks"—otherwise Irene, wife of the Byzantine Emperor Manuel Comnenus—was apparently written to console the German-born empress for her failure to bear a son.[76] Hildegard greeted the empress respectfully, but with the authority that befits a prophet.

> The breath of the Spirit of God says: . . . By a stream that rises from a rock in the East the filth of other waters is cleansed, for it runs swiftly and is more useful than other waters, because there is no corruption in it. So it is with those to whom God grants a day of prosperity and a glowing dawn of honor, and whom the north wind does not oppress with the rough blast of hostile foes. Therefore look to him who has touched you, who seeks a burnt offering from your heart and the keeping of his commandments. Sigh to him, therefore, and may he give you the joy of offspring as you desire, and as you petition him in your need. For the living eye regards you and wishes to have you, and you shall live forever.

We do not know whether Bertha had asked Hildegard especially to pray she would bear a son, and the saint made no rash promise. What is noteworthy in Hildegard's letter, beyond the usual exhortation to trust God, is her analogy between the queen's noble status and the mountain stream, which purifies the land because it flows from the heights. The powerful whom God has exalted to prosperity and honor should likewise set an example of gratitude and virtue for the realm. But, while admonishing the empress and promising

---

76. Bertha of Sulzbach, sister-in-law of Conrad III, married Manuel Comnenus in 1146 and bore one daughter. See Ep. 81, Pitra 542.

the salvation of her soul, Hildegard refused to prophesy her earthly future.

The seer stressed this limitation of her fortune-telling abilities when writing to a woman of much humbler rank, one Sibyl of Lausanne.[77] This matron's circumstances are not clear from Hildegard's two surviving letters to her, but she seems to have been bereaved by a complicated family tragedy. Hildegard called her a "daughter of the woods," so perhaps she had tried to adopt the life of a recluse. Whatever the woman's predicament, Hildegard carefully delimited the role she herself was able to play in it.

> Sibyl, handiwork of God's finger, amend your unstable way of life, and do not exert yourself in mental agitation. You cannot excuse yourself by this means, for God discerns everything. But God does not bid me to explain his judgments upon you, but rather to pray for you, because certain people are now watching out for revenge on account of what your parents did. For sometimes God stretches out his lash even to the third and fourth generations. Yet trust in the Lord that he may deliver you from the sword of your enemies, even though your daughter has been seized by them.
>
> I, however, speak more about the salvation of souls than about the fates of men, so I often say nothing about these things. For the Holy Spirit pours out not revelation to confound people's crimes, but just judgment. Now may God set you in the field of life that you may live forever.[78]

Hildegard's private epistles, compared with her public sermons, reveal that she felt more confident in predicting events

77. Or "Sibylla trans Alpes" as in the ms heading of Ep. 36, Pitra 521. At this period "Sibylla" should probably be taken as a proper name rather than an epithet.

78. Ep. 125, Pitra 560–61. This same letter, with the proper name and the reference to Sibyl's daughter deleted, appears as Ep. 88 in PL 197: 309d–10a, where it is addressed to the provost of a monastery in Koblenz. The editor has conflated Hildegard's letter to Sibyl with another to Bertha, a matron of Fulda (Ep. 43, Pitra 526). As Schrader and Führkötter have pointed out (*Echtheit* 160–71), the so-called Riesenkodex (Wiesbaden, Hess. Landesbibliothek Hs. 2), from which most of the letters in Migne's collection are taken, often falsifies the addresses of otherwise authentic letters in order to exalt the rank of Hildegard's correspondents.

on a grand scale than in foretelling individual fates. To her friend Sibyl she gave no more than the pious counsel, consolation, and prayers that any Christian might offer, although she still wrote with an assured authority. Yet in a second letter to this woman, she displayed another and more spectacular charism.

This time, the hapless Sibyl had been suffering from an issue of blood, like the sick woman described in Mark 5:25–34. In the name of the visionary Light, Hildegard proposed a cure.

> Place your trust in God. But around your chest and your navel set these words, in the name of him who orders all things rightly: "In the blood of Adam death arose; in the blood of Christ death was restrained. In that same blood of Christ I command you, blood, to cease your flowing."[79]

This charm, like many others in the *Book of Simple Medicine*, lies on the borderline between sacraments (in the broadest sense) and sympathetic magic. According to Hildegard's *Vita*, the remedy worked;[80] it is but one of many miraculous cures ascribed to her. Oddly enough, however, her medical books are unique among her writings in that they make no claim to any prophetic or visionary inspiration. The fact that she wrote them on her own initiative, so to speak, suggests that although she took a strong interest in medicine, she considered this aspect of her work less authoritative than her spiritual and ethical teaching. Nevertheless, there can be no doubt that her flair for unconventional healings, like her vivid apocalyptic and her audacious preaching tours, fired the imagination of her peers. Sensational gifts, after all, attract even pious attention more readily than serious calls to a devout and holy life. So Hildegard's renown as a creature blessed among women rested, for Guibert and other saint-watchers throughout the empire, on acts and claims more mysterious than the

79. Ep. 36, Pitra 521.
80. *Vita* 3.40, PL 197: 119cd.

zeal of her teaching. Above all, it rested on her famed experience as a "seer of the living Light."

THEOLOGY AND THE PROBLEM
OF FEMININE AUTHORITY

Hildegard's visions not only supplied her with a message; they also assured an audience for it. Were it not for the visions, she would never have preached or written at all, and she even maintained—echoing a theme as old as Moses—that in spite of them she was hardly eager to prophesy. But it is no less true that, had she not claimed her gift as a mark of divine authority, no one would have listened to her. Many have suggested that, in an age when the Apostle's command that "no woman is to teach or have authority over men" (I Tim. 2:12) was rigorously enforced, it was only through visions that a religious or intellectual woman could gain a hearing. This is not to say that such visions were necessarily rooted in the desire for authority; but the visionary could not help knowing that, although men might perhaps heed a divinely inspired woman, they would have little patience with a mere presumptuous female.

This awareness can explain some of the vehemence with which Hildegard insisted on her inspiration, even to the point of claiming verbal inerrancy. In her *Vita* she told how, at the time of her move to the Rupertsberg, many asked "why so many mysteries should be revealed to a foolish and uneducated woman, when there are many powerful and learned men," and some people wondered whether she had been seduced by evil spirits.[81] Even some of her own nuns rejected her and refused to move to the new foundation. Although only one letter attacking Hildegard is extant, she referred in several places to her detractors. Some resented the severity, others the novelty of her monastic discipline; some questioned her pretensions to divine wisdom; and many must

---

81. *Vita* 2.22, PL 197: 106cd.

have been appalled at conduct unbecoming to her sex, for she remarked in one place that "now, to the scandal of men, women are prophesying."[82] The more vulnerable she knew herself to be, the more emphatically she needed to proclaim that it was not she but the Holy Spirit who spoke. To that end, only the certitude that she was transcribing exact dictation from the living Light could suffice both for herself and for her readers.

The problem of feminine authority was no less troubling for Hildegard herself than for her auditors, since she fully shared her culture's notions of female inferiority. No matter how strong her sense of the grace that animated her, she suffered from an almost equal sense of her own implausibility as a vessel. No doubt, as she struggled to overcome this diffidence, the aristocratic ease born of rank and privilege helped her more than she realized. But, in order to come to terms with her God-given authority, she needed to reconcile it with her gender in a strictly theological fashion. Two complementary means to this end—two strategies of validation, as it were—lay at hand. In the first place, as we have seen, Hildegard took her strongest stand on what seemed to be her worst disability—"feminine frailty." Because the power of God is perfected in weakness, because the humblest shall be the most exalted, human impotence could become the sign and prelude of divine empowerment.[83] In Hildegard's eyes this negative capability compensated for her meager schooling and her poor health as well as for her gender. Her second mode of validation was more oblique, less conscious and deliberate. It lay in accentuating the feminine aspects of the divine, which the following chapters will explore at length. But these two strategies, apparently so opposed, are not unrelated. To see the feminine as a species of incapacity and frailty,

82. Fragment IV.28, p. 71. Cf. *Vita* 2.34, PL 197: 115c–16d; and Ep. 116 from Tengswich, abbess of Andernach (336b–37a), a searching critique offered in ironically courteous terms.

83. Cf. Barbara Newman, "Divine Power Made Perfect in Weakness: St Hildegard on the Frail Sex," in L. Thomas Shank, ed., *Peace-Weavers*, vol. 2 of *Medieval Religious Women* (Kalamazoo, 1987).

yet also as a numinous and salvific dimension of the divine nature: herein lies the characteristic strain of what I have called Hildegard's "theology of the feminine."

Before I turn to examine her visions in detail, it will be useful to see how these two themes were worked out, on a much smaller scale, by a woman closely associated with Hildegard. Her protégée Elisabeth, a young nun at the monastery of Schönau near Bingen, modeled herself from an early age on the seer across the Rhine. In 1152—five years after Hildegard was vindicated by Eugenius III and one year after she published the *Scivias*—the younger nun's visions began. According to her brother, editor, and staunchest supporter, Ekbert of Schönau, the twenty-three-year-old Elisabeth "was visited by the Lord and his hand was with her, doing in her the most marvelous and memorable deeds in accord with his ancient mercies. Indeed, it was given to her to experience ecstasy and to see visions of the secrets of the Lord, which are hidden from mortals' eyes."[84]

Temperamentally, Elisabeth resembled Hildegard in many ways: she shared the older woman's physical frailty, her sensitivity to spiritual impressions of all kinds, and her need for public authentication to overcome initial self-doubt. Just as Hildegard had written in her uncertainty to Bernard, the outstanding saint of the age, so Elisabeth wrote to Hildegard—and, like the abbot of Clairvaux, the abbess of Bingen knew how to console her young protégée while warning her to remain humble. In a characteristic and revealing image, Hildegard told Elisabeth to be like a trumpet, which resounds not by its own effort but by the breath of another.[85] In fact the

84. Elisabeth of Schönau, *Liber visionum* I.1, in F. W. E. Roth, ed., *Die Visionen der heiligen Elisabeth und die Schriften der Äbte Ekbert und Emecho von Schönau* (Brünn, 1884): 1. On Elisabeth see Kurt Köster, "Das visionäre Werk Elisabeths von Schönau: Studien zur Entstehung, Überlieferung und Wirkung in der mittelalterlichen Welt," *Archiv für mittelrheinische Kirchengeschichte* 4 (1952): 79–119; Josef Loos, "Hildegard von Bingen und Elisabeth von Schönau," *Festschrift* 263–72.

85. Ep. 45, PL 197: 217d. This letter probably answers not the epistle of Elisabeth printed in Migne but an earlier letter of hers. For English transla-

analogy fit Elisabeth better than Hildegard herself, for the younger woman lacked her admired mother's independence and originality. Many of her visions were inspired by the queries of Ekbert and other patrons, and often they echo Hildegard's in content, imagery, and style.[86]

By 1158 the author of the *Annales Palidenses* found it natural to link the two visionary nuns in a single notice: "In these days also God displayed the signs of his power in the frail sex, that is, in his two handmaidens Hildegard on the Rupertsberg near Bingen and Elisabeth in Schönau, whom he filled with the spirit of prophecy and to whom, through the Gospel, he revealed many kinds of visions, which are extant in writing."[87] The chronicler's reference to "the frail sex" shows once again that contemporaries could not overlook the issue of gender, whether they found in it occasion for praise or for blame. No less than Hildegard, Elisabeth felt this liability keenly. While she was still in doubt about publishing her visions, she feared that some people would dismiss them as satanic delusions or mere feminine fancies (*muliebria figmenta*).[88] And when, like Hildegard, she felt herself called to prophetic preaching, she needed assurance that God would help her fulfill what she felt to be a masculine role. Hence the angel of the Lord commanded her, "Arise, . . . and stand upon your feet, and I will speak with you; and fear not, for I am with you all the days of your life. Play the man (*viriliter age*) and let your heart take courage."[89]

In one sense, Elisabeth's path should have been easier than Hildegard's simply because the older nun could provide a model for her. Her *Book of the Ways of God* (1156) obviously

---

tions see Kathryn Kerby-Fulton and Dyan Elliott, "Self-Image and the Visionary Role in Two Letters from the Correspondence of Elizabeth of Schönau and Hildegard of Bingen," *Vox Benedictina* 2 (1985): 204–23.

86. The mountain, city, and column described in the *Liber visionum* are particularly reminiscent of *Scivias*, Book III, and the stylized dialogues between the prophet and God or his angel also recall Hildegard.

87. *Annales Palidenses* ad 1158, MGH.SS. 16, 90.

88. Elisabeth, *Liber visionum* I.1 in Roth, *Visionen der heiligen Elisabeth* 1.

89. Elisabeth, *Liber visionum* I.67 in Roth, *Visionen der heiligen Elisabeth* 32. Cf. Ezek. 2:1 , Matt. 28:20, Ps. 26:14.

takes its title, though not its subject matter, from the *Scivias*. Elisabeth gracefully acknowledged this debt in her vision of a pavilion filled with books that, an angel tells her, have yet to be revealed before the Day of Judgment. The angel shows Elisabeth her own volume, still unwritten, with the words: "'This is the *Book of the Ways of God*, which is to be revealed through you after you have visited Sister Hildegard and heard her.' And indeed," Elisabeth added, "so the prophecy began to be fulfilled as soon as I had returned from seeing her."[90] Like Hildegard, too, Elisabeth wrote a treatise against the Cathars[91] and a collection of hortatory epistles to religious. Her best-selling book on St. Ursula fostered the cult of that same legendary saint to whom Hildegard wrote some of her most powerful lyrics. Elisabeth could also trust her patron to support her in the face of difficulties. For instance, when Elisabeth felt herself in jeopardy because someone had been circulating a spurious prophecy in her name, and because various disasters she had predicted did not come to pass, she could write to Hildegard in confidence that the abbess of Bingen would clear her name.[92]

On the other hand, the older visionary had sources of security that her protégée lacked. First, from a secular standpoint, she could count on support from a powerful circle of friends, relatives, and churchmen—including St. Bernard, the archbishop of Mainz, and the pope. Elisabeth had only her devoted brother. Second, Hildegard seems to have had fewer doubts about the authenticity of her call, although she did fear its consequences. Elisabeth began more hesitantly still. Not only did she endure sickness and short-term paralysis, like Hildegard; she also suffered from profound depression, anorexia, suicidal temptations, and demonic appari-

90. Elisabeth of Schönau, *Liber viarum Dei* 6 in Roth, *Visionen der heiligen Elisabeth* 91.

91. See Raoul Manselli, "Amicizia spirituale ed azione pastorale nella Germania del seculo XII: Ildegarda di Bingen, Elisabetta ed Ecberto di Schönau contro l'eresia catara," *Studi e materiali di storia delle religioni* 38 (1967), fasc. 1–2: 302–13.

92. Ep. 45, PL 197: 214d–16d. The passage in which Elisabeth styled herself "magistra sororum quae in Schonaugia sunt" is an interpolation.

tions, which alternated for a long time with her more wholesome visions. Whereas Hildegard stressed that her visions seldom interfered with her normal functioning, Elisabeth experienced hers in ecstasy, usually accompanied by agony. This state of inner turmoil gradually subsided, and, as the visionary became more confident, her writings became more objective—less concerned with her personal sufferings and more closely connected with the liturgical year, the needs of her community, and the theological interests of her friends. Her later works thus reflect not only Hildegard's influence but also the successful resolution of her early conflicts. The conflicts themselves, however, were worked out in her initial *Book of Visions*, where the problem of feminine authority emerges as a persistent theme. Elisabeth's ways of coming to terms with her prophetic role, through the instruction and consolation received in her visions, can serve as a preview of Hildegard's more sustained and ample development of this same problematic.

One obvious reply to detractors was available in the Old Testament, whence exempla of feminine courage had been drawn from time out of mind. Elisabeth did not hesitate to invoke the great mothers of Israel:

> People are scandalized that in these days the Lord deigns to magnify his great mercy in the frail sex. But why doesn't it cross their minds that a similar thing happened in the days of our fathers when, while men were given to indolence, holy women were filled with the Spirit of God so that they could prophesy, energetically govern the people of God, and even win glorious victories over Israel's enemies? I speak of women like Hilda, Deborah, Judith, Jael, and the like.[93]

In the seer's reference to "men . . . given to indolence" we can again recognize Hildegard's complaint about "effeminate times," which justify feminine leaders.

---

93. Elisabeth, *Liber visionum* II.1 in Roth, *Visionen der heiligen Elisabeth* 40. Cf. St. Ambrose on Deborah: "In order to enthuse the souls of women, a woman judged, a woman decided, a woman prophesied, a woman triumphed and, in the midst of the fighting troops, taught men the art of war under feminine command. In the mystery, however, the struggle of faith is the Church's victory." *De viduis* 8.49–50, PL 16: 362–63.

Further support for the notion of empowered women comes from the visions themselves. It is not surprising that Elisabeth, in her distress, should receive comfort from the Virgin; but it is more striking that she should see Mary dressed like a priest, standing beside the altar vested in a chasuble and a glorious crown.[94] In another vision Elisabeth beheld the apocalyptic woman clothed with the sun, who turned out to be neither Mary nor the Church but "the sacred humanity of the Lord Jesus" weeping over the iniquity of the world.[95] Elisabeth's brother was upset by this identification, so at his bidding she asked her next heavenly visitor "why the Savior's humanity was shown to me in the guise of a virgin and not in the form of a man." She received a conventional answer, namely that this vision could refer to the Virgin Mary as well as to Christ. But the initial interpretation was not withdrawn. To Elisabeth's inspired imagination, it appeared that if Christ is both divine and human he must also be female as well as male. Both these visions obliquely validate the seer's authority through and despite her sex. In one of them a woman appears in a powerful male role, and in the other Christ himself appears as a woman.[96]

In a different vein, the *Book of Visions* closes with a text even more reminiscent of Hildegard. Elisabeth had seen Nebuchadnezzar's vision (Dan. 2:31–33) of a great statue with a head of gold, chest of silver, belly of bronze, legs of iron, and feet of clay; and she interpreted this image as the apocalyptic Christ. The feet of clay in her vision represented Christ's human body and soul, and she wanted to know why these were

---

94. Elisabeth, *Liber visionum* I.6 in Roth, *Visionen der heiligen Elisabeth* 6. The vision probably derives from the iconography of Mary in priestly vestments as a personification of the Church. See Ilene Forsyth, *The Throne of Wisdom: Wood Sculptures of the Madonna in Romanesque France* (Princeton, 1972): 23–24 and figs. 112–21.

95. Elisabeth, *Liber visionum* III.4 in Roth, *Visionen der heiligen Elisabeth* 60–61.

96. Cf. Gertrud Jaron Lewis, "Christus als Frau: Eine Vision Elisabeths von Schönau," *Jahrbuch für Internationale Germanistik* 15 (1983): 70–80. On the femininity of Jesus, an important minor theme in twelfth-century writers, see the title essay and references in Bynum, *Jesus as Mother*.

so frail while the iron and bronze, symbolizing the Church, were so strong. The answer she received is this: "all the virtue and strength of the Church grew out of the Savior's weakness, which he incurred through the flesh. The weakness of God is stronger than men. This was well demonstrated by a figure in the first parents, when the vigor of bone was taken from Adam that Eve might be made; that the woman might be confirmed whence the man was made infirm" (*inde firmaretur mulier, unde infirmatus est vir*).[97] Here Elisabeth, like Hildegard, associated the paradox of saving weakness with the reversal of normal gender roles, whereby men become weak and women strong. Earlier she had seen Christ's humanity in the guise of a woman; now that same humanity is represented by the fragile feet of clay, which, paradoxically, confer strength on the woman Ecclesia.

It was through reflection on the humanity of Christ, considered in all its multifarious richness, that Elisabeth came to accept both feminine weakness and feminine strength. Her theology of the feminine, like Hildegard's, has its roots in the charismatic woman's need for authentication in a mistrustful world. But both visionaries finally transcended that need. In the chapters to come we shall see how Hildegard, blending the high traditions of sapiential thought with received ideas about women and weakness, was able to achieve a distinctive, tense, and highly energized interpretation of the Christian faith.

---

97. Elisabeth, *Liber visionum* III.31 in Roth, *Visionen der heiligen Elisabeth* 87.

2

The Feminine Divine

Hildegard's visionary style and self-understanding, as we have seen, derive in fundamental ways from the Old Testament prophets. And her visions of the feminine divine, whom she called Sapientia and Caritas, are no less indebted to the Biblical wisdom literature.

The books of Proverbs, the Wisdom of Solomon, and the Wisdom of Jesus ben Sirach, or Ecclesiasticus, enjoyed a much wider popularity in the Middle Ages than they do in post-Reformation theology. Twelfth-century writers made use of this wisdom literature in a variety of ways. Aside from its obvious didactic content—the aphorisms on friendship, politics, women, morality, and other subjects—they were particularly drawn to the passages that portray Sophia or Wisdom as God's feminine consort and collaborator in the works of creation. Chief among these are Proverbs 8, Ecclesiasticus 24, and Wisdom of Solomon 7–9, texts in which Sophia praises herself or receives praise in a style befitting a goddess. Medieval theologians, following the church fathers, applied these texts to Christology, exemplarist cosmology, and the glorification of Mary. What the Song of Songs was to St. Bernard, the speeches of Sophia were to many others: an inexhaustible font of doctrine welling from poetry with a deep imaginative appeal. The influence of these texts in medieval religious culture is too pervasive and multifaceted to permit the formulation of a single "sapiential theology," yet we may note the existence and convergence of several sapiential traditions, which left their mark more or less deeply on Hildegard's visions.

As scholars have often noted, most medieval allegorical figures are female because most abstract nouns in Latin take the feminine gender.[1] Yet Wisdom or Sapientia is unique, for this is the only personification that remained equally compelling, and indeed ubiquitous throughout the Middle Ages, in both a masculine and a feminine guise.[2] In fact, its long history witnesses a tension between the procedures of personification allegory, in which the persona's traits must be consistent with its grammatical gender, and the special demands of Christian theology, in which Wisdom—a feminine persona in the Old Testament—was very early identified with the masculine Christ (cf. I Cor. 1:24).[3] Certain medieval theologians were sensitive to this problem. For instance, St. Martin of Léon (d. 1221) expected Jews to ask, "If Christ is the Wisdom of God, why is he called a son and not a daughter?" He could only reply that the name of son was "more honorable."[4] But even during the patristic period, while the femininity of Sophia was largely suppressed in the interests of Christology, she nonetheless returned in the guise of *fabula.*

Certain allegorical dames from the late antique classics— Lady Philosophy in Boethius's *Consolation,* Queen Sapientia in Prudentius's *Psychomachia,* and the learned bride in Martianus Capella's obscure but popular allegory, *The Marriage of Philology and Mercury*—gave Carolingian scholars an opportunity to savor the feminine mystique of Wisdom while interpreting it in impeccably Christian terms. Indeed, the Carolin-

---

1. For general discussion see Morton Bloomfield, "A Grammatical Approach to Personification Allegory," *Modern Philology* 60 (1963): 161–71.

2. "The figure who in specific theological contexts will be called *verbum dei* and seen as the masculine *son* of God has always, in another *integumentum,* been identified with Sapientia or Providentia—a feminine hypostasis." Peter Dronke, Notes to Bernard Silvestris, *Cosmographia* (Leiden, 1978): 165, n. iii 17–18.

3. During the formative period of Christology "it becomes evident," according to Jaroslav Pelikan, "that the basis for the fullest statement of the divine in Christ as Logos was provided not by its obvious documentation in John 1:1–14 but by Proverbs 8:22–31 (LXX)"—an aretalogy of Sophia. The fourth-century Arian controversy seems to have broken out over the interpretation of this very passage. *The Emergence of the Catholic Tradition, 100–600* (Chicago, 1971): 186–93.

4. Martin of Léon, *Sermo IV in Nativitate Domini,* cited in Étienne Catta, "*Sedes Sapientiae,*" in *Maria* 6:707, n. 103.

gian period witnessed the rise of a veritable cult of Sapientia, as Alcuin and his confreres raised the banner of Christian humanism over palace school and chapel. Both Alcuin's native church of York Minster and the palace chapel in Soissons were dedicated to the Holy Wisdom, after the example of St. Sophia in Byzantium. In his capacity as liturgist, Alcuin composed a votive *Mass of the Holy Wisdom*, which remained in widespread use through 1570.[5] At the same time, the flourishing cult and iconography of the Virgin gave an ever-increasing place to sapiential themes, reintegrating the feminine Sophia into Christian symbolics in yet another form.[6] It was in the twelfth century that the elements of this rich tradition—theological reflection on Christ, devotion to the Mother of God, classicizing humanism, and liturgical and artistic innovation—fully converged. Texts such as Bernard Silvestris's *Cosmographia*, Alan of Lille's *Anticlaudianus*, and St. Hildegard's sapiential visions bear witness to the fact.[7]

Unlike the two philosopher-poets, Hildegard made no attempt to devise a new mythology. But like their fictive goddesses—Noys, Natura, Prudentia—the figure she called Caritas or Sapientia has to do with the ultimate mystery of creation, the bond between Creator and creature. Wherever such personae appear, we will find the Platonizing cosmology that captivated twelfth-century thinkers: the divine ideas, eternal in the mind of God and bodied forth in creatures; the

5. See Wolfgang Edelstein's valuable study, *Eruditio und sapientia: Weltbild und Erziehung in der Karolingerzeit* (Freiburg, 1965). For the Mass see PL 101: 451 and Marie-Thérèse d'Alverny, "La Sagesse et ses sept filles," *Mélanges dédiés à la mémoire de Félix Grat* 1 (Paris, 1946): 245–78.

6. A popular *Ordo*, composed c. 950 in Hildegard's own diocese of Mainz, prescribed the reading of the sapiential books during the month of August, on the Sundays just before and after the principal Marian feast of the Assumption. Michel Andrieu, *Les Ordines Romani du haut moyen âge* 5 (Louvain, 1961): 89, 357–58; cf. Catta, "*Sedes Sapientiae*," and Georges Frénaud, "Le Culte de Notre Dame dans l'ancienne liturgie latine," *Maria* 6: 157–211.

7. On this literary movement see Brian Stock, *Myth and Science in the Twelfth Century: A Study of Bernard Silvester* (Princeton, 1972); Winthrop Wetherbee, *Platonism and Poetry in the Twelfth Century: The Literary Influence of the School of Chartres* (Princeton, 1972); Peter Dronke, *Fabula: Explorations into the Use of Myth in Medieval Platonism* (Leiden, 1974).

world soul; the deep resonance of macrocosm with microcosm; the fervent hope of access to God through human rationality and virtue. Above all, in Hildegard, we will find the
mystery of the Incarnation, envisioned as the center and final
cause of creation—predestined by God "from before the foundation of the world" (Eph. 1:4). Because this mystery was accomplished by means of a woman, it is evoked in visions that
also highlight the feminine dimension of divine reality. Hildegard saw this as the dimension in which mediation or, at a
higher intensity, union between Creator and creature can be
achieved. Where the feminine presides, God stoops to humanity and humanity aspires to God. If the vision takes on a
moral cast, we see the divinely human Virtues, like the angels
on Jacob's ladder, descending through grace and ascending
again through good works.[8] We might characterize the same
movement metaphysically as the cycle of emanation and return, or existentially as that of revelation and response. Hildegard herself perceived it, in her last vision, as the endless
circulation of the energy of love.[9]

This complex of ideas and images by no means precludes
a more linear understanding of salvation history, cast in the
form of a narrative beginning with creation and the fall, cul-
minating in the death and resurrection of Christ, and con-
cluding with the Last Judgment. When she was following this
narrative pattern, discussing the great and unrepeatable
events of history, Hildegard normally used masculine designations for God—Father and Son, King and Redeemer and
Judge. The feminine designations, on the other hand, evoke
God's interactions with the cosmos insofar as they are timeless or perpetually repeated. Thus, feminine symbols convey
the principle of divine self-manifestation; the absolute predestination of Christ; the mutual indwelling of God in the
world and the world in God; and the saving collaboration between Christ and the faithful, manifested sacramentally in the
Church and morally in the Virtues. In theological shorthand,

8. *Scivias* III.8.13, p. 495.
9. DOD III.10.1, PL 197: 997–98; cf. Fig. 6.

the feminine divine is associated with the principles of theophany, exemplarity, immanence, and synergy. All of these can be seen as conditions or corollaries of the Incarnation. It is essential to remember that, for Hildegard, the advent of the Word-made-flesh was not one event among many but *the* event for which the world was made, an event that is destined to be continually renewed and extended until the whole world has been subsumed in the Body of Christ. Thus, unlike the passion or the resurrection, the Incarnation is not primarily a historical event but an event beyond time and history in the sphere of the eternal, of the feminine divine. What will concern me in the rest of this chapter is the expression of these theological themes through the imagery of Wisdom as bride, mother, and queen.

THEOPHANY AND THE BRIDE OF GOD

A figure of Wisdom first appears in *Scivias* III, where Hildegard saw the Word of God symbolized by a three-sided pillar, crowned with a radiant dove.[10] The three sides, she was told, signify the Word of God as manifested in the ancient law (patriarchs and prophets), the new life of grace (apostles, martyrs, and virgins), and the wisdom of the doctors. On contemplating these mysteries, the seer was overcome by fear and trembling; she heard a voice saying, "What you see is divine," and dared not look any further. At this point, however, there appears the figure of Scientia Dei, the Knowledge of God, standing in a building that represents the heavenly City or the Church. Turning her gaze now to the pillar of the Word, now to the people entering the building, she warns these Christians to remember their Creator. A throng of angels worships her with fear and love, while people identified as those "compelled to come in" (Luke 14:23) look on with pure fright.

In the illuminated Rupertsberg manuscript, Scientia Dei appears as a veiled woman with one hand raised in a gesture

---

10. *Scivias* III.4. On this vision see Peter Dronke, *"Arbor Caritatis,"* in P. L. Heyworth, ed., *Medieval Studies for J. A. W. Bennett* (Oxford, 1981): 228–33.

of forbearance. She is colored entirely with gold leaf and set off by the backdrop of a starry sky. Suppliant angels surround her on either side, flanked by a cluster of reverent people on her right and scoffers on her left.[11] According to the heavenly voice:

> That image denotes the Knowledge of God, for she watches over all people and all things in heaven and on earth, being of such radiance and brightness that, for the measureless splendor that shines in her, you cannot gaze on her face or on the garments she wears. For she is awesome in terror as the Thunderer's lightning, and gentle in goodness as the sunshine. Hence, in her terror and her gentleness, she is incomprehensible to mortals, because of the dread radiance of divinity in her face and the brightness that dwells in her as the robe of her beauty. She is like the sun, which none can contemplate in its blazing face or in the glorious garment of its rays. For she is with all and in all, and of beauty so great in her mystery that no one could know how sweetly she bears with people, and with what unfathomable mercy she spares them.[12]

This vision occurs early in a long series revealing the virtues and their attributes. Scientia Dei, more than any other, embodies a paradoxical union of tenderness, radiance, and terror—recalling the divine fire, which, as Hildegard said in her preface, came upon her not burning but warming like the sunlight. Terrible yet tempered, gentle yet dreadful, she conveys both the awesome beauty of divine things and the saving restraint—the "veiled" quality—that makes epiphanies bearable. With her blazing face and shining garments, she recalls the evangelists' portrait of the transfigured Christ, but still more Sophia in the Wisdom of Solomon.

> For she is the splendor of the eternal light,
> And immaculate mirror of God's majesty,
> And image of his goodness. . . .

11. The only other illustrated *Scivias* ms (Heidelberg, Cod. Sal. X.16, fol. 176ᵛ), which was prepared from independent exemplars without Hildegard's supervision, diverges from the text. Instead of the female figure described in the vision, it represents Scientia Dei as a bearded old man.

12. *Scivias* III.4.15, p. 401.

For she is more beautiful than the sun,
and above all the order of the stars:
compared with the light, she is found before it. . . .

Therefore she reaches from end to end mightily
and orders all things sweetly.

(Wisd. 7:26–8:1)

Theologically, Scientia Dei represents both the providence of God, admonishing sinners with patience because she "knows the quality of each," and the self-knowledge she mediates to all who encounter her. The genitive in her name is double-edged: to "see" the Knowledge of God means in effect to see that one is known by God. The visionary, at first too frightened to gaze on the mysteries before her, was able to endure the revelation when it was mitigated by the *suavitas* of a woman. But, like all theophanies, her vision also reveals and revels in its own incompleteness. In the very act of disclosure, it unveils depths that cannot be disclosed.[13]

Somewhat later in the *Scivias*, Hildegard saw a similar image of Sapientia, representing the activity of divine Wisdom in Church and cosmos.[14] Clad in a golden tunic, with a crown and a jeweled stole to proclaim her royalty, she stands on a platform supported by seven pillars—the traditional iconography of the House of Wisdom (Prov. 9:1). Like Scientia Dei, she is *terribilis et blanda*, "terrible and mild to every creature," and, although she reveals herself to the seer, the mind's eye rebounds from her face and her feet remain concealed from view, because "to God alone her secrets are manifest." Like Wisdom in the eighth chapter of Proverbs, Sapientia is revealed as creatrix and ruler of the world she has made. "Hence she reverently folds her hands before her breast: this is the power that Wisdom sagely binds to herself, directing

13. Cf. George Tavard on the Biblical Sophia: "Wisdom is that which man can know of God's glory, or, equivalently, that of God which is communicable to man." *Woman in Christian Tradition* (Notre Dame, 1973): 24.
14. *Scivias* III.9.25, pp. 538–39.

all her work so that none can resist her at all, neither by cunning nor by force." As Queen Consort, she enjoys the bridal chamber of the Most High, for "she is the display of great beauty gleaming in God . . . united with him in a most tender embrace, in a dance of blazing love."

With this memorable image, the seer reinterpreted the primitive notion of a *hieros gamos*, or marriage of the gods, to proclaim the oneness of the hidden God with his self-revelation—or, alternatively, one might say that this religious insight is "remythologized" back into its primordial form. Idea and image alike derive from the Old Testament, especially the Wisdom of Solomon, which declares that "the Lord of all has loved" Sophia (8:3), and Proverbs, which describes her as "playing before [God] at all times, playing in the sphere of the earth" (8:30–31). Hildegard characterized this "play" as *tripudium*, a festal dance: God and his partner join in an eternal cosmic play, which expands to embrace all creation in the *symphonia* of the saints and angels.[15]

As the Bride of God, Sapientia is identical with her alter ego, Caritas: "Wisdom and Love are one," and again, "Love and the foreknowledge of God agree in one."[16] In the *Book of Life's Merits*, Sapientia is called "a most loving mistress in [God's] lovely embrace," and elsewhere Hildegard wrote that she "pleased the heart of almighty and omnipotent God . . . for she was with him always and shall abide with him forever."[17] Caritas, in the same work, remarks, "I am the most loving consort of the throne of God, and God hides no counsel from me. I keep the royal marriage bed, and all that is God's

15. St. Jerome wrote that in the new Jerusalem, virgins would dance for joy in the streets "et tripudiante saltatu, dicent cum David: Saltabo et ludam in conspectu Domini." *Comment. in Zachariam* II.8.5, CCSL 76a: 809. In a sequence to St. Rupert, Hildegard contrasted the wild leaping of a pagan orgy (*saltatio antiquae speluncae*) with the choral dances of heaven. *Lieder* no. 37: 252–56.

16. *Explanatio Symboli S. Athanasii*, PL 197: 1067bc; DOD III.10.4, PL 197: 1001b.

17. LVM I.46 and IV.38, Pitra 23 and 160.

is mine as well" (cf. Wisd. 9:4, John 16:15).[18] This Virtue "has given the High King the kiss of peace," proclaims an anti-phon, thus referring the familiar liturgical act back to its ar-chetype in heaven.[19]

In such theophanies, erotic symbolism manifests the love not only *of* God but also *in* God. Whereas theologians like Richard of St. Victor described the Trinitarian relations in highly abstract, carefully nuanced terms,[20] Hildegard's visions are charged with the much more primitive and powerful ap-peal of eros. Yet, despite their immediacy, the visions do not remain simple; beginning with a single flash of insight, they complicate themselves as they unfold. For example, at the close of a letter, Hildegard subscribed a blessing that turns into a visionary prose poem.

> May the Holy Spirit cleanse you from all faults of malice
> and win you the friendship of Love, most sweet, most
>   tender,
> who captured the mighty stag
> and poured forth song above all heavens
> and entered the bridal chamber of all the King's
>   mysteries
> and revealed herself in all her beauty
> in the mirror of the cherubim.[21]

Caritas first comes to the seer's mind as a *virtus*, an antithesis to the unwelcome *vitia*; but once called forth she becomes a figure of mythic proportions, the royal bride. Her emblems, the stag (cf. Ps. 41:2) and the mirror, symbolize heavenly de-sire and the splendor of God. By summoning Love's grandeur before the eyes of her friend, Hildegard aimed to lead him from a simple ethical directive to a hope of sharing in the everlasting nuptials.

---

18. LVM III.8, Pitra 108.
19. *Lieder* no. 16: 228.
20. Richard of St. Victor, *De Trinitate*, ed. Jean Ribaillier (Paris, 1958); see especially Book III, trans. Grover Zinn, in Richard of St. Victor, *The Twelve Patriarchs* (New York, 1979).
21. Ep. 142, Pitra 567.

THE MIRROR OF PROVIDENCE, THE
VIRGIN SPRING, AND THE TREE OF LIFE

The "mirror of the cherubim" (cf. Wisd. 7:26) is an image of rich theological content. Pseudo-Dionysius had used mirrors as a metaphor for the celestial hierarchies,[22] and Hildegard drew on this familiar usage in the *Activity of God*, where she heard Christ address the Father as *paternum speculum*, the mirror in whose brightness all the angels shine.[23] As we have seen, she also characterized the medium of her visions as a kind of mirror, the "reflection of the living Light," wherein she could observe all things present and future as they exist in God. Her visionary experience thus lends concrete reality to a conventional metaphor for the world of ideas. Among medieval Platonists, from Augustine to Hildegard's contemporaries, it was a commonplace to regard the empirical world as a mere shadow or reflection of the true life possessed by creatures in the mind of God.[24] Poets and mythographers illustrated the idea with the image of a fountain, at once well of life (*fons vitae*) and mirror of providence. One popular source for this topos was *The Marriage of Philology and Mercury*, in which the heroine prays before her apotheosis to a certain *virgo fontana*, whom John of Salisbury interpreted as Sapientia.[25] Bernard Silvestris, in his *Cosmographia*, characterized the divine intellect or Noys (a feminine persona, despite grammatical gender) as a *fons luminis* mirroring the eternal notions and the hidden decrees of God's will.[26] Endelechia, the world

22. Pseudo-Dionysius, *De coelesti hierarchia* 3.2, PG 3: 173a; cf. Richard of St. Victor, *Benjamin Major* 5.14, PL 196: 187ab.

23. DOD III.10.14, PL 197: 1016a; cf. *Ordo virtutum* 191.

24. See for example Augustine, *In Joannem* 2.1.16, PL 35: 1387; Erigena, *Periphyseon* III.16, PL 122: 667a; Honorius, *Liber XII quaestionum* 1, PL 172: 1178c and *Elucidarium* I.4, 1112b; Rupert of Deutz, *De sancta Trinitate, In Genesim* I.5, CCCM 21: 132–33; Alan of Lille, *Theologicae regulae* 45, PL 210: 641b. The ultimate source is *Timaeus* 29e.

25. *De Nuptiis Philologiae et Mercurii* II.205, ed. and trans. Luciano Lenaz (Padua, 1975): 166; John of Salisbury, *Metalogicon* IV.36, trans. Daniel McGarry (Berkeley, 1962): 262–63.

26. Bernard Silvestris, *Cosmographia* II.13, ed. Peter Dronke, 102; trans. Winthrop Wetherbee (New York, 1973): 73–74.

soul, emanates from Noys in the form of a "liquid, flowing fountain."

Caritas as primordial virgin, or virgin spring, dominates the latest and most complex of Hildegard's sapiential visions. Near the end of the *Activity of God*, she saw Caritas with her two companions, Humilitas and Pax, presiding over the "living fountain" that both quickens and reflects all creatures.

> And I saw three images in the middle of the south side [of the building]. Two stood in a limpid well fenced by a round, finely crafted wall of porous stone, as if they were rooted in the well—just as trees sometimes appear to grow in water. One of these was dressed in purple but the other in such dazzling white that I could not gaze on them to the full. The third stood outside the well upon the stone, clothed in a white robe, and her face shone with such brightness that it made me turn my face away. And before them the blessed orders of saints appeared like clouds on which they gazed with love.[27]

Although the seer perceived three figures, one of them speaks for all, as in Abraham's celebrated vision of the Trinity (Genesis 18). Caritas explains that creation is itself theophany: in the utterance of the Word, divine Love gives life to the forms that have always glimmered in her unseen mirror. And in prophecy the seer is granted a privileged glimpse into that selfsame luminous source.

> The first figure said, "I, Love, am the glory of the living God. Wisdom has done her work with me, and Humility rooted in the living fountain is my helper, and Peace is her companion. And by the splendor that I am, the living light of the blessed angels glows, for, as a ray of light flashes from its source, so this splendor shines in the blessed angels. Nor could it do otherwise, since no light lacks radiance. It was I who wrote humanity, which is rooted in me like a reflection in water. Hence I am the living fountain, because all created things were reflected in me; and, according to this reflection, mankind was made with fire and water, as I myself am fire and living water. . . .
>
> "And my glory overshadowed the prophets, who by holy

27. DOD III.8.1, PL 197: 979b.

inspiration predicted things to come, as all that God wished to make was foreshadowed in him before it came to be. But Reason utters her voice, and the sound of the voice is like thought, and the spoken word like a work. Now from this shadow there issued the book *Scivias*, through the form of a woman who was but a shadow of strength and health, because these vital forces were not at work in her.

"Thus, the Spirit of God is a living fountain that he distributes among all his works, which also draw life from him and possess their vitality through him, like reflections in water. And no being can plainly see whence it lives, but each merely senses that which moves it. . . .

"Indeed, the purity of the living God is a leaping fountain, resplendent with his glory. In that splendor, God with great love embraces all things, whose reflections appeared in the leaping fountain before he bade them come forth in their own forms. And all creatures shone resplendent in me, Love, and my splendor made their features visible as a reflection reveals a form. And in Humility, my helper, creation came forth through the bidding of God. In that same humility, God bowed down to me to restore the dry leaves that had fallen, in that bliss by which he can do all that he wishes. For he had formed them from earth, and thence he delivered them after their fall."[28]

This Caritas is more abstract than Hildegard's visions of the divine Bride: she is married now to the God of the philosophers. The gleaming font suggests both inexhaustible vitality and the light of knowledge, recalling the Psalmist's image: "With you is the fountain of life, and in your light we shall see light" (Ps. 35:10).[29] Within this splendor, the ambiguous *umbra* connotes foreshadowing as well as overshadowing: both the preexistence of all beings through their exemplars in the divine Wisdom and the inspiration that reveals these exemplars to the prophets. Taking her own experience as a model, Hildegard understood *obumbratio* paradoxically as illumination: the prophet, a "mere shadow," is overshadowed by the divine light, which enables her to see that light in

28. DOD III.8.2, PL 197: 979c–81a.

29. An even more immediate source for the image may be the Pentecostal hymn "Veni Creator," in which the Holy Spirit is invoked as "Fons vivus, ignis, caritas / Et spiritalis unctio."

which all being is foreshadowed. Equally suggestive is the analogy that likens the speaker, the voice, and the spoken word to divine rationality, thought, and work, recasting an old similitude for the Trinity and applying it to prophetic creation.[30] Even the *Scivias*, revealed "through the form of a woman," embodies one such utterance of the divine Voice, a lesser incarnation of the Word. So Hildegard, as a feeble woman empowered by the glory of God, can compare herself to the Virgin Annunciate overshadowed by the Holy Spirit.

Together with the woman and the fountain, the vision evokes yet a third image of fecundity: the tree of life. The archetypal Adam is not only "written" on the face of the waters—"like a shimmering flame," as the seer would tell Guibert—but also "rooted" in it like a tree. And Caritas refers to lost souls as "dry leaves that had fallen" from the family tree of mankind. This conception probably derives from the tree of Jesse iconography, which represents the patriarchs and prophets in organic unity with Christ. But the arboreal image has many other Biblical associations. Psalm 1 compares the blessed man to a tree growing beside streams of water; Ezekiel (17:24) prophesies that God will wither the green tree and make the dry tree flourish (an image frequently applied to the Virgin); and Wisdom in Prov. 3:18 is called a tree of life, a metaphor carried to great lengths in Ecclesiasticus 24. Sapientia has "taken root among the honored people"; she is "exalted like a cedar in Lebanon, and like a cypress on Mount Zion" (24:16–17). Trees of charity also abound in medieval art and literature.[31] Caritas in this vision is rooted as an evergreen tree in the well that she herself is.

The images need not be visually coherent: they are not meant to be elements in a single picture but successive flashes of perception. Through the sheer abundance of its imagery,

---

30. Cf. Augustine, *De Trinitate* IX.12, and Hildegard's Ep. 14, PL 197: 170d: "Rationalitas etiam tres vires habet, scilicet sonum, verbum, sufflatum. In Patre Filius est, ut verbum in sono, Spiritus sanctus in utroque, ut sufflatus in sono et verbo."

31. Dronke, *"Arbor Caritatis"*; Manfred Lurker, *Der Baum in Glauben und Kunst* (Baden-Baden, 1976).

the vision attempts to convey the plenitude of being that creatures possess in God. Caritas, rising from the water like a celestial Venus, gives the whole theophany a feminine name and form.

THE ETERNAL COUNSEL

From the exemplarist point of view, it seems fitting that if all created things preexist eternally in the mind of God, the same should be true a fortiori of the incarnate Word. Hence it is not surprising that in the twelfth century, which witnessed such a resurgence of Christian Platonism, theologians like Rupert of Deutz and Honorius first propounded the absolute predestination of Christ: the doctrine that God would have become man even if man had never sinned.[32] This "Scotist" view of the Incarnation, championed in the later Middle Ages by Robert Grosseteste, the Oxford Franciscans, and Duns Scotus, stands in contrast to the more familiar and widespread view set forth in Anselm's *Cur Deus Homo*, namely that God became man because thus, and not otherwise, could the fall of Adam be redeemed. Although Hildegard did not ask the hypothetical question "whether God would have become man if man had not sinned," she shared the absolutist view of her fellow German Benedictines. The Incarnation was, for her, the "eternal counsel" of Ps. 32:11—the divine purpose for which the world was made. Thus, at the beginning of *Scivias* III, she prayed for strength "to utter the divine purpose that was ordained in the ancient counsel, how you willed your Son to be incarnate, to become a man in the order of time, willing this before all creation in your simplicity . . . that your Son . . .

---

32. On this doctrine see J.-M. Bissen, "La tradition sur la prédestination absolue de Jésus-Christ du VIIᵉ au XIVᵉ siècles," *France franciscaine* 22 (1939): 9–34; Rudolf Haubst, *Vom Sinn der Menschwerdung. "Cur Deus Homo"* (Munich, 1969), pt. III; James McEvoy, "The Absolute Predestination of Christ in the Theology of Robert Grosseteste," in *Sapientiae Doctrina* (Louvain, 1980): 212–30.

might be truly clothed in humanity, assuming the form of man for the sake of man."[33]

In the Word begotten before all ages, the Father already intended his Son's incarnation and his mystical body, the Church. Hence Hildegard could pray that its empirical members might, so to speak, be united with their exemplars in that Body of Christ which preceded time.

> O eternal God,
> now be pleased
> so to burn in that love
> that we may become those limbs
> that you made in the same love
> when you begot your Son
> in the primeval dawn
> before all creation.[34]

In Hildegard's lexicon of symbols, the rising sun so frequently denotes the Virgin that the "primeval dawn" in this lyric inevitably calls her to mind as the Mother predestined before the world began.

The fulfillment of God's ancient counsel through Mary, as well as the traditional identification of Christ with Sophia, led Hildegard to link the idea of his predestination preeminently with the feminine. It is this doctrine that underlies one of her most alluring visions, as described around 1158–1161 in a letter to Adam, Cistercian abbot of Ebrach.

> And I saw one like a lovely maiden, her face gleaming with such radiant splendor that I could not perfectly behold her. Whiter than snow was her mantle and more shining than the stars, and her shoes were of the finest gold. In her right hand she held the sun and moon and tenderly embraced them. And on her breast was an ivory tablet in which there appeared the form of a man, the color of sapphire; and all creation called this maiden Lady. Now she spoke to the form that appeared in her bosom, saying, "With you is the beginning in the day of your

---

33. *Scivias* III.1, p. 329. Cf. II.1.11, p. 118: "Quod Verbo Dei incarnato illud magnum et antiquum consilium visum est."

34. *Lieder* no. 2: 214.

virtue, in the splendor of the holy ones; I bore you from the
womb before the morning star."[35]

(Ps. 109:3)

Caritas reveals herself here at her most sublimely feminine;
one could almost call her *courtoise*.[36] Elsewhere the texts name
her as a neutral *imago* or *forma hominis*; but here she is, like
the Virgin, a *pulcherrima puella*.

The verse she utters, "I bore you from the womb before the
morning star," had been used in the early Church as a proof
text for the eternal generation of the Word.[37] But its phrasing
obviously suits a mother better than a father, so the verse
readily acquired Marian connotations. In the divine office it
occurs as an antiphon for Christmas and again for Candle-
mas, or the Purification of Mary.[38] Such a transposition, like
the reading of sapiential lessons on feasts of the Virgin, naturally suggests a parallel between the eternal generation and
the temporal birth of Christ—and thus between his divine
Father and his human mother. In Hildegard's vision Caritas
is, as it were, the eternal archetype of Mary, hence both maid
and lady. As a divine yet maternal being, she mediates between Christ's timeless and his temporal birth.

In an earlier vision of the Trinity, Hildegard had seen the
eternal Son as a "human form, the color of sapphire"—a hue
she associated with the divinity and predestination of the
Word (cf. Exod. 24:10).[39] This related image indicates that
what Caritas displays on her ivory tablet is the Child of Mary,
not as an infant but as the One "born before the morning
star." The vision also recalls the iconographic type known as
the Virgin of the Sign (cf. Isa. 7:14), in which Mary stands
with her arms raised in prayer and the Christ Child portrayed

---

35. Ep. 30, PL 197: 192d.
36. Cf. Peter Dronke's exaggerated but provocative remarks on the
"courtly" aspects of this vision in *Medieval Latin and the Rise of European Love-
Lyric*, 2nd ed. (Oxford, 1968), I: 66–69.
37. See for example Ambrose, *De fide* 4.8, PL 16: 634.
38. Frénaud, "Le Culte de Notre Dame" 193, 198.
39. *Scivias* II.2, p. 124. Cf. Christel Meier, "Die Bedeutung der Farben im
Werk Hildegards von Bingen," *Frühmittelalterliche Studien* 6 (1972): 266–69.

in a medallion over her breast. Such iconography represents the Incarnation not as a fulfilled event but as the expectation of the prophets—in other words, the predestination of Christ.[40]

This mode of portraying the Virgin may also have inspired an unusual miniature of Sapientia and Christ that sheds particular light on Hildegard's vision. Executed in Hildesheim about 1160, the painting takes its place in a cycle between the creation of Eve and the Annunciation to Mary. It depicts a crowned figure of Sapientia with uplifted face and arms, supporting a semicircular medallion with a bust of Christ (Fig. 1).[41] Around her are ranged the patriarchs and prophets with scrolls foretelling the Incarnation, and on her scapular is inscribed the text of Prov. 8:30 (now effaced): "I was with him, fashioning all." This Sapientia, like Hildegard's Caritas, is a mysterious persona prefiguring Christ and Mary but distinct from both; she embodies God's decision to create a universe in order that he might enter it as a man.

The doctrine of absolute predestination, as taught by other medieval theologians, almost always occurs in a sapiential context. As early as the ninth century Erigena, influenced by the exemplarism of the Eastern fathers, opined that the Word had descended in order to reunite the primordial causes that inhere in his divinity with their created effects, by means of his humanity.[42] Christ thus mediates cosmic unity by completing the cycle of emanation and return, so that both temporal creatures and eternal exemplars are "saved" by their reunion in the Word. In the *Periphyseon* Erigena associated these *causae primordiales* with the Platonic ideas, of course, but also with the *virtutes*—goodness, wisdom, reason, power, justice, and the like—that play such a significant role in Hildegard's

40. "Maria, Marienbild," *Lexikon der christlichen Ikonographie* III: 159–60; figs. 6 and 11.

41. Albert Böckler, *Deutsche Buchmalerei vorgotischer Zeit* (Königstein, 1953): 53; Ernst Guldan, *Eva und Maria* (Graz and Cologne, 1966): 47–48, 171–72, and figs. 23, 24, 26.

42. Erigena, *Periphyseon* (*De divisione naturae*) V.24, PL 122: 912ab; McEvoy, "Absolute Predestination" 222, n. 23.

Fig. 1. *Sapientia and the eternal counsel.* Divine Wisdom, surrounded by patriarchs and prophets, upholds a medallion revealing Christ to come. Hildesheim Missal, fol. 11ʳ. Courtesy of Rheinisches Bildarchiv and Freiherr von Fürstenberg.

theology.[43] These virtues, ideas, or causes are also identified with the divine names of the Pseudo-Dionysius; in later Orthodox thought they are most commonly known as uncreated energies. It would not be amiss to regard Hildegard's Virtues in the same light, although her treatment of them is less philosophically sophisticated.

While it is unlikely that she knew Erigena's work directly, Hildegard may well have known Honorius's *Clavis physicae*, a digest of the *Periphyseon*. Quoting Maximus the Confessor, Honorius said that "insofar as the human intellect ascends through charity, so far the divine wisdom descends through mercy; and this is the cause and substance of all virtues. Therefore, every theophany, that is every virtue, which begins to be formed in this life in the righteous, . . . is accomplished both by God and by themselves."[44] A similar notion of synergy underlies Hildegard's vision of the living fountain, which alludes to the emanation and return of the Virtues through the incarnate Word. "Love and Humility," states the gloss, "dwell in the all-pure being of God, whence the streams of blessedness flow. For these two Virtues reveal the only Son of God, made known throughout the world for the deliverance and restoration of man. . . . For Love and Humility came down to earth with the Son of God, and brought him back to heaven when he returned."[45] Such formulations, which could be paralleled from the seer's descriptions of numerous other Virtues, express a basically Eastern or Erigenean theology of grace strongly overlaid by Western allegorical conventions. The latter, with their insistence that the Virtues must be feminine personae, only reinforced Hildegard's already strong

43. Erigena, *Periphyseon* II.36, PL 122: 615d–16a. Causae itaque primordiales sunt, quod et in praecedentibus dixeram, quas Graeci ideas vocant, hoc est, species vel formas aeternas et incommutabiles rationes, secundum quas, et in quibus visibilis et invisibilis mundus formatur et regitur.

44. Honorius, *Clavis physicae* 13, ed. Paolo Lucentini (Rome, 1974): 10. Honorius was citing *Periphyseon* II, PL 122: 1205cd, and Erigena in turn was quoting Maximus the Confessor's *Ambigua* on Gregory of Nazianzen's *Sermo de hospitalitate*.

45. DOD III.8.3, PL 197: 981d–82a.

tendency to associate the feminine with the mediation of grace and the predestination of Christ.

In the text just cited, however, the Incarnation is still seen in the context of sin. Honorius, the popularizer of Erigena, had already carried the question further. Following the old Irenaean dictum that "God became man so that man might become God," he stated baldly that "the cause of Christ's Incarnation was the predestined deification of man. . . . And therefore it does not follow that sin was the cause of his Incarnation; rather, it follows that sin could not change the purpose of God concerning the deification of man."[46] This optimistic assertion presupposes that grace is fully capable of bridging the chasm between God and humanity, a belief justified by the Biblical promise that we shall "become partakers of the divine nature" (II Pet. 1:4). Where sin is deemphasized, the accent falls instead on the necessary fulfillment of God's loving will, an approach that harmonizes well with the outlook of the sapiential books. Wisdom—expressing herself freely in creation, delighting in the children of men (Prov. 8:31), resting in the holy city (Ecclus. 24:15), and raising up prophets and friends of God (Wisd. 7:27)—could even be seen as a figure of the incarnate Christ as he might have come, were it not for the tragedy of sin. Thus, Rupert of Deutz, citing Augustine's argument that all the elect would have been born to Adam and Eve even if they had never fallen, applies the same reasoning a fortiori to Christ: "what should we think of that head and king of all elect angels and men, but that he above all did not require sin as a necessary cause in order to become a man among men, to enjoy the delights of his love among the sons of men?"[47]

Honorius and Rupert, by raising the hypothetical question of an unfallen world, highlighted the sapiential context in which many of their less audacious contemporaries also

46. Honorius, *Libellus octo quaestionum*, PL 172: 1187c. See Bissen, "La tradition sur la prédestination absolue," for Byzantine antecedents of this motif.

47. Rupert of Deutz, *De gloria et honore Filii hominis*, super Matt. 13, CCCM 29: 415. Cf. Augustine, *De civitate Dei* XIV.23, CCSL 48: 444–45.

viewed the predestination of Christ. The *Glossa ordinaria* indicates how widely a moderate version of the doctrine was taught and accepted. Under Ecclus. 24:14, where Sophia proclaims, "I was created from the beginning and before the ages," the glossator referred to "the mystery (*sacramentum*) of the Incarnation, foreknown and predestined before the ages."[48] This tendency is also evident in popular devotional works, especially from Benedictine milieus. The illustrated text *De laudibus sanctae crucis* (*In Praise of the Holy Cross*) is subtitled, "Dialogue . . . on the fact that the Lamb was slain from the foundation of the world."[49] In the *Speculum virginum* (*Mirror of Virgins*), a favorite manual for nuns, the predestination of Christ and Mary is set within the general context of exemplarism.

> Therefore, if all things existed in the Wisdom of the Word of God, waiting to be unfolded in their different species according to their preordained nature, manner, and order, how could the Mother not preexist with the Son, whose conception and birth opened the way for the whole rational creation to be sanctified, unified, and restored to peace? How could she be absent, in whom an eternal decree had laid the foundation of an eternal building, the celestial Jerusalem?[50]

This text, which Hildegard might easily have known, closely connects the ideas of exemplarity and eternal predestination with Sapientia, Mary, and "the Jerusalem above, which is our mother" (Gal. 4:26).[51] Almost interchangeably, these three feminine figures point to the Incarnation and its fruit, the society of the redeemed, as the final cause of creation.

Using the same symbolic language, Hildegard expressed this predestinarian optimism when she wrote that Christ's

---

48. *Glossa ordinaria*, PL 113: 1208d.

49. On this work see Albert Böckler, *Die Regensburg-Prüfeninger Buchmalerei des 12. und 13. Jahrhunderts* (Munich, 1924): 33–41.

50. London BL Arundel MS. 44, fol. 41ʳ.

51. The *Speculum virginum*, written in the first half of the twelfth century, was especially popular in the Rhineland. On the text and its manuscript tradition see Matthäus Bernards, *Speculum virginum. Geistigkeit und Seelenleben der Frau im Hochmittelalter* (Cologne and Graz, 1955).

bride, "the heavenly Jerusalem, who was to be adorned by the supreme architect, almighty God, appeared in his presence as the matrix (*materia*) of all things before the creation of the world."[52] Hildegard used the word *materia* in several senses, to denote matter, material cause, motive, or means; but the root senses of *mater* and *matrix* (womb or, more abstractly, substrate) are near at hand.[53] The same constellation of meanings occurs in a vision of Caritas as divine mother, in which the train of thought proceeds from the eternal counsel to the creation of the world.

> And I heard a voice saying to me, "This maiden whom you see is Love, who has her dwelling place in eternity. When God wished to create the world, he leaned down in the tenderest love and provided all that was needed, as a father prepares an inheritance for his son. And thus in a mighty blaze he ordained all his works. Then creation recognized its Creator in its own forms and appearances. For in the beginning, when God said, 'Let it be!' and it came to pass, the means and the matrix of creation was Love, because all creation was formed through her as in the twinkling of an eye."[54]

When this text introduces masculine theological symbols, describing the world as an inheritance laid up by the Father for the Son, Caritas is transformed from a feminine persona into the more neutral *materia creaturae*.[55] She can now be regarded mythologically as the mother and womb of being, like Silva

---

52. Ep. 47, PL 197: 227d.

53. The *Oxford Latin Dictionary* defines *materia* (meaning 8) as "the condition whereby an action or situation is effected, means, occasion, etc." See medieval examples in the *Novum glossarium Mediae Latinitatis* for the sense of "that which provokes an action or gives occasion for it; motive." Hildegard's usage of the terms *materia* and *forma* should not be interpreted in an Aristotelian sense, which would be alien to her metaphysics.

54. Ep. 30, PL 197: 193a.

55. Cf. *Causae et curae* 1, p. 1: "When God wished to make the world, therefore, he made it from nothing; but the *materia* of the world existed in his will. For when the will of God revealed itself to accomplish the work, the *materia* of the world at once proceeded from his will even as God wished, as a dark and formless globe." "Material cause" might be an appropriate translation here. In DOD II.5.17, PL 197: 916c, the heaven and earth of Gen. 1:1 are glossed as *lucida materia* and *turbulenta materia*.

in Bernard Silvestris's *Cosmographia,* or allegorically as a trope to indicate that God created the world from no substance but his own.

But the trope remains irrepressibly feminine in context. The three archetypal mothers in Hildegard's visions—Caritas, Mary, Ecclesia—all bring God into the world in the flesh. Thus, Christ is predestined of eternal Love, who creates the world to provide the substance of his body; in the fullness of time he is born once of the Virgin and continually of the Church, until his mystical body is fulfilled. Through these concordant images of maternity, Hildegard expressed her conviction that the universe exists for the sake of the incarnate Christ. The eternal feminine, in her several guises, links God's coming into the world with the world's own coming to be.

WISDOM AS CREATRIX AND
ANIMA MUNDI

It is surely no accident that, while masculine imagery of the Creator tends to stress God's transcendence, feminine metaphors place the accent on immanence. As creatrix, Hildegard's Sapientia is no unmoved mover, ordering the universe from on high or even—like the Creator in contemporary paintings—molding the nascent world in almighty hands. On the contrary, she creates the cosmos by existing within it, her ubiquity expressed through the image of ceaseless or circular motion.

> O power of Wisdom!
> You encompassed the cosmos,
> encircling and embracing all
> in one living orbit
> with your three wings:
> one soars on high,
> one distills the earth's essence,
> and the third hovers everywhere.
> Praise to you, Wisdom, fitting praise![56]

56. See Appendix B, no. 1; discussion in Peter Dronke, *Poetic Individuality in the Middle Ages* (Oxford, 1970): 157.

Hildegard's keen sense of divine immanence led her to envisage the creative power not as a force propelling the world from without but as an ambience enfolding it and quickening it from within. The three wings evoke the three Persons of the Trinity: the Father enthroned on high, the Son rising from the earth, and the Spirit hovering everywhere.[57] Still more, the all-pervading presence recalls the motif of Sophia's cosmic odyssey.

> I have circled the vault of heaven alone,
> and pierced the depth of the abyss,
> I have walked amid the waves of the
>   sea,
> and stood upon all the earth.
> (Ecclus. 24:8–9)

At one point Hildegard sensed this affinity between Wisdom and the cosmos so strongly that she identified the two. Expounding a verse from the Song of Songs—a book to which she paid surprisingly little attention on the whole—she explained that "when Solomon felt himself imbued with wisdom, he spoke to her as to a woman in the familiar language of love." Proceeding further, she declared that the bridegroom and bride, or Solomon and Sapientia, are types of the Creator and the cosmos. Wisdom explains:

> As I ordained all things when I circled the vault of heaven, so also in Solomon I spoke of the Creator's love for creation, and the creature's for the Creator. He adorned her when he made her, for he loved her greatly; and she sought a kiss from him when she obeyed him. . . . And I compare the mutual love of Creator and creature to the love and fidelity in which God united man and woman to bring forth children. And as every creature came forth from God, so too every creature looks to God in its service, doing nothing without his command—just as a woman looks up to her husband to fulfill his bidding and strives to please him.[58]

57. Barbara Grant, "Five Liturgical Songs by Hildegard von Bingen," *Signs* 5 (1980): 564.
58. LVM V.39, Pitra 197.

Classic interpreters of the Song of Songs understood the Bride as the Church, the soul, or the Virgin Mary; but Hildegard saw in her the world wedded to its Maker. So intimate in her view is the bond between divine Wisdom and the creature's response, that Sapientia and "Creatura" merge. The marriage, then, represents the total activity of God in the world—shaping Wisdom, nurturing Love, divine energy seeking the creature's cooperation to sustain her union with him, which is already given in the mere fact of being. And herein lies another reason for the feminine gender. As Hildegard's use of the marriage analogy shows, she shared her contemporaries' view of the female as essentially receptive, submissive, and obedient. For this reason the cosmos must naturally be "feminine" vis-à-vis the Creator. But the seer transcended this stereotype insofar as she assimilated this limited view of the female with the perspective of the sapiential books of Scripture, in which the feminine is also a dimension of God.

Sapientia eludes all precise definition, for the obvious reason that her gender makes it impossible to identify her with any fixed point of dogma. Yet neither does she exclude or supplant these fixed points. She is, rather, a unique perspective on them—a whole realm of associations, images, and spiritual perceptions that may bear on aspects of Christ, or Mary, or the Trinity, but cannot finally be reduced to these. In her manifestation as the divine presence in the cosmos, she is like the Shechinah of Jewish mysticism, or the Spirit of the Lord that "filled the whole earth" (Wisd. 1:7), or the goddess Natura sung by the philosopher-poets.[59] Caritas in the *Book of Life's Merits* is both the élan vital, the elemental force that invigorates nature, and the spiritual force that instills new life in the soul. "I am the air," she sings, "I who nourish all green and growing life, I who bring ripe fruit from the flower. For I am skilled in every breath of the Spirit of God, so I pour out the most limpid streams. From good sighing I bring weeping,

---

59. See George Economou, *The Goddess Natura in Medieval Literature* (Cambridge, Mass., 1972).

from tears a sweet fragrance through holy actions."[60] Such is
"Love's Answer to Envy" in the dramatic context of this passage: envy stunts the verdant grass with his poison, but the
more he rages the more it grows. Natural and spiritual life are
one, and love is unquenchable in both.

In a sequence on the Holy Spirit, it is Caritas as the third
person of the Trinity who makes the universe fruitful and one.

> O mighty passage, penetrating all
> in the heights, upon the earth,
> and in all deeps,
> you bind them and gather them
> all together.
> From you the clouds have their flowing,
> the ether its flight,
> the stones their moisture,
> the waters spurt forth in streams,
> and the earth exudes verdure.[61]

Nothing is more distinctively Hildegardian than this sense of
universal life, of a world aflame with vitality. But, perhaps
because of her sense of direct contact with God, she could not
help but see this life as divinity itself. So there is no goddess
Natura apart from God, no carefully graded scale of emana-
tions as in the works of Bernard Silvestris. The same "fiery
life" that is Caritas, "self-moving and active, is God [the Trin-
ity], one life in three energies."[62]

In medieval parlance, what Bergson would call the élan
vital was known as the anima mundi, the Platonic world soul:
"Vegetable in trees, sensible in beasts, rational in human
beings."[63] A few theologians, notably Peter Abelard and Wil-

60. LVM III.8, Pitra 107.
61. *Lieder* no. 19: 232–34.
62. DOD I.1.2, PL 197: 744a.
63. This inscription—"vegetabilis in arboribus, sensibilis in pecoribus, ra-
cionabilis in hominibus"—appears on a banderole held by Anima mundi in
the only known pictorial representation of her, which illustrates Honorius's
Clavis physicae; see Marie-Thérèse d'Alverny, "Le cosmos symbolique du douzième siècle," *Archives d'histoire doctrinale et littéraire du moyen âge* 28 (1953):
facing p. 46. The standard work is Tullio Gregory, *Anima mundi* (Florence,
1955).

liam of Conches, tried in the face of strong opposition to equate this anima mundi with the Holy Spirit. Plato, Abelard said in his *Christian Theology*, "rightly posited the world soul, that is the Holy Spirit, as the life of the universe," for "in God we live and move and have our being" (Acts 17:28).[64] Because the world soul "foresees the causes of all things that appear" (*Timaeus* 37b), it possesses the fullness of divine knowledge and is rightly inferred to be God.[65] Moreover, philosophers say that the world soul animates all bodies with life unless the hardness of their nature impedes it. "This is a beautiful poetic fiction," according to Abelard, because "the love of God, which we call the Holy Spirit, . . . gives life to some . . . and in others the same Spirit is said to remain empty because the hardness of their depravity resists it."[66] Thus, the anima mundi is divine because it is all-pervading, all-knowing, and life-creating, like the Holy Spirit or the love of God. Similarly, for William of Conches:

> The world soul is a natural energy by which some things possess movement alone, others growth, others sensation, others discernment. . . . But, as it seems to me, this natural energy is the Holy Spirit, that is, a divine and generous harmony. . . . It is rightly called a natural energy because by divine love all things grow and flourish. It is rightly called the world soul because by divine love and charity alone all things in the world live and possess life.[67]

Hildegard never mentioned the world soul by name, either because she did not know the term or perhaps because she knew the Cistercians had condemned the doctrine as one of Abelard's errors.[68] Nevertheless, the most celebrated of all her

---

64. Abelard, *Theologia christiana* I.72, CCCM 12: 101–2.

65. Abelard, *Theologia christiana* I.95: 111–12.

66. Abelard, *Theologia christiana* I.109: 117.

67. "Des commentaires inédits de Guillaume de Conches et de Nicolas Triveth sur la *Consolation de la philosophie* de Boèce," ed. Charles Jourdain in *Excursions historiques et philosophiques à travers le moyen âge* (Paris, 1888): 36–37.

68. Bernard of Clairvaux, *De erroribus Abaelardi* IV.10, PL 182: 1062b; "William of St. Thierry," *Disputatio adversus Petrum Abaelardum* V, PL 180: 265.

visions is, in effect, a revelation of Caritas in the guise of anima mundi.

At the outset of her work *On the Activity of God* (c. 1163), Hildegard saw "a beautiful and wonderful image, like a human form, in the mystery of God." On her head she wears a golden circlet, above which appears the bearded face of an older man. The figure has four magnificent wings, and, in the curvature of the upper pair, the heads of a fiery-eyed eagle and a man peer out to the left. The central figure's tunic glows like the sun; in her hands she holds a shining lamb; and under her feet a black monster and a serpent lie prostrate. According to the heavenly voice that glosses the vision, this figure is Caritas: "In the strength of unfailing divinity dwells Love, beautiful in election and marvelous in the gifts of the heavenly Father's mysteries, revealing man."[69] The gloss proceeds to allegorize other details. The golden circlet represents the Catholic faith; the head of the older man, God's kindness; the upper wings, love of God and neighbor; the two heads, contemplative and active lives; the lower wings, Love sustaining the just and the sinful; the shining garment, Christ's pure body; the lamb, his gentleness; the monster with the serpent, discord and the devil. All the aspects and activities of Caritas, then, relate to Christ and the Christian life (although the gloss does include a digression on the divine foreknowledge and angelic light).

But while the gloss concerns incarnate Love in the Church, the speech of Caritas herself is a paean to the élan vital. Like the Biblical Sophia or the Egyptian Isis, she sings her own praise.

> I am the supreme and fiery force who kindled every living spark, and I breathed forth no deadly thing—yet I permit them to be. As I circled the whirling sphere with my upper wings (that is, with wisdom), rightly I ordained it. And I am the fiery life of the essence of God: I flame above the beauty of the fields; I shine in the waters; I burn in the sun, the moon, and the stars. And, with the airy wind, I quicken all things vitally by

69. DOD I.1.3, PL 197: 744cd.

an unseen, all-sustaining life. For the air is alive in the verdure and the flowers; the waters flow as if they lived; the sun too lives in its light; and when the moon wanes it is rekindled by the light of the sun, as if it lived anew. Even the stars glisten in their light as if alive.[70]

Love established the pillars that uphold the earth, the "wings of the winds," which also "blaze like the breath that moves man without ceasing." Nothing in the macrocosm lacks its correlative in the microcosm; nothing in the world is mortal or meaningless.

> I also am Reason. Mine is the blast of the resounding Word through which all creation came to be, and I quickened all things with my breath so that not one of them is mortal in its kind; for I am Life. Indeed I am Life, whole and undivided— not hewn from any stone, or budded from branches, or rooted in virile strength; but all that lives has its root in me. For Reason is the root whose blossom is the resounding Word. So, because God is rational, how could it be possible for him not to work? Now every work of his blossoms through man, whom he made to his image and likeness; and he sealed all creatures after their measure in man himself. For God desired from eternity that his work, man, should come to be, and when he had completed that work, he gave man all creatures so that he could work with them, just as God himself had made man as his own work.

Life, reason (*racionalitas*), and work (*opus*): here again, in altered form, is the triad from the vision of the living fountain. "Work," or "activity," as in the title *De operatione Dei*, is the natural and inseparable expression of divine love. Thus, God's image and likeness, as Hildegard said in another text, makes man "the workman of divinity" (*operarius divinitatis*) within the macrocosm that the human being mirrors.[71] Caritas acts analogously in both.

> I flame above the beauty of the fields to signify the earth— the matter from which God made man. I shine in the waters to indicate the soul, for, as water suffuses the whole earth, the

---

70. DOD I.1.2, PL 197: 743–44.
71. *Vita* 2.35, PL 197: 116c.

soul pervades the whole body. I burn in the sun and the moon to denote reason, and the stars are the innumerable words of reason.[72]

This splendid vision, which Hildegard said "made all her organs tremble" and brought on one of her rare ecstasies,[73] superabounds with meaning. Caritas explains her own speech; the usual "voice from heaven" interprets it yet again; and each detail receives cosmic, microcosmic, incarnational, and ecclesial reference. The iconography, so brilliantly transcribed by the artist of the thirteenth-century Lucca ms. (frontispiece; Bibl. Gov. cod. lat. 1942), adds yet another dimension. While the miniature faithfully reproduces the seer's vision, adding only the scarlet hue of face, hands, feet, and robe to symbolize the "fiery force," the image is obviously inspired by Trinitarian iconography. In one familiar type of the Trinity, the so-called *Gnadenstuhl* or Throne of Grace, the Father, depicted as an old man, holds a lamb or crucifix representing the Son, while the Holy Spirit appears in the form of a dove. In the Lucca miniature, the wings of Caritas replace those of the missing dove and at the same time form a mandorla shape around the figure, as in a *Majestas Domini* composition. Although the bearded head and the lamb are supposed to represent "kindness" and "gentleness," it is scarcely possible not to read them as emblems of the Father and the Son; and in that case the fiery central figure can only be the Holy Spirit. The viewer can then identify Caritas, the subject of the vision, either with the central figure alone or with the entire Trinity, majestically trampling the devil underfoot.

WISDOM'S VESTURE

Creation, Hildegard observed, is "Wisdom's vesture": it reveals the hidden God just as a person's clothes hint at his body.[74] In a much earlier vision, *Scivias* I.3, she had seen the

72. DOD I.1.2, PL 197: 744b.
73. *Vita* 2.35, PL 197: 116b.
74. DOD III.9.14, PL 197: 996b.

universe in the form of a cosmic egg, whose components embody as well as symbolize the manifold works of God. Kent
Kraft has convincingly shown that in this vision, too, the underlying form is the mandorla, the almond-shaped enclosure
that, by an iconographic shorthand, signals Christ in majesty.
By superimposing an ordered and ornamental scheme of the
cosmos upon the human form of God, the vision presents the
whole world as his apparel. "Just as man has been endowed
with the *dignissimo indumento visibilis speciei*, the 'most worthy
garment of visible beauty,' so Christ too has donned similar
garb. But His apparel in the vision is not merely the human
form alone, the form in the mandorla behind the image, but
the entire body of the universe. The stars and the planets, the
winds and the waters, and the earth itself are His cloak and
vesture."[75] Images of clothing, which occur frequently enough
in Scripture, naturally lend themselves to illustrate the relation between God's invisible essence and his visible glory,
whether in the world or in humanity. Hildegard's contemporary Gerhoch of Reichersberg made succinct and felicitous use
of the motif when he said of Christ:

> As if naked you came from on high into this world . . . for you
> came into all creation when you assumed all creation in man,
> who is himself every creature. And you caused the Gospel to
> be preached to all creation; and believing and obeying it in
> man, all creation became as your vesture. Hence you, who
> went forth as if naked from the Father, put on in the world the
> tunic woven from above, that is the holy Church.[76]

For Hildegard, the motif of Wisdom's vesture had similar
connotations, with a special relevance to the feminine. Not
only did she find the theme appealing as a metaphor, but she
also took a personal delight in rich garments—in fact, she was
once criticized by a fellow abbess for allowing her nuns to

75. Kent Kraft, *The Eye Sees More than the Heart Knows: The Visionary Cosmology of Hildegard of Bingen* (Ph.D. Diss., University of Wisconsin, 1977):
256–57.

76. Gerhoch of Reichersberg, *Comment. in Psalmos* 7, PL 193: 730a.

wear jewelry and allegorical headgear of her own devising![77] Be that as it may, her visionary forms are no less richly appareled. In one vision she saw Sapientia dressed in a robe of white silk and a green tunic studded with pearls, wearing a lavish display of golden jewelry. The colors have both a theological and a moral significance: green denotes the fruitful, life-creating power of Wisdom; white, the sweetness of divine love in the Incarnation; and golden chains, the obedience of all nature to its God. Creatures have their being in Wisdom "as the finest, most elegant beauty, gleaming in the radiant splendor of her essence. And the person who fulfills God's commandments is a soft, shining white robe for Wisdom, and a green mantle through good intentions and vigorous deeds, made beautiful by many kinds of virtue."[78] Because Wisdom is both a cosmic and a microcosmic figure, her garb can represent the workmanship of either God or man; or else she herself may be depicted, like Athena, as a weaver who meshes things divine and human in her web.

A Biblical precedent is Solomon's ideal wife, the "valiant woman" of Proverbs 31, who earns her husband's praise by making fine garments of wool, linen, and purple for her family. For Augustine this woman was Ecclesia; Aelred of Rievaulx likened her to the Virgin; Adam of Perseigne in the thirteenth century saw her as Ecclesia, Mary, and Sapientia.[79] Hildegard adopted the least common of these readings; for her too the valiant woman was Wisdom. "In her secret zeal she has sought gentleness like wool and piety like linen," and by her heavenly works "she has protected the sons of men lest they walk naked before God, nor does she allow them to be idle; for she shows them many works to do, as she herself is wont to work always."[80] In this piece of allegory, man is again Sapientia's workman, but she is his solicitous mother;

77. Ep. 116, PL 197: 336cd.
78. DOD III.9.2, PL 197: 985bc.
79. Augustine, *Sermo 37*, CCSL 41: 446–73; Aelred, *Sermo 25 de beata Maria*, PL 195: 353d; Adam, *Sermo 5 in Assumptione*, PL 211: 734.
80. LVM IV.38, Pitra 160–61.

she clothes her children with righteousness that they may in turn clothe her. "Wisdom is justified by all her children" (Luke 7:35)—or, equivalently, "by her deeds" (Matt. 11:19).

Thus, the motif of Wisdom's clothing combines two of Hildegard's favorite sapiential themes: theophany, or the revelation of divine beauty in visible form, and synergy, or the cooperation of grace with human effort through the Virtues. This is particularly clear in the seer's explanation of why Caritas, like Solomon's "queen clothed in variety" (Ps. 44:10), changes her garb from one vision to the next.[81] Her many garments show that all the Virtues have their origin in Love, revealing her beauty in one guise after another, "for Love fulfills the whole will of God, adorned now with this apparel, now with that. The Virtues acting in humanity make Love's beauty visible, for all good things come about through love."[82] Conversely, when men and women stain their spirits with sin, the Bride's robes become soiled as well. Although Caritas is divine, she dwells in the world, and her clothes cannot be immaculate until human beings become pure. Yet, although she cannot always remain in gilded vesture, she can always purify her robe through the penance she inspires: "Every ordinance of Wisdom is sweet and gentle, for, when her robe is spotted with dirt, she washes it in the blood of the Lamb, who is merciful" (cf. Apoc. 7:14).[83]

This bedraggled Sapientia is bound to recall another lady in similar straits—Boethius's Philosophia, her robe torn by the dissensions of philosophers.[84] The numinous lady in splendid, yet torn or soiled, apparel is indeed a familiar medieval figure. In Alan of Lille's *Complaint of Nature*, Natura laments that her sublime dress has been rent by homosexuals.[85] Hil-

81. Cf. Richard of St. Victor: Probatio enim charitatis est exhibitio operis. Nam opera bona ejus sunt vestimenta. In vestitu, inquit, deaurato. In vestitu opera justitiae, in auro intellige claritatem sapientiae. Vestimenta ergo aurea, opera sunt discreta. *Adnotatio in Ps. 44*, PL 196: 323a–24a.

82. DOD III.10.3, PL 197: 1000cd.

83. DOD III.9.14, PL 197: 996c.

84. Boethius, *Consolation of Philosophy*, book I, prose 3.

85. Alan of Lille, *De planctu Naturae*, prose IV, ed. Thomas Wright in *Anglo-Latin Satirical Poets of the Twelfth Century* (London, 1872), II: 467.

degard herself envisaged Iustitia and Ecclesia in like disarray on account of sins against them.[86] Such figures forcefully illustrate human power, for good or ill, to change the face of creation through moral actions. And insofar as that face is female, Wisdom's clothing represents the feminine raised as it were to an exponential power. What the feminine divine is to the hidden God, splendid apparel should be to the female: an outward and visible sign of the inward, invisible glory. Perhaps that is why clothing, for Hildegard, became a leitmotiv connected with every significant female in her works, from Eve in her tunic of skins to the woman clothed with the sun.

THE CHASTISEMENTS OF CHARITY

As an epiphany of the Creator's love, Sapientia reveals herself by her words and actions as well as her appearance. In the Old Testament, she is by no means a static or merely decorative figure. Wisdom cries out in the streets, calling people to repentance; she reproves foolishness and vice, teaching discipline instead; she threatens those who despise her with calamity and death, but promises every reward to those who love her (Proverbs 8). Her counterpart, the "foolish woman" or harlot, lures men to their death with the promise of stolen pleasures (Prov. 9:13–18), but Wisdom prepares a rival banquet.

> Wisdom has built herself a house,
>   she has hewn out her seven pillars.
> She has slaughtered her beasts,
>   she has mixed her wine,
>   and she has set her table.
> She has sent out her maids to call
>   to the tower, and to the walls of the city:
> "Whoever is simple, let him come to me!"
>   and to the foolish she has said,
> "Come, eat of my bread,
>   and drink of the wine I have mixed for you.

---

86. DOD III.10.8, PL 197: 1007b; Ep. 52, PL 197: 269b–71d.

> Forsake childishness, and live,
> and walk in the ways of prudence."
> (Prov. 9:1–6)

Although patristic and medieval exegetes liked to read this text as an allegory of the Incarnation,[87] its lively dramatic flavor was not lost on them. St. Bernard, in particular, transferred some of Sophia's more human traits to his own favorite persona, Caritas—the figurative mistress of his "School of Charity" at Clairvaux. Her astringency especially could be useful. In his epistles, Bernard frequently invoked the persona of Caritas to excuse his less ingratiating remarks, as if to say, "It is not I who dare to speak thus, but Love." Not Bernard but Caritas dared to trouble a friend's contemplative leisure; not he but Caritas had the courage to instruct a pope, the severity to refuse a favor, the audacity to intervene in a quarrel, the temerity to presume on a forgotten friendship.[88]

As a literary device, such personification could be highly effective in the hands of an accomplished rhetor, while providing a psychological buffer zone between the speaker and the unpleasant message. The most vivid example occurs in Bernard's early letter to Fulk of Langres, an apostate from the Augustinians. After heaping the runaway with reproaches, the abbot suddenly took refuge behind the superhuman figure of Caritas as *mater dolorosa*.

> Charity would have you feel sorrow that then you may begin to have less cause to be sorry; she would have you know yourself to be shameful so you may then have less cause for shame. Our good mother Charity loves us all and shows herself differently to each one of us, cherishing the weak, scolding

87. For the house of Wisdom as the body of Christ see Augustine, *De civitate Dei* XVII. 20, CCSL 48: 588; Leo, Ep. 31, PL 54: 792; Gregory, *Moralia in Job* 33.15, PL 76: 693–94; Honorius, *Sermo de dedicatione*, PL 172: 1101; "Anselm," *Homilia Prima in Ecclus.*, PL 158: 586c. Cf. Bernard's sermon "De domo divinae Sapientiae, id est Virgine Maria," no. 52 in *Opera*, ed. Jean Leclercq and Henri Rochais (Rome, 1957–1977), 6¹: 274–77.

88. Epp. 12 to Guy of Chartreuse, 15 to Pope Honorius, 91 to Oger of Mont-St. Eloi, 228 to Eustace, occupier of the see of Valence, and 328 to Hugh, abbot of Prémontré, in *The Letters of St. Bernard of Clairvaux*, trans. Bruno James (London, 1953): 42, 50, 136, 306, 407–8.

the restive, exhorting the advanced. But when she scolds she is meek, when she consoles she is sincere. She rages lovingly, her caresses are without guile. She knows how to be angry without losing patience, how to be indignant without being proud. It is she, the mother of angels and men, who brings peace not only on earth, but even in heaven. It is she who brings God to men and reconciles men with God . . .

And it is this mother whom you have wounded, whom you have affronted. Yet although you have affronted her, she does not contend with you. Spurned by you she calls you back, showing by this how truly it has been written of her: "Charity is patient; charity is kind" (I Cor. 13:4). Although wounded and affronted by you yet, should you return to her, she will meet you as an honoured mother. She will forget how you repudiated her and throw herself into your arms, rejoicing that her son who was lost is found; who was dead has come to life again.[89]

Here is a classic instance of the twelfth-century "feminization" of religious language: Caritas the mother replaces God the Father in welcoming the prodigal son back home. And her authority is beyond question because "God is Charity" (I John 4:8).

Bernard's influence on Hildegard is nowhere clearer than in her treatment of this Virtue.[90] After her initial correspondence with the abbot of Clairvaux, she enjoyed close contact with a number of Cistercian communities, including Ebrach, Salem, Eberbach, Heilsbronn, Maulbronn, and Kaisheim. In the year of St. Bernard's death (1153), the Cistercian general chapter dared to ask her "what in us and our order is displeasing to you, or rather to the eyes of God."[91] Predictably,

89. Ep. 2 in *Letters of St. Bernard* 10–11.

90. This influence should not, however, be exaggerated. Despite Hildegard's familiarity with the Cistercian ethos, one searches her works in vain for many of the order's hallmarks, e.g., devotion to the humanity of Jesus, ascetic austerity, theology of contemplation, and reflections on the psychology of love.

91. Ep. 144, PL 197: 380bc. Migne's text is incomplete, but the remainder can be found in Ep. 3, Pitra 334–35, and the complete text in J. M. Canivez, ed., *Statuta capitulorum generalium ordinis Cisterciensis* (Louvain, 1933), I: 53–56. The date of this letter is disputed. In Alberic's chronicle (MGH.SS. 23: 842), the abbots' request and Hildegard's reply are described under the year

the seer answered *in persona Dei* and managed to find a pleth-
ora of faults, notably presumption, instability, hypocrisy, and
schism. Her letter blends her own brand of erotic imagery
with a distinctly Bernardesque portrayal of Caritas, giving the
Cistercians a taste of their own medicine. Caritas mourns for
her wayward children yet remains a perpetual virgin, like Mater Ecclesia in the orthodox polemics against heresy. Those
who tear themselves away from her embrace defile not her
but themselves, arousing her bridegroom's sorrowful wrath.

> O sons of Israel, why have you corrupted tender Love, who
> gazes far into my depths and flows forth in works abounding?
> Because she flows within me, from her in turn flow the living
> waters. She resembles a budding branch (*virga*), for, as a vir-
> gin's embraces are the most tender because of her integrity,
> even so Love's embraces are more tender than those of any
> other Virtue. But now she mourns, because audacious men
> tear her to pieces with their loquacious grumbling. Hence she
> flees from them to that height whence she came, and weeps
> because her children, whom she suckled at her fertile breasts,
> fall sick and will not be cleansed from the corruption of their
> flighty minds.
>
> O wretched men! Why do they take on themselves the mis-
> ery of alienation and exile, tearing themselves away from the
> royal wedding feast of the new bride? She is always ready for
> her bridegroom as a virgin is for her husband, when she has
> not yet been united with him in intercourse but still remains
> untouched in her virginity. Yet these men separate themselves
> from that bride, whence they are darkened and shadowed by
> clouds as if they had ruptured heaven.[92]

The plaint of Caritas recalls not only Bernard's letters but also
his sermon on Song 1:5 ("My mother's sons fought against
me"), which decries discord and contention in the Church.[93]
But Hildegard's Caritas is less active, less powerfully maternal

---

1153, but Pitra has given the unexplained date c. 1172. I see no reason to
question Alberic's dating; it seems natural that the general chapter would
have appealed to Hildegard in the year of Bernard's death, when the memory
of the two saints' mutual esteem was still fresh.

92. Ep. 144, PL 197: 380cd.

93. Bernard of Clairvaux, *Sermo 29 super Cantica, Opera* 1: 202–9.

than Bernard's; she is still the shining virgin of the fountain,
not pursuing but fleeing from those who abuse her.

Caritas, of course, is only one of many Virtues who figure
in Hildegard's visionary world. But she is pivotal, for it is she
who, reflecting both the cosmological and the moral aspects
of the wisdom tradition, links the sapiential theology of the
philosopher-poets with the more conventional didactic allegory favored by monastic authors. The reader is apt to be
struck by the disparity between Hildegard's more grandiose
visions, which are comparable to the most innovative twelfth-
century poetry, and the old-fashioned personifications, which
hark back to Hermas and Prudentius. Her penchant for har-
monizing the new and the old in spiritual culture reminds one
of Alan of Lille, who, a generation later, began as a writer of
cosmographical epics and ended his days as a Cistercian. But
this sense of discrepancy is by and large an illusion of perspective. The same alternation of sublime and merely pru-
dential discourse occurs in the wisdom books themselves,
and therein lies the chief point of the personification. Sapientia, as we have seen, is the feminine link between Creator and
cosmos; but she is also arbiter of the moral law, the one who
teaches men and women to distinguish between good and
evil, discretion and folly. The lyrical passages exalting her person and work do not merely elevate an otherwise pedantic
discourse; rather, they weld the ideal of ethical living insep-
arably with the vision of divine love and beauty, which, in
elusive but ever-alluring form, leads upward and on. Di-
vorced from the moral ideal, Sapientia would be a merely
mythic figure of a sort profoundly alien to the Judeo-Christian
tradition. The same may be said of Hildegard's Caritas. She
is God's love for the world as well as the world's for God. She
is the love that beckons us to wonder but also the love that
summons us to work.

Aside from her comprehensive use of moral allegory in the
Play of Virtues and the *Book of Life's Merits*, Hildegard sometimes presented her correspondents with parables, or morality plays in miniature, in which Caritas interacts with the
other Virtues who "make Love's beauty visible." Such para-

bles were becoming common in twelfth-century spiritual writings, supplementing the older and staler Virtue-Vice pairings of the *Psychomachia* tradition. For instance, the "four daughters of God" began to emerge in commentaries on Ps. 84:11: "Mercy and Truth have met together; Justice and Peace have kissed each other." St. Bernard, Hugh of St. Victor, and Rupert of Deutz all personified these Virtues in dramatic contexts, heralding Langland's consummate treatment of the theme two centuries later.[94]

The full-fledged morality play was invented by Hildegard herself, but its way was prepared by a type of devotional meditation that also involved personified Virtues and Vices. In the pseudo-Anselmian treatise *De custodia interioris hominis* (*Keeping Watch over the Inner Self*), Fear of Death and Love of Eternal Life come to visit the house of the soul, which they find guarded by the four cardinal virtues, and inspire it to meditate on hell and heaven.[95] A simpler parable of this genre occurs in Hildegard's letter to Duno, prior of St. Michael's in Bamberg (c. 1169–70). She encouraged the leader of that troubled community by recommending to him three virtues (Caritas, Humilitas, and Obedientia), who enact an edifying scene with Superbia.

> Now understand this, man! In a certain house were sitting two men: one was a knight and the other a slave. And two wise and beautiful maidens came to that house and knocked at the gate, and said to those men, "In distant lands, we have heard a rumor of you that was not good—namely that you have spoken against the King in many questionable affairs. And the King said of you, 'Who are those filthy men? And who am I?' So listen now to our advice, that you may gain the victory."

94. Bernard of Clairvaux, *Sermo 1 in festo Annuntiationis, Opera* 5: 13–27; Hugh of St. Victor, *Miscellanea* II.63, PL 177: 623c–25d; Rupert of Deutz, *De glorificatione Trinitatis* IX.6, PL 169: 186–87. On this theme see Arthur Långfors, "Le thème des quatre filles de Dieu. Excursus bibliographique," *Notices et extraits de la Bibliothèque nationale et autres bibliothèques* 42 (1933): 172–282.
95. *Memorials of St. Anselm*, ed. R. W. Southern (Oxford, 1969): 354–60.

An interpretation follows:

> In the house of your heart, man, sit the knight Obedience and the slave Pride. And at the gate of your mind, Love and [Humility] are knocking, to keep you from doing all the evil that lies in your power. Now see that the knight vanquishes the slave, lest the beauty of Obedience lie prostrate beneath the feet of a slave. For Pride says, "It is impossible to loose the chains with which I bind people." But as for you, answer as you hear Love speaking to you: "I sat inviolate in heaven and kissed the earth. And Pride swore an oath against me and wished to fly above the stars, but I cast him into the abyss. Now trample upon the slave with me, my child, and abide in me, Love. And embrace Humility as your lady, and you shall never be confounded, nor ever die."[96]

It is worth noting that, while all four dramatis personae are grammatically feminine, Hildegard described Caritas and Humilitas as *puellae* but referred to Obedientia and Superbia as *viri* (*miles* and *vernaculus*). Such deviations from grammatical gender indicate that she did not feel bound by the rules of language (which, in any case, she claimed not to know) but exercised considerable freedom in her personifications.[97] She also took liberties with class, following the rule that Virtues must be noble and Vices base: so Obedience and Humility enjoy the high rank of knight and lady, whereas Pride is reduced against his character to servitude. Like many of Hildegard's visions, the story on a literal plane is incoherent. The knight must be less obedient than his name, or else he would need no rebuke, and the slave is not serving but waiting to be trampled underfoot. Even in the course of this brief parable, the characters alter before our eyes: the slave Pride is suddenly unmasked as Lucifer, who wished to set up his throne

96. Ep. 93, Pitra 547–48. The second *puella* must be Humilitas rather than Obedientia as in Pitra's text, for she has a speech beginning "Ego humilitas" and is named as *domina* at the end of the letter.

97. A curious sidelight on this problem is provided by Bengt Hasselrot, "Les vertus devraient être soeurs, ainsi que les vices sont frères," in *Actes du 4ᵉ Congrès des Romanistes Scandinaves, Revue romane*, special issue 1 (Copenhagen, 1967): 35–44.

above the stars (Isa. 14:13); and Caritas, the King's handmaid, turns out to be the Word, who "kissed the earth" in the Incarnation and cast Satan into the abyss. Her exhortation to "abide in me" fittingly recalls Christ's farewell sermon (John 15:4), although the injunction "embrace Humility as your lady" restores the feudal and courtly context of the narrative. The several inconsistencies show the fluidity of Hildegard's mind at work, conflating allegorical levels that more systematic writers would have preferred to distinguish. She had particular trouble keeping the Virtues in their place; they are always rising above themselves.

Very similar is the parable addressed to Henry, bishop of Beauvais (1149–1162)—a fine sample of Hildegard's prophetic appeal to the clergy. In this visionary text, the virtue of Pura Scientia—evidently the same as Scientia Dei in *Scivias* III.4 and 9—appears to the seer with a message for her correspondent. Like Caritas in Bernard's letter to the apostate Fulk, the Virtue clearly speaks as the writer's mouthpiece—or vice versa, assuming that the intended reader took the epistle as the prophetic document it was meant to be.

> I saw the beautiful figure of a Virtue, Pure Knowledge. Shining bright was her face, her eyes were blue as jacinth, and her vesture like a mantle of silk. Over her shoulders she wore a bishop's pallium the color of rubies. And she summoned the King's fair consort, Love, saying, "Come with me!" And they both came and knocked at the gate of your heart, saying:
> "We wish to make our home with you! So beware that you do not resist us, but be strong in withstanding vices, worldly troubles, and those shifting winds that mount up in tempests like noxious smoke or like waters stirred by a storm. These are the anxieties of human minds possessed by anger and other passions. Do not keep silent from weariness, but let your voice resound like a trumpet in the rites of the Church, and purify your eyes in knowledge so you will not be sluggish to shake off the worthless dust of your burden. For you are covered with dew of the night (Song 5:2). Persuasive Pride urges you not to wash yourself, but our will is otherwise. We want you to cleanse yourself of all darkness and not to fear the many threats of your enemies who speak lies and slander about you.

O knight, give us a dwelling place in your heart, and we will bring you with us to the palace of the King."[98]

Because the *Scivias* visions portray Scientia Dei as watching particularly over sinners in the Church, she becomes an appropriate symbol for the pastoral office. Hence, in this vision she wears episcopal vestments and offers herself as a model for the bishop—even though Hildegard argued ex professo that "women must not approach the service of the altar."[99] Nevertheless, as an emissary of the living Light, Pura Scientia appeals to the bishop by means of God's mouthpiece, the prophet. One is reminded of Elisabeth of Schönau's vision of Mary in priestly vesture. Despite the strictures of an all-male priesthood, feminine exempla for the apostolic role were not uncommon. Abelard had praised the faithful women at Christ's tomb as "apostolas super apostolos," and Rupert of Deutz hailed the Virgin as "magistra magistrorum."[100] In all three of these cases, however, the women represent the prophetic or didactic rather than the sacramental role of the clergy. The same is true of Pure Knowledge in this vision. As a heavenly double for the seer herself, she significantly uses the same metaphor Hildegard had proposed to Elisabeth: "let your voice resound like a trumpet." Thus, the epiphany of a numinous female in vestments embodies the prophet's sense of mission as well as her message. From the recipient's point of view, Pura Scientia represents both the virtues of his office and the grace that will enable him, if he so chooses, to fulfill it.

Another parable, in some ways the most interesting of the three, reveals some unexpected sides of Hildegard's character. Addressed to a monk, it features Caritas and her corresponding Vice, Love of the World (Amor Saecularis), together with a third woman, Philosophia.

98. Ep. 23, PL 197: 180c–81a.
99. *Scivias* II.6.76, p. 290.
100. Abelard, Ep. 7 "De origine sanctimonialium," PL 178: 232b; Rupert of Deutz, *In Cantica* I.6, CCCM 26: 24.

A certain fair and noble lady [Caritas] had a chamber lined with gold, and she often chose two maidens with elegant features [Benevolentia and Largitas] to live with her. But a great throng, seeing this lady, praised her beautiful face and wished to dwell with her. She said to them, "I will give you gifts that will please you, but it would be of no use either to me or to you if we lived together. For I do not wish to give my nobility and beauty to dogs and foxes for derision."

But a wrinkled woman [Amor Saecularis], whose face was black and scarlet, wanted to be like this noble lady, and unworthily laid claim to her nobility and beauty. This wrinkled woman walks in the mountains and runs about everywhere, seeking praise and honor, but she gets none. Instead, everybody says, "That disturbed, unruly woman is from the devil, and everyone should drive her away."

Another woman, a merchant, collected wares of every kind that were lovely to look on, and she took pains to let people see and hear of these unknown marvels. Then she set a very pure, beautiful crystal before the fiery sun, which enflamed it so that it gave light to all. . . . Now the merchant woman is Philosophy, she who established every art and discovered the crystal of faith, which leads to God.[101]

In this text, Love of the World parodies divine Love as the foolish woman apes Wisdom in the book of Proverbs. The rivalry of the two women, one godly and one from the devil, lends vivacity to the traditional contrast between charity and cupidity. In the portrait of Amor Saecularis, we also catch a glimpse of that age-old figure of folklore, the she-devil or witch. Hildegard told the Cistercian monks, in the letter cited previously, that by forsaking Caritas the virgin they have fallen prey to her enemy—"the twisted woman, all swarthy and wrinkled, who grinds her teeth and goes her viperish way, horrid in all her doings." This woman, like a new Circe, makes pigs of those who should have been holy and elect, renouncing the world.[102]

But Caritas too has diminished in the presence of her rival. Elsewhere the most divine and universal of the Virtues, she now reveals a disconcerting snobbery. Again, because of her

101. Ep. 135, PL 197: 363a–c.
102. Ep. 144, PL 197: 381a.

instinctive association of virtue with nobility, Hildegard described Caritas as a lady (*domina*) and Amor Saecularis as a mere woman (*mulier*). The one is beautiful, highborn, and secluded, while the other is vulgar in every sense. The noble lady's refusal to consort with "dogs and foxes" (or to cast her pearls before swine) plainly reflects the seer's aristocratic pride. Her community at Bingen, like most of the older Benedictine houses, accepted only girls of excellent family. When the abbess of Andernach reproached Hildegard for this policy, she defended it with zest, invoking the principle of hierarchy among people, beasts, and angels.[103] This letter makes the same point more obliquely, presenting Caritas as a respecter of persons who chooses the noble and leaves the mob outside her golden chamber to resist the enemy alone. Differences of class coincide, in metaphor as in reality, with the felt difference between divine love in the cloister and demonic or false love in the world.[104]

But the third woman, Philosophia, provides an alternative. For the sapiential humanists of the time, she was of course not a merchant but a queen.[105] Illuminated Bibles often show her with her Boethian attributes—books in her right hand and a scepter in her left—enthroned in the initial *O* of Ecclesiasticus: "Omnis sapientia a Domino Deo est."[106] Another favorite convention, derived from Martianus Capella, is the depiction of Philosophia as *fons artium*, or mother of the seven liberal arts.[107] Alcuin called her "the supreme wisdom" and "mistress of all virtues,"[108] and Erigena, commenting on Mar-

---

103. Ep. 116, PL 197: 337b–38c.

104. On divine order and social class in Hildegard's thought cf. Peter Dronke, *Women Writers of the Middle Ages* (Cambridge, 1984): 165–67.

105. See Marie-Thérèse d'Alverny, "Le symbolisme de la Sagesse et le Christ de Saint Dunstan," *Bodleian Library Record* 5 (1956): 232–44; "Alain de Lille et la *Theologia*," in *L'homme devant Dieu: Mélanges Henri de Lubac* (Paris, 1964), II: 112.

106. See for instance the Bamberg and Grandval Bibles, produced at Tours not long after Alcuin's death, and the eleventh-century Bible of St. Martial of Limoges, cited in d'Alverny, "La Sagesse et ses sept filles."

107. For a delightful illustration of this motif see Georg Swarzenski, *Die Salzburger Malerei*, 2nd ed. (Stuttgart, 1969), plate 115, fig. 392.

108. Alcuin, *De dialectica*, PL 101: 966a; and *De grammatica*, 849c.

tianus, made the extraordinary claim that "no one enters into heaven except through philosophy."[109] Such notions were still current and fashionable in Hildegard's day. Her contemporary Herrad of Hohenbourg gave this learned queen a distinguished place in her illustrated *Hortus Deliciarum* (*Garden of Delights*).[110] In a miniature from that work, Philosophia appears with a scroll that reads, "All wisdom is from the Lord God. Only the wise can do what they desire." Plato and Socrates sit at her feet, and the three branches of philosophy— ethics, logic, and physics—are designated by three heads above her crown. From her breast flow seven streams to nurture her daughters, the seven liberal arts, who stand in an arcade beneath. To leave no doubt about this mother's true identity, a caption at the left reads, "The Holy Spirit is the inventor of the seven liberal arts."

Such is the background of Hildegard's "merchant woman." The appellation is an odd one, perhaps faintly disparaging to the marketplace of human knowledge, with which Hildegard claimed to have no traffic. It is even more odd to find the prophet of pure inspiration exalting a figure of such noted humanistic credentials. But, like her sister abbess Herrad, she assimilated the divine Sophia with the classical Philosophia, though not quite so thoroughly. Note that Philosophia holds not the traditional handful of books but the crystal of faith— an emblem of focused and concentrated light. In this image of *intellectus quaerens fidem*, Philosophia best represents human wisdom contemplating the Wisdom of God, gazing into her crystal just as Caritas gazes on the sapphire form of Christ. Although faith, surpassing the arts, is the highest gift that Philosophia can offer, it is nonetheless striking that *she* can offer it. We can take her as a model for the enlightened

109. Erigena, *Annotationes in Marcianum*, ed. Cora Lutz (Cambridge, Mass., 1939): 64.
110. Herrad of Hohenbourg, *Hortus Deliciarum*. A Reconstruction by Rosalie Green, Michael Evans, et al. (London, 1979). The original manuscript is no longer extant.

secular life, as Caritas in this parable is for the monastic life. Those who are too common to gain admittance to the house of Caritas, but too wise to consort with the wicked Amor Saecularis, can still live a holy life through the love of wisdom illumined by faith.

At this point, we may safely leave Philosophia peering into her crystal ball as we pause to summarize the ways Hildegard's thought is refracted through these diverse visions, parables, and proclamations. We have seen, thus far, that the feminine divine is the revelation of the hidden God—particularly in the archetypal world, in nature, and in the life of the soul. She is divinity proposing, revealing, creating, assisting, and alluring; she is also the inner dynamism of the world obeying, receiving, responding, and cooperating. Through her the heavens declare the glory of God, the prophets are overshadowed by the living Light, and the faithful participate in the Virtues. Her bearing is regal toward the cosmos, erotic toward God, maternal toward men and women; her epiphanies aim to inspire the love of wisdom through the beauty of holiness. She is the faithful mirror of divine intentions but also of human actions; it is her vesture that men and women adorn through good works or disfigure through sin. Intimate with God, she is supremely accessible to the faithful, for her consummate work, her *operatio*, is the union of Creator and creature. As the "counsel of the Lord which stands forever" (Ps. 32:11), the feminine divine brings the world into being that God may be born in it and leads it back to God through the Word-made-flesh. Under the first aspect, she is the archetype of Mary; under the second, she is the eternal and preexistent Church.

It should be abundantly clear that the feminine divine, as manifested under the names of Sapientia and Caritas, is a wholly positive symbol. The same may be said of the Biblical Sophia. Yet, paradoxically, no books of Scripture are so filled with misogyny as the wisdom literature. "Better is the iniquity of a man than a woman who does good," says the Wisdom of Sirach (Ecclus. 42:14).[111] The beauty of women is a snare and a delusion (Ecclesiasticus 9); the daughter is a burden to her father (42:9–10), and the harlot a slayer of the simple (Proverbs 7). As for the wife, "it is better to live in a desert land than with a contentious and fretful woman" (Prov. 21:19). And, of course, "from the woman came the beginning of sin, and by her we all die" (Ecclus. 25:33). Needless to say, the ascription of positive symbolic value to the feminine is no safeguard against misogyny, any more than the glorification of the lady in courtly lyrics testifies to a decent regard for actual women.

As we have already seen, Hildegard herself also used the feminine to symbolize various types of physical and moral weakness—a usage far more widespread (despite the cult of courtesy) than the elite forms of symbolic theology we have examined so far. The question to which we must now turn is a crux: how far was she able to maintain her sapiential outlook—in cruder terms, her idealism—when she turned to contemplate woman in her fallen state? Given her strong sense of the demonic, the weight of sin, and the downward pull of the flesh, we can expect ambivalence at the very least. The issue arises sharply in Hildegard's treatment of Eve, whom she believed to be the first historical woman and the first victim of Satan's misogyny.

111. See M. L. Arduini, "Il tema 'vir' e 'mulier' nell' esegesi patristica e medioevale di Eccli. XLII.14," *Aevum* 55 (1981): 246–61.

3

The Woman and the Serpent

For Hildegard, as for medieval Christians generally, the story of Paradise lost recounted in Genesis served as the touchstone for all meditation on man and woman. It explained their origin, end, and present plight, as well as their relations with God, Satan, and one another. Although the seer nowhere offered a full-scale commentary on the Genesis story, she returned time and again to the figures of Adam and Eve. Their creation, marriage, and banishment appear in one of her earliest visions (*Scivias* I.2) and still occupied her on her deathbed. Adam and Eve occupy a central place in the saga of cosmic history: their adventures provide a sequel to the fall of Lucifer and a prologue to the Incarnation, for, in the seer's eye, these events were three acts of one drama. But the fall also comprises a tragic and pathetic narrative in its own right, which Hildegard retold with mythopoeic grandeur and poignancy. In the vision of Eve and Adam in Paradise, she saw both the paradigm of human sexuality as it was intended by God and its ultimate purpose: the Incarnation of the Word. Conversely, the fallen couple supplied her with an image and etiology of all the moral and physical ills that she saw (often though not always) to be grounded in sexuality gone wrong.

Hildegard's treatment of Eve, then, is predictably fraught with tensions. On the one hand, the paradigmatic woman must embody all the sapiential values that inhere in the feminine per se. But, on the other, Hildegard could not escape the influence of the Augustinian tradition, which linked original sin with concupiscence or desire, and the related monastic tradition, with its esteem for virginity. These traditions, formed and perpetuated as they were by male celibates, are notorious for their tendency to identify sex in general with the female sex in particular, and thus to condemn Eve and her daughters as the abiding source of temptation.[1] Because Hildegard by and large shared the antierotic bias of her Benedictine heritage, it is fascinating to watch her attempts to sidestep the antifeminist corollaries that it usually entailed. Insofar as she succeeded, she did so partly through her sapiential theology, partly through reliance on insights alien to the Augustinian tradition—for instance, folk wisdom, medical lore about women, and theological motifs that derive ultimately from Greek or Jewish rather than Latin sources. She could also make shrewd use of her instinctual and empirical perceptions. Nevertheless, the tensions in her view of the concrete, embodied feminine are far from thoroughly resolved.[2]

In the following pages I shall look at texts dealing with Eve, and in the next chapter I shall consider Hildegard's views on women generically, particularly as they concern questions of gynecology, erotic sensibility, and marriage. Most of the texts in which Eve appears present her dialectically vis-à-vis Mary, Adam, or Satan. In the divine order, she is the mother of mankind and hence, proleptically, of Christ; in the natural and social order, she is the partner of man; and, in the fallen world, she is the victim of the devil's envy. After the fall it is no longer possible to segregate the effects of sin, nature, and grace as long as woman continues to express her sexuality in marriage, for only through virginity can she fully overcome "the venom of the ancient serpent." As a sexual being, woman is (like man) tainted at the source, yet even in her fallenness she is capable of receiving and revealing grace.

1. The literature on this subject is immense, but the reader may wish to consult especially George Tavard, *Woman in Christian Tradition* (Notre Dame, 1973); and Rosemary Ruether, ed., *Religion and Sexism: Images of Woman in the Jewish and Christian Traditions* (New York, 1974); as well as the works cited in ch. 1, n. 8.

2. Cf. the chapter on Hildegard in Peter Dronke, *Women Writers of the Middle Ages* (Cambridge, 1984); and Elisabeth Gössmann, "Das Menschenbild der Hildegard von Bingen und Elisabeth von Schönau vor dem Hintergrund der frühscholastischen Anthropologie," in Peter Dinzelbacher and Dieter Bauer, eds., *Frauenmystik im Mittelalter* (Ostfildern, 1985): 24–47.

MADE IN GOD'S IMAGE

A question central to medieval anthropology, and one that was still contested in Hildegard's time, was whether Eve no less than Adam had been created in God's image and likeness (Gen. 1:26). Certain of the church fathers, like John Chrysostom, had identified the image of God with universal sovereignty and thus inferred that it belongs only to the male, because "man dominates all and woman serves."[3] Other theologians distinguished between "image" and "likeness" as between two degress of resemblance, the greater pertaining to Adam and the lesser to Eve. Abelard, reckoned by some as a twelfth-century feminist, nonetheless held that man enjoys a "more express likeness" to the Trinity because he excels woman in the divine attributes of power, wisdom, and love.[4] The Cistercian Arnold of Bonneval believed similarly that "man is made to the image of God, woman to the likeness, . . . man according to a fuller intensity of spirit, woman according to a more lax desire for contemplation."[5] The canonist Ivo of Chartres remarked, on the basis of I Cor. 11:7, "Woman veils herself because she is not the glory or the image of God."[6] Most twelfth-century theologians, however, held to the equality of the sexes in this regard. Among them are Hervé of Bourg-Dieu, Peter of Celle, and Gilbert Porreta.[7] Rupert of Deutz stated plainly that "God made woman no less than man to his own image."[8] What is at issue here is not only the valuation of woman but the broader question of what it means to be made in the image of God. Unlike Chrysostom, who based his notion on the social order, virtually all Western

---

3. John Chrysostom, *Homily 8 on Genesis 1*, no. 4, PG 53: 73.
4. Abelard, *Expositio in Hexaemeron*, PL 178: 760d–61d.
5. Arnold of Bonneval, *De operibus sex dierum*, PL 189: 1534ab.
6. Ivo of Chartres, *Panormia* VII.44, PL 161: 1291ab.
7. Hervé of Bourg-Dieu, *In Epistolam I ad Corinthios*, PL 181: 927c; Peter of Celle, *De panibus* 10, PL 202: 975b; Gilbert Porreta, Troyes Cod. lat. 626, fols. 113^v–114^r, cited in Robert Javelet, *Image et ressemblance au douzième siècle* (Paris, 1967), II: 207, n. 540. For a summary of these positions see Javelet, *Image et ressemblance* I: 236–45.
8. Rupert of Deutz, *In Genesim* II.7, CCCM 21: 191.

writers followed Augustine in placing the locus of the image in the rational mind.[9] Hence the issue of woman's equality or inferiority hinged on each theologian's opinion of her mental and spiritual capacities in relation to man's.

Hildegard, however, took a fundamentally different approach to the problem. According to Gerhart Ladner, the twelfth century witnessed a growing awareness of the "incarnational," as opposed to purely spiritual, image of God.[10] Hitherto the body had played a lesser part in Western thought about the image, except for the isolated speculations of Erigena.[11] But a new interest in the predestination of Christ led to a recognition of Adam's physical, as well as intellectual, resemblance to the Word made flesh. Bruno of Segni, an early exponent of this new approach, affirmed that the Creator "gave man such a bodily image as he had decreed before time that the Son, who is indeed God, should receive. Thus, not only our inward but also our outward man may be in some way similar to God."[12] The thirteenth-century Cistercian Hélinand of Froidmont remarked that "before the Incarnation of the Word only the inward form was like God; but since the Incarnation of the Word, even the outward form of man has become the form of God."[13] On the face of it, this reference to Christ's physical form would seem inimical to woman's equal participation in the *imago Dei*. But for Hildegard, who used the feminine expressly to symbolize the eternal counsel,

9. Augustine defined the image of God as "ipsa ratio vel mens vel intelligentia," *De Genesi ad litteram* III.20, CSEL 28¹: 86. This view is reiterated by Alcuin, *De animae ratione* 5, PL 101: 641a; Rabanus Maurus, *Comment. in Genesim* I.7, PL 107: 460b; Angelomus of Luxeuil, *Comment. in Gen.* 1, PL 115: 122d; and Remigius of Auxerre, *Comment. in Gen.* 1, PL 131: 57a. See Gerhart B. Ladner, *Ad Imaginem Dei: The Image of Man in Mediaeval Art* (Latrobe, Pa., 1965): 86–87, n. 54.

10. Ladner, *Ad Imaginem Dei* 42, 108–9.

11. Erigena, citing Gregory of Nyssa, called the body *imago animae* and hence *veluti secunda imago* [*Dei*]. *Periphyseon (De divisione naturae)* II.27 and IV.11, PL 122: 585d, 790c.

12. Bruno of Segni, *Expositio in Genesim*, PL 164: 158ab.

13. Hélinand of Froidmont, *De cognitione sui* 8, PL 212: 729d.

woman's role as vessel of the Incarnation was the very seal of her creation in the image of God. Following an old analogy, she asserted that "man is like the soul and woman like the body," and, by extension, "man signifies the divinity and woman the humanity of the Son of God."[14] Herein lies the clue to Hildegard's surprisingly radical anthropology, which would exalt not the male but the female as the representative human being. Adam symbolizes, but does not share, the divine nature. In contrast, Eve both symbolizes and bestows the divine humanity, insofar as she prefigures Mary. It is not by her appearance but by her gift that the woman represents Christ's human nature and bears the stamp of his image.

Typically, Hildegard conveyed her sense of the first woman's nature less through straightforward exposition than through a series of images. And no sooner does one of these yield its weight in concepts than the concepts dissolve into new images, enhancing or correcting the first. The final product is less a doctrine than an iconography, albeit rich with doctrinal meaning. In order to see Eve through Hildegard's eyes, then, it is helpful to begin where she did, with things seen. Three distinct but subtly related images—the garment, the mirror, and the cloud—most often characterize Eve, and in her person all womankind. The garment and the mirror, as we have seen, are also sapiential images linked with the feminine divine. All three symbols designate motherhood as well as theophany—or, more precisely, motherhood *as* theophany. Woman's primary significance in the divine scheme of things is to reveal the hidden God by giving him birth. In the meantime, she gives birth to his image in every child that she bears. But for this work she must collaborate with man; so Eve's special iconographic symbols represent her secondarily in her role as helpmeet and complement to Adam.

14. DOD II.5.43, PL 197: 945d; I.4.100, 885c. For the subsequent development of this theme see Caroline Bynum,"' . . . And Woman His Humanity': Female Imagery in the Religious Writing of the Later Middle Ages," in Caroline Bynum, Steven Harrell, and Paula Richman, eds., *Gender and Religion: On the Complexity of Symbols* (Boston, 1986).

THE GARMENT AND THE MIRROR

In a central passage from *On the Activity of God*, Hildegard set forth her incarnational concept of the divine image as a preface to her treatment of the sexes.

> Now when God looked upon the man he was well pleased, for he had created him after the tunic of his image and after his likeness, to proclaim all his marvels through the trumpet of a rational voice. For man is the consummate work of God. It is he who knows God, and for his sake God created all creatures, and, in the kiss of true love, enabled him to proclaim and praise him through reason.[15]

The disparate metaphors of "tunic" and "trumpet" here denote the divine image and likeness respectively. The latter resides in the rational soul, with its capacity to acknowledge God in speech and song, while the former refers to the bodily form—or, as Hildegard said elsewhere, "the tunic of [Christ's] humanity, which he was to assume from the form of a woman."[16] In this garment, the flesh of the incarnate Word, Love and Wisdom will be fully and finally vested.[17]

Although both sexes partake equally in the image and likeness, as both share the structure of soul and body, the garment pertains especially to the woman because it is so closely connected with the Incarnation. Thus, in an eccentric commentary on the wedding at Cana, Hildegard interpreted Jesus' enigmatic words to Mary—"Quid mihi et tibi est, mulier?" (John 2:4)—as a question about that which God and the woman share. Instead of taking Christ's words as a reproach, she paraphrased: "Woman, what do you and I, the Creator of

15. DOD I.4.100, PL 197: 885b.
16. Ep. 47, PL 197: 223a.
17. The so-called *assumptus homo* Christology, one of the three options discussed in Peter Lombard's *Sentences*, is based on the metaphor of clothing. In Augustine's formulation, the theory maintains that man "was assumed [by the Word] that he might be changed for the better and reformed by him, like a garment worn by a person, but in a fashion unspeakably more excellent and fitting . . . for he did not become human by changing himself into a man, but by clothing himself in man." *De diversis quaestionibus* 83, question 73, PL 40: 84–85.

all, have in common? Humanity is mine, that I might create all things; and yours as well, that it might be my garment."[18] In other words, human nature belongs to the woman by God's gift and to him reciprocally by hers.

The miracle of the Incarnation was foreshadowed from the beginning, because Mary would clothe the Son of God in flesh just as Eve clad the sons of Adam. Hildegard contrasted the "naked" angels, which consist of pure spirit and light, with the more fragile human spirit, which needs a robe of clay.[19] To receive this clothing every man must depend on woman, on his own mother but ultimately on Eve, the mother of all living. And in return for this robe of flesh, man offers woman the protection and support that she needs.

> Woman is weak and looks up to man to provide for her, just as the moon receives its strength from the sun. For this reason she is subject to man and should always be prepared to serve him. For by the work of her knowledge she covers man, because she was fashioned from both flesh and blood, unlike the man, who was originally clay. On this account, even in his nakedness, he looks to woman to clothe him.[20]

Woman's function as weaver is literal as well as metaphorical: man receives not only the garment of flesh from the mother's womb but also garments of linen and wool from her hands. Discussing the division of labor between the sexes, Hildegard intimated that man is of the earth, earthy, so his portion is to till the earth from which he was taken. But woman, created as flesh from flesh, was made the mother of all flesh. In addition, she is distinguished by her skilled handiwork (*artificiosum opus manuum*), probably referring to the

---

18. *Expositiones evangeliorum*, Pitra 261. More commonly the saying was interpreted as a rhetorical question of the form "What have I to do with thee?"

19. *Scivias* III.1.16, p. 345: "God preserved the splendor [of the fallen angel] for the clay that he formed into a human being, covering him with the lowly element of earth so that he would not exalt himself in the likeness of God; for the one he had created shining in great brightness, but not covered with so frail and wretched a form as man is, was unable to stand in his pride."

20. DOD I.4.65, PL 197: 851c, as emended from Ghent, Universiteitsbibliotheek Cod. 241, fols. 164–65.

feminine arts of spinning, weaving, sewing, and embroi-
dery.[21] This fusion of symbolic and social contexts is typical of
Hildegard's perspective. Woman's work is socially indispensable, but it is also a revelation of God's work. Just as the cosmos is Wisdom's vesture, or God's visible glory, so the body
born of woman is the glory of the soul—or would be, had
there been no fall.

The exposition of Gen. 1:27 continues with a discussion of
Eve as Adam's partner.

> But the man had no helper like himself. So God gave him
> one, and this was the mirror image of woman (*speculativa forma*
> *mulieris*), in which the whole human race lay hidden until it
> should come forth in God's mighty power, just as he had
> brought forth the first man. Male and female were joined to-
> gether, therefore, in such a way that each one works through
> the other. The male would not be called "male" without the
> female, or the female named "female" without the male. For
> woman is man's work, and man is the solace of woman's eyes;
> and neither of them could exist without the other.[22]

The tantalizing phrase *speculativa forma* defies translation. *Spe-*
culatio can denote contemplation as well as reflection; thus,
Hildegard called the knowledge of good and evil *speculativa*
scientia, reflective or contemplative self-awareness.[23] Insofar
as Eve is Adam's mirror, he looks at her and recognizes his
own image and likeness. But he also sees in her the mother
of his children, who are reflected in their mutual gaze like the
endless figures that appear, one behind another, when two
mirrors stand face to face with a sole figure between them.

---

21. *Causae et curae* 59. The association here may be clarified by a text from
Rupert of Deutz: "Nature herself teaches that it befits man to work the earth,
for it is more suitable for woman to engage in serviceable handiwork for
man's body. Therefore the text, 'that he may work the earth from which he
was taken,' is properly interpreted to mean that woman too should work to
care for the man from whom she was taken." *In Genesim* III.31, CCCM 21:
272.

22. DOD I.4.100, PL 197: 885bc.

23. *Scivias* III.2.9, p. 356: "Just as a person looks at his face in a mirror to
see whether it is beautiful or blemished, so in knowledge he examines the
good and the evil in a past action that he inwardly considers."

Adam and Eve, answering one to another, allow the image of God to become visible in myriad reflections, corresponding to all the unborn generations still in the womb. The mirror in this text, then, denotes woman as both the complement of man and the primordial mother.[24]

As we have already seen, Hildegard described her visionary light as a kind of mirror, and she praised the disclosure of Love's beauty in "the mirror of the cherubim." An emblem of revelation, the mirror also implies self-awareness, for the beholder is always part of the vision he or she beholds in it. In this sense each choir of angels is a mirror or "seal of reflection" (*speculativum sigillum*) to the next, in an ascending hierarchy of vision: the divine mysteries that each lacks in itself it perceives in the higher, as it reveals its own to the lower.[25] Man too is a mirror created even more perfect than the angels, for he reflects the entire cosmos, which is sealed in him: "man is the mirror of all the miracles of God."[26] What Adam is to the world and the angels are to their fellows, so Eve is to Adam: a mirror in which his own glory is reflected and thereby redoubled. All that he is and does is embodied in her, so that by contemplating her he beholds himself and his world imbued with new radiance.[27] Eve too, as the serpent notices, "looks to another as the angels look to the Lord."[28] In Hildegard's view, all salvation is contingent upon this act of turning away from self to contemplate another, for God so ordered the cosmos that "the higher parts have gained splendor from

24. On this image cf. Maura Böckeler, *Das Grosse Zeichen* (Salzburg, 1941): 27–34; Margot Schmidt, "Hildegard von Bingen als Lehrerin des Glaubens; *Speculum* als Symbol des Transzendenten," *Festschrift* 95–157; Heinrich Schipperges, "Das Schöne in der Welt Hildegards von Bingen," *Jahrbuch für Ästhetik und allgemeine Kunstwissenschaft* 4 (1958–59): 83–139.

25. DOD III.6.6 and III.10.14, PL 197: 960d and 1016b.

26. *Causae et curae* 65. Cf. Ep. 51, PL 197: 261b: hominem speculum honoris sui et miraculorum suorum constituit [Deus].

27. Cf. Godfrey of Admont's remark that, although a man can reflect inwardly on the divine image that he bears, yet he beholds it "plenius et perfectius" when he contemplates woman, who was taken from him. *Homiliae dominicales*, PL 174: 360cd.

28. Ep. 47, PL 197: 222d.

the lower, and the lower from the higher."²⁹ So, by the mu-
tuality of their gaze, Adam and Eve reflect the life of the Trinity and the unfallen angels, and escape the sin of Lucifer, who
wished to be a lamp instead of a mirror.³⁰ As man and woman
reflect on each other and shine before each other, each grows
in wisdom and the world is enriched. For the increase of love
and knowledge, it is not good for man to be alone.³¹

Hildegard called man "the solace of woman's eyes" because
Eve looks to Adam with hope and longing: he will bring the
potential life within her to fruition. Conversely, when Adam
contemplates Eve, he sees the reflection of things to come,
and rejoices in his prophetic knowledge.

> For when Adam looked at Eve, he was utterly filled with wis-
> dom, for he saw the mother through whom he would beget
> children. But when Eve looked at Adam, she gazed at him as
> if she were seeing into heaven, as a soul that longs for heavenly
> things stretches upward, for she set her hope in the man.³²

If she is a mirror, it is his form that she reflects. If she is a
fountain, it is he who draws water: "Although man has
greater strength than woman, yet woman is a fountain of wisdom and a wellspring of deep joy, which man draws out to
perfection."³³ In this sense the seer can say that "woman is
man's work." Yet in practice the distinction is relative, for just
as each looks to the other in contemplation, so each works
through the other in procreation.

The sexual act itself defines both the complementarity of

29. *Scivias* II.1.6, p. 115.
30. LVM VI.15, Pitra 226. Lucifer enim velut speculum cum omnibus or-
namentis suis constitutus erat; sed ipse lux, et non umbra ejusdem lucis esse
voluit.
31. See LVM IV.3, Pitra 148: Omne instrumentum Deus sic instituit, quod
unumquodque in aliud respiciat. Quanto plus enim alius ab alio sapit, quod
in se nescit, tanto plus scientia illi adest. Cf. DOD III.6.5, PL 197: 959d:
Plenum namque gaudium utilitatis ex se ipso homo habere non potest nisi
illud ab alio percipiat.
32. *Causae et curae* 136.
33. Ep. 13, PL 197: 167b.

the sexes and the priority of the male. God created Adam
before Eve not because he is morally, intellectually, or ontologically superior but because his work precedes hers in the
act of generation. He is like the summer, which fructifies the
earth, and she like the winter, which stores and ripens its
produce.[34] Hildegard, in fact, so insisted on this complementarity that she even misquoted the Biblical text she was expounding to prove it. St. Paul remarked that "man was not
made from woman, but woman from man. Neither was man
created for woman, but woman for man" (I Cor. 11:8–9). To
be sure, he redressed the balance with a reminder of mutual
dependence: "As woman was made from man, so man is now
born of woman. And all things are from God" (I Cor. 11:12).[35]
But the seer could not admit the Apostle's implicit doctrine of
"he for God only, she for God in him," and she so accentuated
his second idea that she inadvertently denied the first.

> "Woman was created for man's sake," and man was made
> for woman's. For as she is from man, so too man is from her,
> lest one be sundered from the other in the unity of procreation.
> For in one activity they perform one act, just as the air and the
> wind work together. . . . The wind stirs the air and the air
> enfolds the wind, so that every green plant in their sphere is
> under their sway. What does this mean? Woman cooperates
> with man, and man with woman in the act of generation.[36]

In this text there is no hint of either inequality or corruption
in sexuality; intercourse appears as a wholly natural and reciprocal act. The verdant foliage and the analogy of the wind,
a sign of the Spirit, evoke marriage in Paradise.

34. DOD II.5.43, PL 197: 945cd.
35. A typical exegesis is that of Hervé of Bourg-Dieu: "Woman is the glory
of man when he rules and she obeys; man is ruled by wisdom, woman by
man." *In Epistolam I ad Corinthios*, PL 181: 926c.
36. *Scivias* I.2.12, p. 21. The edition records no variant ms readings or
attempts to correct the misquotation, which is noted by Marie-Thérèse d'Alverny in "Comment les théologiens et les philosophes voient la femme," *Cahiers de civilisation médiévale* 20 (1977): 123, n. 103.

THE BRIGHT CLOUD AND THE SHADOW

One of the early *Scivias* visions deals with Eve and Adam at the moment of their fall, an event depicted in an extraordinarily cryptic miniature of the Rupertsberg manuscript (Fig. 2). In the lower-right corner, two flowering trees suggest Eden. Above them, a naked Adam lies sleeping with open eyes. His right hand is cupped to his ear, which hearkens to the flames rising from hell-mouth below. From Adam's left side issues a stylized cloud shaped like a wing or a drooping tulip blossom (described as a *candida nubes* in the text, but painted leaf-green). A number of golden flowerlike stars gleam within it. Out of hell-mouth billows a dark cloud of smoke, veined like a tree trunk and branching into eight tongues at the summit. The lowest one takes the form of a serpent's head and spews streams of venom into the starry cloud. In the upper register, the remaining tongues seek to pierce heaven, where more golden stars flower in the sky, but a thick firmament prevents them. At the four corners of the miniature appear the emblems of earth, water, fire, and air.

Some of the strangeness of this image results from the compression of two normally distinct scenes, the creation of Eve and the temptation, into a single miniature. But despite its unusual features, the image is remotely derived from the familiar creation of Eve iconography.[37] It illustrates the following text:

> Then I saw as it were a great throng of living torches, very bright, kindled by a bolt of a fiery lightning from which they acquired a glowing splendor. And behold! there appeared a lake, very broad and deep, with a mouth like a well belching forth fiery smoke and a terrible stench. From the lake, too, came a hideous cloud of mist, which billowed out to touch something like a vein with deceiving eyes. Through it, the foul

37. See Henri Leclercq, "Adam et Ève," *Dictionnaire de l'archéologie chrétienne et de liturgie* (1907), I.1: 509–19; Herbert Schade, "Das Paradies und die *Imago Dei*. Eine Studie über die frühmittelalterlichen Darstellungen von der Erschaffung des Menschen als Beispiele einer sakramentalen Kunst," in *Probleme der Kunstwissenschaft* (Berlin, 1966), II: 79–182.

Fig. 2. *Eve over-shadowed by the devil.* Adam listens to counsel from hell-mouth while a belching serpent-tongue infects Eve. Eibingen *Scivias,* Abtei St. Hildegard; facsimile of Wiesbaden, Hessische Landesbibliothek, Hs. 1 (now missing), vision I.2. All photographs from this ms courtesy of Brepols, Turnhout, Belgium.

cloud breathed upon a shining cloud, filled with stars upon
stars, which issued from the beautiful form of a man in a region
of light. Thus, the foul cloud cast the shining cloud and the
human form out of that region.

After this a luminous splendor surrounded the place; and
all the elements of the world, which had formerly lain in great
peace, became turbulent and displayed frightful terrors.[38]

At the center of this panoramic scene, midway between
hell and heaven, appears the mother of all living. In lieu of
the conventional woman emerging from Adam's side, Hildegard envisioned Eve as a bright starry cloud to which the artist—for excellent reasons—gave the aspect of a tender green
leaf. *Viriditas* for Hildegard was more than a color; the fresh
green that recurs so often in her visions represents the principle of all life, growth, and fertility flowing from the life-creating power of God. In Peter Dronke's words, this *viriditas* is
"the greenness of a paradise which knows no Fall," "the
earthly expression of the celestial sunlight."[39] According to
Hildegard's gloss, the visionary form signifies "Eve with her
innocent spirit, taken from the innocent Adam and pregnant
with the whole multitude of mankind in her body, shining in
the foreordination of God."[40] In the miniature, only the iconographic context hints at the meaning and enables us to recognize the enigmatic form as a woman.

As the text explains, the stars within Eve's body denote the
children to be born of her, radiant as the angels that shine like
living stars above her. To an eye familiar with this convention,
by which stars represent angels or saints,[41] the miniature reveals at a glance that the bright cloud is a potential heaven on
earth. Both the vision and the image represent, in a highly
condensed and graphic form, the widely held belief that man-

38. *Scivias* I.2, p. 13.

39. Peter Dronke, "Tradition and Innovation in Medieval Western Colour-
Imagery," *Eranos Jahrbuch* 41 (1972): 82, 84.

40. *Scivias* I.2.10, p. 19.

41. According to Alan of Lille, "per lunam Ecclesia, per stellas sancti fi-
gurantur," because "stella a stella differt in claritate" (I Cor. 15:41). *Distinctiones*, PL 210: 955c–56a.

kind was made to replace the lost angels in heaven.[42] Juxtaposed with the scenes of Satan in hell and the good angels confirmed on high, like torches kindled by a flash of lightning, the star-spangled cloud intimates that Eve's children will replace those stars that have fallen.

This symbolism, though obscure on account of its compression, is clarified by comparable images elsewhere in the seer's works. In *Scivias* III.1, Hildegard saw Lucifer and his angels as a shower of stars, which, turning from the Luminous One on his throne toward the northern void, lose all their brightness in falling. But their lost light is not quenched; it returns instead to the Father of lights, who clothes it in flesh for his second son, Adam.[43] Elsewhere, Christ himself is compared to a "burning star ablaze among shadowy clouds."[44] This image, predictably, derives from the sapiential books. In Ecclus. 24:7 Sophia proclaims, "My throne is in the pillar of cloud," and, according to the standard commentary of Rabanus Maurus, "the cloud may signify the flesh of the Savior."[45] Stars shining through clouds, then, indicate divine splendor gleaming through the veil of the flesh.

With regard to Eve, the shining cloud has still further connotations. In Hildegard's vision of Mother Church, the region between the navel and the thighs is clothed in a similar cloud that signifies the secular life, because lay men and women produce children to bring the Church to her fullness.[46] Eve's motherhood thus prefigures that of Mater Ecclesia. The bright cloud, like the mirror, can evoke the womb, with its hidden but glorious contents. As a cloud modestly conceals the rising sun, which it carries, it can serve as a symbol of chastity in

---

42. Augustine adopted this notion to justify his view that Adam and Eve would have reproduced sexually in Paradise even if they had not fallen. See *De Genesi ad litteram* IX; Gregory, *Homiliae in Evangelia* II.34, PL 76: 1249cd; Paul Salmon, "Der zehnte Engelchor in deutschen Dichtung und Predigten des Mittelalters," *Euphorion* 57 (1963): 321–30.
43. *Scivias* III.1.16, pp. 344–45.
44. *Scivias* I.3.31, p. 59.
45. Rabanus Maurus, *Comment. in Ecclus.* VI.13, PL 109: 925d.
46. *Scivias* II.5.23, p. 195.

marriage, a sort of bridal veil. Hildegard may have known Isidore's etymology of *nubes* "from *obnubendo*, that is, covering heaven, whence also brides are called *nuptae* because they veil their faces."[47] Such a veil would suit the first bride and mother well. Moreover, according to St. Ambrose, the "light cloud" of Isa. 19:1 is a figure of the Virgin.[48] Hildegard wrote that when God first took Eve from Adam, "in his foreknowledge he already held the Life by which all life subsists, and foresaw when it would descend into the woman through whom man would enter into the glory of the celestial Paradise."[49] In creating the first Eve, mother of humanity, he envisioned the second Eve, Mother of God. This idea is exemplified in a late-twelfth-century miniature that shows Christ as Creator flanked by six medallions depicting the works of the Hexaemeron (Fig. 3). Before his body he holds a seventh medallion in which Mary, a seated *orans* with nimbus, mantle, and face upturned in an attitude of prayer, exactly mirrors the gesture of the newly created Eve. A strong diagonal line connects the medallions showing the first day of creation, its conclusion with the birth of Eve, and its predestined consummation in Mary.

Not only the brightness of the cloud but also its very matter suggest the motherhood of Eve. Clouds, in Hildegard's view, are compounded of water and air or ether—a substance purer and subtler than ordinary air, occupying the heavenly sphere midway between fire and water. Allegorically, the ether denotes pure penance, which placates the wrath of God as ether mitigates the fury of water and fire.[50] Hence Eve's "ethereal" nature implies the virtues of purity, moderation, and sweetness. Her physical constitution, "airy" as opposed to "earthy," also makes the first woman permeable and spacious. Like the clouds of heaven, her body offers room enough

---

47. Isidore of Seville, *Etymologiae* XIII.7.2, PL 82: 476b.
48. Ambrose, *Expositio in Lucam* 10.42, CCSL 14: 357.
49. Ep. 47, PL 197: 222d.
50. DOD I.4.5, PL 197: 809ab. This ether is not to be confused with the Aristotelian quintessence; see Hans Liebeschütz, *Das allegorische Weltbild der heiligen Hildegard von Bingen* (Leipzig, 1930): 67–68.

Fig. 3. *Eve and Mary: "Firstborn before all creation."* The six medallions surrounding Christ demonstrate the six days of creation. The enthroned Virgin, imitating the gesture of Eve before her fall, already occupies the central place. Illustration to Josephus, *Antiquitates Iudaicae*, Paris, BN lat. 5047, fol. 2ʳ. Courtesy of Bibliothèque Nationale.

to lodge many stars: "The first mother of mankind was made like the purest air, for, as the ether enfolds the inviolate stars, so she—inviolate, incorrupt, without pain—held the human race within her when she was told to increase and multiply."[51] In a reflective moment Hildegard described herself too as a woman of the airy temperament, to which she ascribed both her frailty and her openness to the Spirit—as if what in other women is a capacity for motherhood had in her become a capacity for God.[52]

The ambiguous brightness of clouds, at once revealing and concealing, is a sapiential image that figures in many Biblical theophanies: the pillar of cloud in the desert (Exod. 13:22), the vision of Ezekiel (Ezek. 10:3–4), the Transfiguration (Matt. 17:5, "a bright cloud overshadowed them"), and the Ascension (Acts 1:9). In Ecclus. 24:6 Sapientia declares, "I made a never-failing light to rise in heaven, and like a cloud I covered all the earth." But the cloud of theophany par excellence is the overshadowing of Mary at the Annunciation: "The Holy Spirit shall come upon you, and the power of the Most High shall overshadow you" (Luke 1:35). *Obumbratio* is, however, a profoundly ambivalent metaphor. On the one hand, it can denote grace, shelter, refreshing coolness, protection from too dazzling a light; but, on the other, it suggests sin, ignorance, error, and death.[53] In fact, the image of the darkened mirror or the sun overshadowed by clouds is a frequent metaphor for fallen nature.[54]

If the shining cloud signifies Eve, overshadowing is a nat-

51. *Causae et curae* 104.

52. DOD III.10.38, PL 197: 1038a: Ipsa enim cum inspiratione Spiritus sancti officialis existit, et complexionem de aere habet; ideoque de ipso aere, de pluvia, de vento, et de omni tempestate infirmitas ei ita infixa est, ut nequaquam securitatem carnis in se habere possit, alioquin inspiratio Spiritus sancti in ea habitare non valeret.

53. For a convenient summary of these meanings see "umbra" in Alan of Lille, *Distinctiones*, PL 210: 985–86.

54. Cf. Gerhoch of Reichersberg: "the sun of justice so detests the cloud of sin that covers the whole earth that it seems just for it to withdraw its brightness, because it cannot form the likeness of its image in the mirrors of filthy human hearts unless the filth is first wiped away." Ep. 27, PL 193: 614b.

ural metaphor for her fall, making it a negative type or diabolic parody of the Virgin's conception. In *Scivias* I.2, the inversion expressed aurally by the words *Ave* and *Eva* becomes
a visual experience. As Mary would one day be overshadowed
by the bright power of God, satanic darkness now overshad-
ows Eve in equal and opposite fashion. Hildegard saw the
shining cloud defiled by a hideous one: the foul mist of hell
poisons the radiance of heaven. By this assault, Satan's envy
triumphs over Eve's naïveté, and, through her, over all her
progeny. "For death entered into the woman because, hearing
the serpent's words, she overshadowed the whole world."[55]
Ultimately, what the serpent wants to darken is Wisdom herself and all her works: "Through the devil's deception arose
that first, original sin, like a cloud of mist rising from foul air
to cover the whole earth, hiding the pure light of day and
corroding the works of Wisdom as if it despised them."[56] Behind the trouble in Eden lies the primeval war of Satan on
Sapientia.

EVE AND SATAN

The notion that death entered the world through the devil's
envy (Wisd. 2:24), though Scriptural and widely taught, plays
an unusually critical role in Hildegard's understanding of the
fall. When she expounded the Genesis story in narrative
rather than symbolic terms, the distinctiveness of her reading
became even more apparent. Unlike her contemporaries, she
showed virtually no interest in the psychology of Eve and
Adam, and scarcely considered the question of their guilt.
Her approach was ontological, cosmic, and mythical, where
the prevailing exegetical trends were psychological and
moral. Even her use of the Augustinian tradition was selective
and sparing.

Augustine, formulating a doctrine that would prevail in the

55. *Prooemium Vitae S. Disibodi* II, Pitra 353.
56. DOD I.4.37, PL 197: 833bc, as emended from Ghent Cod. 241, fol.
145.

West for a thousand years, had ascribed to Adam and Eve both moral and existential freedom. God created them with the potential either to sin or not to sin, and, in consequence, to die or not to die as their choice determined. As fully responsible agents, they sinned and reaped the punishments they deserved: death and corruption. Because Adam chose to disobey God's will, he was punished with a kind of poetic justice when a part of his body, the sexual member, began to disobey his own will. Thus, concupiscence, or unruly desire, originated as a penalty for sin; but it also became the means by which sin perpetuates itself, because the inescapable lust of intercourse infects each newly conceived child with the same disease.[57] This view of original sin minimizes the devil's role in order to place responsibility squarely on the protoplasts. Satan's innuendos against God, said Augustine, could not have beguiled Eve "unless there were already in her mind a certain love of her own power and a certain proud self-presumption."[58] But while sin originated with Eve and Adam, Augustine in effect made God responsible for its continuance by identifying the just punishment for sin as the very means that brings more sinners into the world. Aside from this difficulty, his theory is somewhat lopsided in that his discussion of the "disobedient member" obviously pertains to male rather than female sexuality. The woman participates in the penalty through her suffering in childbirth, but not necessarily in the guilty pleasure that transmits sin.[59] Later and less subtle theologians would compensate for this apparent bias

57. Augustine, *De nuptiis et concupiscentia* I.7 et passim; *De peccato originali* 38–45. Peter Brown has explored the revolutionary character of Augustine's teaching in "Sexuality and Society in the Fifth Century A.D.: Augustine and Julian of Eclanum," in Emilio Gabba, ed., *Tria Corda: Scritti in onore di Arnaldo Momigliano* (Como, 1983): 49–70.

58. Augustine, *De Genesi ad litteram* XI.30, CSEL 28[1]: 363.

59. "Whether, indeed, such pleasure accompanies the commingling of the seminal elements of the two sexes in the womb, is a question which perhaps women may be able to determine from their inmost feelings; but it is improper for us to push an idle curiosity so far." Augustine, *De nuptiis et concupiscentia* II.26, trans. Peter Holmes in *Saint Augustine: Anti-Pelagian Writings*, vol. 5 of *Nicene and Post-Nicene Fathers* (New York, 1887): 293.

against the male by laying the whole burden of temptation and rampant lust on the female.

Taking their cue from Augustine, commentators agreed with one accord that, if Adam and Eve had not fallen, they would have experienced sex without pleasure and birth without pain. The bishop of Hippo saw the three curses of lust, agony in childbirth, and death as inextricably related. In Paradise, he maintained, the first parents would have come together "with no anxious burning of lust, with no labor and pain of childbirth," and when the predestined number of saints was fulfilled, God would have changed their animal bodies into spiritual ones with no intervening death.[60] This scenario allowed Augustine to defend sexuality and marriage against their Manichaean despisers, while safeguarding his doctrine of concupiscence as the just penalty for sin. His suspicion of pleasure prevailed well into the twelfth century. According to one widespread view, Adam and Eve would have coupled without delight, like two clasping hands.[61] Rupert of Deutz remarked that sinless parents would have engendered citizens for the republic of heaven out of charity, instead of rutting like beasts to perpetuate their own names.[62] It was Abelard who first revolted against the idea that pleasure per se was sinful, and even argued that Adam and Eve might have joined in intercourse before their fall; but his views were, for obvious reasons, suspect.[63]

Medieval exegetes transmitted Augustine's view of original sin with monotonous regularity, but twelfth-century writers

---

60. Augustine, *De Genesi ad litteram* IX.3, CSEL 28[1]: 271–72.
61. See for instance Honorius, *Elucidarium* I.74, ed. Yves Lefèvre (Paris, 1954): 374; William of Champeaux, *Glosulae glos. ad Romanos* 5, Bamberg Cod. Bibl. 129, fol. 13, cited in Michael Müller, *Die Lehre des hl. Augustinus von der Paradiesesehe und ihre Auswirkung in der Sexualethik des 12. und 13. Jahrhunderts bis Thomas von Aquin* (Regensburg, 1954): 48, n. 22.
62. Rupert of Deutz, *In Genesim* II.9, CCCM 21: 193–94.
63. Abelard, *Expositio in Hexaemeron*, PL 178: 781cd; Müller, *Lehre des hl. Augustinus* 66–75. See also Reinhold Grimm, "Die Paradiesesehe. Eine erotische Utopie des Mittelalters," in Franz Hundsnurscher and Ulrich Müller, eds., *Getempert und Gemischet. Festschrift Wolfgang Mohr* (Göppingen, 1972): 1–25.

took an increasing interest in the psychological and forensic aspects of the fall. On the basis of I Tim. 2:14 ("Adam was not seduced, but the woman was seduced into transgression"), many writers held that Eve really believed the serpent's lies, while Adam merely yielded to her feminine wiles. This view was reinforced by the Philonic allegory of Adam as reason and Eve as sensuality, which had been introduced to the West by St. Ambrose in his treatise *On Paradise*. Allegorically, Philo had claimed, the senses are deluded more easily than the mind, whereas literally, "woman is of a nature to be deceived rather than to reflect greatly."[64] Most commentators assumed that the serpent approached the woman first because she was either more presumptuous or less intelligent than the man. According to Arnold of Bonneval, she believed the serpent because he told her what she wanted to hear.[65] Rupert proposed curiosity as her sin, making Eve a new Pandora: as she strolled through the garden with wandering feet and eyes, thinking too much about the outside world, she gave occasion to the serpent lurking beyond the walls.[66]

While Hildegard often referred to original sin in language reminiscent of Augustine, some of her assumptions about the first parents are significantly different from those of the medieval Augustinians. To begin with, she placed a much greater emphasis on Adam and Eve's prelapsarian glory, in keeping with the so-called maximalist tradition of the rabbis.[67] In this view the first couple had been graced with supernatural perfections: they could see the glory of God with their physical eyes; they knew every language, whether human or angelic; their dreams were full of prophetic truth; and they shone with splendor like the sun, robed in garments of light.[68]

64. Philo, *Questions and Answers on Genesis*, trans. Ralph Marcus in *Philo*, supp. 1, vol. 46 of Loeb Classical Library (London, 1953): 26. For similar notions see *De opificio mundi* 59 and *Legum allegoria* II.11.

65. Arnold of Bonneval, *De operibus sex dierum*, PL 198: 1545.

66. Rupert of Deutz, *In Genesim* III.2, CCCM 21: 236.

67. See J. M. Evans, *Paradise Lost and the Genesis Tradition* (Oxford, 1968), ch. 3. Rabbinic sources on Adam are cited in Louis Ginzberg, *The Legends of the Jews*, trans. Henrietta Szold (Philadelphia, 1954), I: 59–62.

68. Ep. 47, PL 197: 222c; *Solutiones* 3–4, 1041b–d; *Causae et curae* 45–46, 82.

For Hildegard, the most distinctive feature of their perfection was the state of integrity—wholeness of mind and body—which includes but transcends physical virginity. Its symbol is the song of Adam, "whose voice rang with the sound of all harmony and the sweetness of the whole art of music."[69] In Paradise, Adam and Eve were indeed free from lust, but their union would not have been without pleasure. Rather, husband and wife would have lain side by side, "and they would gently perspire as if sleeping. Then the woman would become pregnant from the man's perspiration (*sudor*), and, while they lay thus sweetly asleep, she would give birth to a child painlessly from her side . . . in the same way that God brought Eve forth from Adam, and that the Church was born from the side of Christ."[70] For Hildegard *sudor*, as Dronke has noted, "has the associations not of the sweat of effort but of the distillation of a perfume, a heavenly quality, out of anything that is fertile or beautiful on earth."[71]

Eve's childbearing would have been as pure and undefiled as that of Mary, who was also said to give birth "from the side" and not from the womb.[72] And just as her own creation from Adam's rib prefigured Ecclesia's birth from the side of the Crucified, Eve's motherhood would have conformed to this incorrupt pattern.[73] To this way of thinking, only the Virgin's conception and childbearing reveal true "nature" as God ordained it from the beginning; it is the motherhood of fallen

---

69. Ep. 47, PL 197: 220c.

70. Fragment IV.29, p. 72; cf. Augustine, *De peccato originali* 40.

71. Dronke, *Poetic Individuality* 157.

72. Fragment IV.7, p. 68.

73. Cf. Godfrey of Admont: "If Eve, as a figure of [Mary], had adorned a bridal chamber for the Holy Spirit in the temple of her heart, through the discipline of humility and obedience, grace would not have been lacking, and while the power of the Most High overshadowed her, no heat of concupiscence would have burned the soul consecrated to God. She would indeed have conceived by her husband, as the earth watered by showers puts forth herbs and buds in fertile increase; and, with no passion of desire, her husband would have used the conjugal embrace only to sow the seminal reasons." *De operibus sex dierum*, PL 189: 1564–65. On the typology see Sebastien Tromp, "De nativitate Ecclesiae ex corde Jesu in cruce," *Gregorianum* 13 (1932): 489–527.

Eve and her daughters that is "unnatural." Hildegard here combined an extreme typological (or sapiential) view of Eve with a standard rejection of sexuality in its present state. Yet, unlike most of her contemporaries, in her Edenic idyll she preserved a gentle eroticism. However corrupt the sexual attraction that we now experience, she maintained that in origin the pleasure of love is neither an evil nor a punishment. This outlook is even clearer in a text describing the creation of Eve, where Hildegard stated that "Adam experienced a great love in the slumber that God sent upon him. And God made a form for the man to love, and thus woman is the love of man. And as soon as the woman was formed, God gave the man the power of creation that by his love, who is woman, he might beget children."[74]

This affirmation of eros in Paradise (albeit of an idyllic rather than ardent stamp) is inconsistent with the view that pleasure as such is a penalty. And although Hildegard deplored concupiscence as vehemently as any, she seemed concerned to avoid the implication that it is a punishment imposed by God. At the same time, she wished to minimize Eve's guilt as far as possible. The only solution left is to blame Satan, which she did with consistency and force. In this way she escaped both Augustine's inclination to a vindictive view of divine justice and the misogyny based on his influential reading of Genesis. Her Eve is more sinned against than sinning, not so much tempted as victimized outright, and, if any misogyny comes into play, it is Satan's. Medieval readers who wanted women "to be despicable on account of Eve's transgression," like the critics Hildegard addressed in her *Scivias* prologue, might find the exemplar of their sentiments in the devil.

Satan's grudge against Eve is grounded in envy of her

---

74. *Causae et curae* 136. This motif may also be of Jewish origin; a midrash in the *Torah Shelemah* states that Adam enjoyed Eve's intimacy in a dream while she was being created, or otherwise he would never have known how to love. Midrash Abakir, cited in Menahem Kasher, *Encyclopedia of Biblical Interpretation* (New York, 1953), I: 114.

motherhood. As the *Scivias* vision demonstrates, her children are meant to replace his angels in heaven, and, moreover, she is the vessel of Wisdom's counsel, which he hates. The important motif of Satan's jealousy is most clearly stated in Hildegard's commentary on the woman clothed with the sun (Apocalypse 12), whom she identifies against all precedent as Eve.[75] What Satan envies is the woman's clothing—whether of flesh or of light Hildegard did not say. But Eve's garment serves to evoke her fertility as against Satan's nakedness and sterility.

> When the devil saw the woman clothed, knowing in his envy that he had been cast out of heaven, he wondered inwardly why God had given her clothing, and drew himself up in rage. . . . This must be understood as follows. The ancient dragon, seeing that he had lost the place where he wished to set up his throne (for he had been cast down to the netherworld), sharpened his wrath against the woman, because he recognized that through childbearing she was the root of the whole human race. Hating her mightily, he said to himself that he would never cease to pursue her until he had drowned her in the sea, as it were; for in the beginning he had deceived her.[76]

In the same vein, Hildegard observed that the devil loves homosexuality because of his loathing for mothers: "because of the primal hatred he felt for the woman's fecundity, he persecutes her still lest she give birth; but he prefers men to pollute themselves in perversion."[77] At another time, she saw a host of demons raging against women and crying, "These are fit for the propagation of the world as the earth is for seeds. So let us make haste to seduce them, lest they give birth to warriors against us."[78] Such is the cause of enmity between the woman and the serpent (Gen. 3:15). For Hildegard, this

---

75. The woman was normally interpreted as the Church until Ambrosius Autpertus introduced a Marian reading. For a history of exegesis see Ewald Vetter, "*Mulier amicta sole* und Mater Salvatoris," *Münchner Jahrbuch der bildenden Kunst* 9–10 (1958–59): 32–71.

76. DOD II.5.16, PL 197: 915bc.

77. LVM III.98, Pitra 141.

78. LVM I.114, Pitra 50.

conviction did not remain merely theoretical but led to practical action. For instance, believing that the ancient serpent and his minions, "the malignant spirits of the air," lay in ambush for women in childbirth, she advised mothers to protect childbed and cradle with powerful demon repellents, such as jasper or fronds of fern.[79]

The tendency to magnify Satan's guilt, without denying that of Adam and Eve, forms an integral part of the maximalist exegesis of the fall.[80] But Hildegard was extreme even for this school. Apropos of the disaster in Paradise, she remarked that Satan "knew he could conquer the woman's softness more easily than the man's strength, seeing too that Adam burned with such powerful love for Eve that, if the devil himself conquered her, Adam would do whatever she told him."[81] Eve's "softness" and Adam's "strength" are scarcely moral qualities at all; Adam is "strong" because he was taken from earth, and Eve "soft" because formed from his flesh.[82] Such formulations correspond to the standard etymologies that derive *vir* from *vis* and *mulier* from *mollities*, and, beyond these, the ingenious rabbinic traditions that base the contrasts between man and woman on the difference of earth from flesh.[83]

Eve's softness makes her more vulnerable, but, with her usual optimism, Hildegard managed to find a saving grace in this very frailty. In his great mercy, God had ordained that if the human race could not forbear sinning, at least their sin would spring from weakness and not strength, and so be more amenable to healing. Physical traits are correlated, if not confused, with traits of character. Yet the issue of guilt seemed almost irrelevant when Hildegard wrote that "if Adam had

79. LSM IV.10, PL 197: 1257b; I.47, 1148ab.

80. Evans, *Paradise Lost* 87–88.

81. *Scivias* I.2.10, p. 19.

82. *Causae et curae* 47: Caro et cutis Adae fortior et durior fuit quam hominum nunc sit, quia Adam de terra formatus fuit et Eva de ipso.

83. Isidore of Seville, *Etymologiae* XI.2.17–18, PL 82: 417a. According to rabbinic lore, only woman wears perfume because meat needs preservatives to keep it fresh, but the dust of the earth needs none. Similarly, an angry man is placated more easily than a woman because earth in water softens faster than bone. Ginzberg, *Legends of the Jews* I: 67.

sinned before Eve, that transgression would have been so grave and incorrigible, and man would have fallen into such great, unredeemable stubbornness, that he neither would nor could have been saved. Hence, because Eve transgressed first, the sin could more easily be undone, since she was weaker than the male."[84] Here again, the ambiguous frailty of woman makes her more susceptible to both temptation and redemption, just as her "airiness" opens her to both the Holy Spirit and the demonic powers of the air.

Eve is also the shortest route to the heart of Adam because of his blameless love for her—a fact that Satan recognizes and exploits. In Eden, said Hildegard, "the serpent came and breathed upon the woman with his eloquence, and she accepted it and bowed to the serpent. And she gave the thing she had tasted from the serpent to her husband, and it remained in the man; for it is man who brings all acts to their completion."[85] Behind this cryptic account lies an ancient legend in which the serpent breathes poison on the forbidden fruit before offering it to the woman. In the Jewish *Apocalypse of Moses*, Eve confesses to her children that the devil "went and poured upon the fruit the poison of his wickedness, which is lust, the root and beginning of every sin, and he bent the branch on the earth and I took of the fruit and I ate."[86] This mythical motif, suitably glossed, found its way into the classic Western exegesis through Ambrose, who wrote that Satan "vomited a certain poisonous wisdom into this world, so that men might take falsehood for truth and let their love be captured by appearance."[87] Alcuin too used the metaphor of poison, as did Rupert.[88]

The ideas of lust, death, deception, and satanic vomit

---

84. *Causae et curae* 47.

85. Ep. 104, PL 197: 325d–26a.

86. *Apocalypsis Mosis* xix.3, trans. L. S. Wells in R. H. Charles, ed., *Apocrypha and Pseudepigrapha of the Old Testament* (Oxford, 1913), II: 146. For other instances of this motif see Louis Ginzberg, "Adam," *Jewish Encyclopedia* I: 179.

87. Ambrose, *De Paradiso* 12.55, CSEL 32¹: 312.

88. Alcuin, *Interrogationes et responsiones in Genesim* 6, PL 100: 517d–18a; Rupert of Deutz, *In Genesim* III.3, CCCM 21: 237.

merge in Hildegard's vision of the stinking cloud with the tongue of a serpent, spewing venom into Eve. Thus, "the ancient serpent's maw devoured Eve," as Abstinence warns the faithful in the *Book of Life's Merits*—"and through Eve it vomited out great filth."[89] This filth, here as in the *Apocalypse of Moses*, consists chiefly of lust or the "taste of flesh" (*gustus carnis*). Because it was acquired from the serpent, carnal passion is "slippery, fickle, and deceitful, just like the serpent's counsel."[90] Poisoned words and poisoned fruit have their counterpart in the "poison of semen," which first congealed in the blood of Adam after the fall.[91]

Hildegard's Eve neither persuades nor seduces Adam, although the episode of her beguilement furnished most exegetes with an arsenal of misogynist barbs. Instead, Eve simply catches the devil's disease, as it were, and passes it on by contagion. By preferring this medical analogy to forensic and legal models of the fall, Hildegard again distanced herself from the Augustinian tradition, with its potential for antifeminism. In her view, the fall represents the onset of a terminal illness caused by the poisoned apple, corrupting and disrupting all the bodily humors. Like her contemporary Hugh of Folieto, who wrote a treatise *On the Medicine of the Soul*, she began with a moralized theory of the humors, but incorporated it into a view of the fall so holistic that it is virtually impossible to separate the medical from the moral and mythical aspects.[92] Loss of visible splendor, spiritual blindness and amnesia, lust, shame, depression, rage, frailty, and perversion of the senses are only a few of the symptoms.[93] The in-

89. LVM II.5, Pitra 64.
90. Ep. 104, PL 197: 326a.
91. *Causae et curae* 36.
92. For a comparison of the two moralizing *physici* see Raymond Klibansky, Erwin Panofsky, and Fritz Saxl, *Saturn and Melancholy* (London, 1964): 110–11.
93. Ep. 47, PL 197: 220–24; *Causae et curae* 143–46; *Solutiones* 3–6, PL 197: 1041b–42c. For rabbinic parallels see *Genesis Rabbah* xi; *Baba Batra* (Talmud) 58a; *Targum Yerush. Gen.* 3.7; *Apocalypsis Mosis* xx; *Pirke R. Eliezer* xiv; *Vita Adae et Evae* xxxiv.1.

sidious poison causes melancholia, the source of all diseases and evil passions, to coagulate in Adam and thus perverts his blood and seed.[94] Eve suffers equivalent harm, losing the primal glory and the vision of God; and she incurs the special penalties of menstruation and labor pangs.

> When the torrent of greedy desire invaded Eve, all her veins opened into a river of blood. Hence every woman has tempests of blood within her. . . . But all woman's veins would have remained intact and healthy if Eve had remained for the full time in Paradise. For when she looked upon the serpent, assenting to him, her vision, which had seen heavenly things, was blinded, and when she listened to him with agreement, her hearing, which had heard heavenly things, was blocked; and, in the taste of the apple, the splendor that shone in her was darkened.[95]

Although the Biblical curse of Eve does not expressly include menstruation, Jewish exegetes often referred to it as an effect of the forbidden fruit, together with the first stirrings of lust.[96] Christian commentators seldom mentioned it, though Rupert of Deutz brooded glumly that "the more fertile a woman is, the more wretched she is." He added that even when a woman is not afflicted in childbirth, she is forced to suffer the pain of menstruation, "for woman is the one and only animal who menstruates."[97] To Hildegard, the "tempests of blood" loosed in Eve represented a deep wound to her integrity, which would be further violated by the loss of virginity. And the pain she suffers in menstruation, beginning at the very moment of her fall, heralds the agony of childbirth.

Authors expounding Gen. 3:16 (Vg: "I will multiply your afflictions and your offspring: in pain shall you bring forth

94. *Causae et curae* 36.
95. *Causae et curae* 102–3.
96. Ginzberg, *Legends of the Jews* V: 101, n. 85.
97. Rupert of Deutz, *In Genesim* III.22, CCCM 21: 260; cf. Isidore of Seville, *Etymologiae* XI.140, PL 82: 414b.

children") could furnish harrowing descriptions of labor.[98] But none ascribed to it the same apocalyptic nature as Hildegard, who wrote that every daughter of Eve must give birth in fear and trembling, "in such pain as when the earth shall be changed at the end of time."[99] Yet the analogy, probably inspired by Paul's reference to the approaching doom (I Thess. 5:3), also has its positive side. Eve's pains, viewed sub specie aeternitatis, are not merely punitive but also proleptic. When Christ was born at last, Hildegard stated, the long-expectant prophets rejoiced in the Spirit like a newly delivered mother; and, at the end of time, universal birth pangs will engender a new heaven and a new earth.[100] The Church and the cosmos are in labor until the end; and woman, who personifies both, bears in her body the pain with which Satan has tainted all fruitfulness.

Even the curse of menstruation has its redemptive aspect. Popular lore, as reflected in medical writings like the *Trotula*, dubbed a woman's period her *flores* by analogy with the "fruit of the womb"; and Hildegard likewise would transmute Eve's river of blood into every woman's "native foliage and flowering," the ground of her fertility.[101] Her pain should therefore be an occasion for mercy as well as judgment. In the *Scivias* Hildegard said in the person of God, "I do not disdain this time of suffering in woman, for I gave it to Eve when she conceived sin in the taste of the fruit. So a woman during her period should be treated with the great medicine of mercy."[102]

98. For example, Arnold of Bonneval: "Offspring are multiplied at the urge of lust, and because sin is not acknowledged in the assault of impurity, it is suffered in pain when the woman's womb is shaken; when the chains of nature are ruptured from within, the afterbirth comes forth as the infant wails, the trembling hands of the midwives meet the clinging babe—truly, it is a miserable business!" *De operibus sex dierum,* PL 189: 1564bc.

99. *Causae et curae* 105.

100. DOD II.5.31, PL 197: 928ab; *Scivias* III.12.

101. *Causae et curae* 105. For the "menstrua, quae vulgus flores appellat," see "Trotula," *Diseases of Women,* trans. Elizabeth Mason-Hohl (Los Angeles, 1940): 2; Paul Diepgen, *Frau und Frauenheilkunde in der Kultur des Mittelalters* (Stuttgart, 1963): 141.

102. *Scivias* I.2.20, p. 27.

The divine voice goes on to grant menstruating women permission to attend church, although men wounded in battle are to abstain lest they violate the integrity of Christ's temple.[103] The message is clear: a man who has shed blood in warfare is unclean, like the fratricidal Cain, but a woman shedding her own blood is not. Even though Eve's wound is a punishment for sin, it is nonetheless God-given and therefore sacred. Hildegard's treatment of Eve forms a curious contrast with Augustine's view of Adam. According to the Latin doctor, God punished the man with a pleasure that results in the perpetuation of guilt. According to the German prophet, he punished the woman with a pain that results in fertility and mercy. It would seem that Hildegard's view is the more straightforward and the more flattering to God.

The myth of Paradise lost conveys pathos as well as promise. Hildegard's interpretation, with its strong tragic sense balanced by startling optimism, is epitomized in two of the more recondite legends she recorded. In the bestiary that forms part of her *Book of Simple Medicine*, she recounted an exotic bit of lore about the lion, which occurs neither in the *Physiologus* nor in the patristic Genesis commentaries.[104] According to this legend, the lioness bears her cubs stillborn and goes away in sorrow, until the lion comes along and rouses them to life with a roar. Afterward the whole family roars together. Thus it was with Adam and Eve at the birth of their first child.

> Adam and Eve did not lift their voices in a lament before any human being was born. But after the first infant was born, at

103. Cf. Gregory, *Responsiones* to Augustine of Canterbury, question 8, cited in Bede, *Ecclesiastical History of the English People*, ed. and trans. Bertram Colgrave and R. A. B. Mynors (Oxford, 1969): 92–93: "a woman must not be prohibited from entering a church during her usual periods, for this natural overflowing cannot be reckoned a crime: and so it is not fair that she should be deprived from entering the church for that which she suffers unwillingly."

104. The only analogue that I have been able to find occurs in a Manichaean *Book of Scholia* composed c. 600 by one Theodore bar Khoni, who wrote that Adam wept "like a lion that roars and ravens" (cited in Evans, *Paradise Lost* 67). According to *Physiologus*, trans. Michael Curley (Austin, 1979), the lion's vivifying roar signifies the resurrection.

once he cried out wailing to the highest elements. Hearing the unfamiliar voice, Adam ran and listened to the voice of this lamentation, and then he too cried for the first time along with Eve—just as the lion, the lioness, and the cub roar together when they are roused.[105]

The mythical detail contributes both poignancy and grandeur to the tale of our exile. In the *Activity of God,* Hildegard further observed that after their banishment Adam and Eve "became corruptible along with the other fruits of the earth; and in their fall and eviction the whole created world was overshadowed, as if a ray of sunlight shone through a thick cloud."[106] The gates of Eden, too, were hidden by a cloud and sheltered by the cherubim with the flaming sword (Gen. 3:24) to keep Satan from any further mischief there. Because of this protection, "Paradise itself is not darkened in the shadow and ruin of sins," despite human misery.[107] It remains hidden and inviolate, a garden enclosed, "giving the parched land a powerful sap"—at once a reminiscence of Eve before her fall and a type of the woman yet to come.

105. LSM VII.3, PL 197: 1315ab.
106. DOD II.5.15, PL 197: 914cd.
107. *Scivias* I.2.28, p. 32.

4

Daughters of Eve

Outside the gates of Eden, one can no longer speak hypothetically about the world or the women in it. When Hildegard wrote about the daughters of Eve—living women in their concrete psychosexual being—the prophet turned physician; and the reader may be startled to find pages of frank, original discussion of female physiology and passion, with scarcely a nod toward theological interpretation.[1] Most of this material occurs in the *Causes and Cures*, where subjects like sexual desire, intercourse, conception, and childbirth are treated in great though disorganized detail, and in the *Book of Simple Medicine*, which supplies herbal and mineral remedies for such conditions as sterility, amenorrhea, and prolonged labor—as well as antiaphrodisiacs and charms against love magic.

Such a candid, morally neutral treatment of sex might seem implausible, or at least unseemly, on the part of a cloistered virgin, and in large part it was this that led Bertha Widmer to reject the *Causes and Cures* as spurious.[2] We must recall, however, that Hildegard's worldview in principle—and very

---

1. This material has been briefly reviewed by Bernhard Scholz, "Hildegard von Bingen on the Nature of Woman," *American Benedictine Review* 31 (1980): 361–83; and Michela Pereira, "Maternità e sessualità femminile in Ildegarda di Bingen: Proposte di lettura," *Quaderni storici* 44 (1980): 564–79.

2. Bertha Widmer, *Heilsordnung und Zeitgeschehen in der Mystik Hildegards von Bingen* (Basel, 1955): 20. As grounds for rejecting the work, Widmer cited its naturalistic approach, determinism, use of Germanic words, and a single reference to Plato (p. 51). But the philosopher is mentioned only in passing, not cited as an authority; and the Germanic words are almost exclusively the names of plants and of diseases, indicating that Hildegard drew on vernacular folk traditions rather than learned medical lore. I will discuss the issues of naturalism and determinism later.

nearly in fact—excluded nothing known to her age. And the modern reader must be reminded that medieval discussions of sex were far less euphemistic than any until recent times.[3] Yet the material remains problematic. First, as Widmer has pointed out, the paucity of moral and theological comment is baffling in a writer so given to edification, and, where it does occur, it is so ambivalent as to verge on self-contradiction. Hildegard seems to have believed, for example, that no conception can take place without the cooperation of both God and Satan. Second, and no less disturbing, is the strain of determinism that runs through her treatment of sexual behavior and conception, in marked contrast with her more typical insistence on human freedom.

It takes no psychoanalyst to suggest that Hildegard, like most people most of the time, felt ambivalent about sexuality—the area of human behavior that is most intimately personal, yet at the same time most deeply affected by forces beyond our consciousness and control. Alongside this normal ambivalence, we will see the authoritative force of a tradition overwhelmingly hostile to sexual enjoyment, and to women as sexual beings, confronting the intuition of a female visionary whose experience disposed her to perceive the workings of divine Wisdom throughout created nature. Hildegard's gender and her awareness of the misogyny in her culture undoubtedly contributed to her fresh approach. Yet these factors should not be overemphasized, nor should her lingering uneasiness about sex be ascribed solely to Augustinian influence. In effect, the question of sexuality manifests, in its extremest form, the tension between ascetic renunciation and frank appreciation of created goods. Such a tension is inherent in any worldview that affirms both the transcendence of divine Spirit and the real but limited goodness of matter. We

3. Kathleen Casey has observed that medieval society, "despite all efforts by the clerical culture (if not by the clerics themselves) had neither particularly innocent, nor particularly repressed, nor particularly delicate in its language." "The Cheshire Cat: Reconstructing the Experience of Medieval Women," in Bernice Carroll, ed., *Liberating Women's History* (Urbana, 1976): 238.

find it in Augustine himself when he discusses aesthetic pleasures and the sensual dimension in his love for God.[4] The
spiritual ways of Affirmation and Rejection, in the words of
Charles Williams, must pay one another homage;[5] and it is far
easier to imagine that Hildegard held her contrary attitudes
in a sort of delicate balance than that this most holistic of
thinkers managed to compartmentalize them. What she did
not do, unfortunately, was work out a coherent resolution.

The difference between her conflicting expressions coin-
cides, to a degree, with a distinction between two genres.
Hildegard tended to declare her moral prescriptions (or those
of the voice from heaven) in her visionary works, while she
gave vent to more naturalistic thoughts, without visionary
sanction, in her medical works. It is characteristic of medieval
scientific writings, whether Christian or Islamic, to treat sexual functioning frankly without regard for sexual ethics,[6] and
to this rule Hildegard provided only rare exceptions. Peter
Dronke has ascribed her apparent double-mindedness to an
acute conflict between theological/moral and medical/scien-
tific approaches to life.

> As a medical writer, her whole inclination is to look at human
> beings in their empirical reality: they are organisms that can
> be accounted for in terms of physical principles. Not that she
> demarcates physical principles in any irrevocable way from
> metaphysical ones. Yet whenever she is writing of the human
> being (rather than of the soul or spirit), Hildegard's emphasis
> tends to be what in later periods would be called a materialist
> and deterministic one. The same holds true, for instance, and
> in a similar way, of the scientific and especially the medical
> writings of Avicenna. Yet Hildegard, like Avicenna, is also a
> committed mystic, one for whom the transcending of the
> physical world is of supreme importance. This, for both think-

4. Augustine, *Confessions*, book X, 6.33–34.
5. Charles Williams, *The Descent of the Dove: A Short History of the Holy
Spirit in the Church* (London, 1939): 57–58.
6. Helen Lemay, "Human Sexuality in Twelfth- through Fifteenth-Century Scientific Writings," in Vern Bullough and James Brundage, eds., *Sexual
Practices and the Medieval Church* (Buffalo, 1982): 188.

ers, was a source of keen tension: in the words of Marlowe's Faustus—"O Ile leape up to my God: who pulles me downe?"[7]

On the basis of this formulation, Dronke believes he can discern two opposing strains in the *Causes and Cures*: one is "positive" and tends toward affirmation of the world, materialism, physical and astral determinism, and acceptance of human sexuality; the opposite, "negative" strain tends toward asceticism and a "Manichaean" insistence on the stark oppositions between God and Satan, purity and corruption, fallen nature and the supernatural. Both tendencies, in fact, coexist throughout Hildegard's oeuvre. Given the tension, however, we must beware of premature judgment. One might just as well characterize the materialistic strain as negative, from a spiritual point of view, for it implicates man and woman in a web of influences that seems to leave little or no leeway for freedom. The opposite strain, on the other hand, offers a much wider scope for moral striving, albeit at the price of a psychologically, if not ontologically, dualistic view of the world.

Before we examine the medical works, a prefatory look at sexuality in the *Scivias* should indicate the dimensions of the problem. In this early work, rejection of sexuality predominates. As we have already seen, Hildegard's vision of Mother Church represents the married by means of a cloud—the symbol of Eve—which decently covers the figure's loins. In Ecclesia's bosom, by contrast, shines a radiant sunrise denoting virginity; and between the two lies "a thick darkness, more horrible than human tongue can tell."[8] This barrier, representing the fall, divides the spiritual from the carnal; above it, celestial desire rises toward heaven, and below, earthly lust (*concupiscentia*) limps along the way of all flesh. While sexuality can be redeemed in the sacrament of marriage, it is plainly inferior to the virgin state, and unhallowed desire is so foul that it deserves no image but unspeakable horror. To underline this point, Hildegard dealt with marriage in her vision of

7. Peter Dronke, *Women Writers of the Middle Ages* (Cambridge, 1984): 171.
8. *Scivias* II.5.12, p. 186.

the fall, instead of treating it together with the other sacraments (baptism, confirmation, priesthood, and Eucharist) in her section on the Church.[9] Even among the married, intercourse without regard for procreation is considered a "diabolical act," because it was Satan who engineered the fall into lust in the first place, and its ubiquity enables him to claim mankind as his own. "Because intercourse does not take place without the devil's persuasion," he can boast that "my strength lies in the conception of man, and therefore mankind is mine."[10] Again, it was Satan who, "opening [Eve's] womb, belched all his filth into her body (*materia*) to set his mark on all the children of man, for they are venomously sown in the fire of lust."[11] Yet, despite such outbursts, Hildegard admitted—as orthodoxy required—that married love is at least tolerable when it is consummated "as human nature teaches . . . with human discipline, for the love of children."[12]

In a much more surprising passage, she even forgot about the fall long enough to compare the three causes of Adam's creation—namely the will, power, and goodness of God—with the three causes of procreation—the male's desire (*concupiscentia*), potency (*fortitudo*), and affection (*studium*).[13] This Trinitarian analogy, which seems to be original with Hildegard, is at best anomalous in a writer who normally branded concupiscence as a devilish vice. No less oddly, the same passage from the *Scivias* implies that the primary impulse of women is to resist men's desire. Countering the widespread belief that woman was more lustful than man,[14] Hildegard stated that virgins do not feel ardent desire, and, were it not

9. She evidently regarded monastic vows as a sacrament of equal rank, because they are discussed along with holy orders in *Scivias* II.5. Hildegard did not consider penance or unction as sacraments; in her time the sacramental system was still quite fluid.

10. *Scivias* I.2.15, p. 24. For the *opus diabolicum* see I.2.20, p. 27.

11. LVM I.38, Pitra 19.

12. *Scivias* I.2.20, p. 27.

13. *Scivias* II.3.22, p. 147.

14. Cf. Adelard of Bath, *Quaestiones naturales* 42, ed. Martin Müller in *Beiträge zur Geschichte der Philosophie und Theologie des Mittelalters* 31 (1934): 42–43; William of Conches, *Philosophia* IV.14, PL 172: 89; Brian Lawn, ed., *The Prose Salernitan Questions* B.7 (London, 1979): 4.

for woman's natural moisture, "she would not voluntarily accept man but, scorning him, she would not consent to his will."[15] Underlying this pronouncement may be a sense that the loss of virginity is a humiliation that no woman would endure if she could help it. But the hint that women have a natural purity contradicts more frequent remarks on the universality of lust, and neither of these notions sorts well with the idea that male passion bears the image of God. It would be pointless to look for a synthesis that Hildegard herself, at this juncture, had not achieved.

For a more thorough discussion of these matters, we must turn to the *Causes and Cures*. It is useful to remember that this work as we have it is little more than a series of haphazardly compiled jottings, probably written over a number of years and never assembled in a definitive form.[16] Unlike the visionary writings, it was not intended to inspire, admonish, or edify, and, because in it Hildegard was speaking in her own person, she could feel free to set down her opinions and observations as they changed over time. Some of her comments aim at mere description; in others, etiological or therapeutic concerns are paramount. We cannot expect to find a "theology of the sexual life" as such, but, within the context of ambivalence established by the *Scivias*, the material can lend itself to theological reflection.

In the previous chapter I considered the three faces of Eve as sexual partner, as mother, and as victim. Pragmatically, these aspects of womanhood are mirrored in Hildegard's investigation of female passion, as the complement of masculine ardor; female physiology, as dominated by the vocation of motherhood; and female suffering, as the result of both natural and unnatural causes.

WOMEN'S SEXUALITY AND CHARACTER

Medieval physicians, following the theorists of late antiquity, took as their starting point the doctrine of the four elements

---

15. *Scivias* II.3.22, pp. 147–48.
16. *Echtheit* 58; cf. Gertrude Engbring, "Saint Hildegard, Twelfth Century Physician," *Bulletin of the History of Medicine* 8 (1940): 770–84.

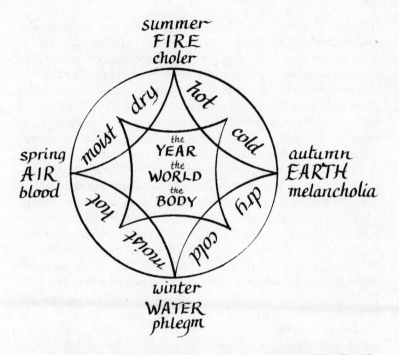

Fig. 4. *Table of temperaments.* This table from Isidore of Seville's *De natura rerum* correlates the four humors or temperaments with the four elements and the four seasons, each characterized by a blend of two primary qualities. Adapted from PL 83: 981–82, courtesy of Beata Riedlmayer.

and their qualities (hot, cold, moist, and dry), together with the four resultant mixtures or temperaments. Figure 4 illustrates the system of correlations as found in a well-known book by Isidore of Seville: each element is associated with a season of the year and a humor, or bodily fluid, characterized by its two salient qualities.[17] Women, according to conventional wisdom, were colder and moister than men; in the words of William of Conches, "the warmest woman is colder

17. Isidore of Seville, *De natura rerum* 11, PL 83: 981–82. For a moralized version of the humoral table see Hugh of Folieto, *De medicina animae*, PL 176: 1185. A full discussion can be found in Raymond Klibansky, Erwin Panofsky, and Fritz Saxl, *Saturn and Melancholy* (London, 1964), ch. 2.

than the coldest man."[18] Accordingly, the two warmer elements, fire and air, were assigned to the male, and the colder ones to the female: "Scientists call these two elements [fire and air] masculine, but water and earth feminine. For the former lie above, the latter below; the former are active, the latter passive."[19] This statement of Alberic of London well illustrates the hierarchical assumptions underlying the distinction of sexes, in keeping with Aristotle's dictum that the male represents active form and the female passive matter.[20]

We have seen that Hildegard accepted the analogy comparing man and woman to soul and body, and she also agreed that the female nature is colder than the male.[21] At her most conventional, she noted that woman is "weak and fragile and a vessel for man," and, because of her delicate constitution, she needs less exercise and should spend more time sitting than walking or standing.[22] However, Hildegard soon diverged from the norm by ascribing the earthy complexion to the man, on account of Adam's formation from earth, and the airy temperament to the woman. Such anomalies alert us to the fact that, where the heavenly voice and the Church were silent, Hildegard recognized no authority beyond her own perceptions. For instance, no previously attested writer asserted that woman "has a divided skull and a thin skin, so that the infant in her womb can get air."[23] By the "divided skull" (*diversa calvaria* or *divisum caput*), Hildegard apparently meant that the space between a woman's scalp and brainpan expands during her period, so that the blood vessels in the

18. William of Conches, *Philosophia* I.23, PL 172: 56.
19. Alberic of London ("Third Vatican Mythographer"), ed. G. H. Bode, in *Scriptores rerum mythicarum latini tres* (Celles, 1834), I: 163.
20. Aristotle, *De generatione animalium* I.20, 729a. Cf. IV.1, 765b: "a male is male in virtue of a particular ability, and a female female in virtue of a particular inability."
21. *Causae et curae* 77; "fertilis natura feminae frigidior est et magis sanguinea quam natura viri." Blood is supposed to be one of the warm humors, but Hildegard's use of humoral theory was often unorthodox. Undoubtedly she had women's menstrual bleeding in mind.
22. *Causae et curae* 60, 87.
23. *Causae et curae* 59, 87.

brain can release the menstrual blood for her purgation, and, at the end of the period, the two layers of the skull come to- gether again and constrict the veins, thus ending the flow.[24] It is this menstrual blood that makes woman fertile, and her porous skin that allows the embryo to breathe.

Woman's temperament, which sensitizes her to any spiri- tual forces that happen to be "in the air," also makes her body more sensitive to the physical environment. Because of her maternal biology she retains the "ethereal" nature of Eve, though no longer in its purity. In a remarkable simile that recalls her image of the prophetess as God's trumpet, Hilde- gard compared woman's body to a lyre—or better, perhaps, an aeolian harp. Women are "open like a wooden frame in which strings have been fastened for plucking; or, again, they are like windows through which the wind blows (*fenestrales et ventosae*), so that the elements affect them more vehemently than men, and the humors too are more abundant in them."[25] Hildegard believed that her own sicknesses came upon her "from the air, from the rain and the wind, and from all stormy weather"[26]—and especially from the Föhn, that warm south wind that Germans even today consider noxious.[27] During one near-fatal bout in the 1150s, she felt her whole body af- flicted with an "airy pain" that dried up her blood and mar- row, while her womb or stomach (*venter*) "seethed from the heat of an aerial fire."[28]

On the physiological level, this airiness affects the quality of woman's passion. Desire, according to Hildegard's biology, is caused by a hot, fiery wind (*ventus delectationis*), which is- sues from the marrow and descends to the loins, warming the blood with the taste of pleasure. In a man, "because the loins are somewhat narrow, tight, and confined, that wind cannot diffuse itself very widely in them and burns there powerfully

24. *Causae et curae* 107–8. See Paul Diepgen, *Frau und Frauenheilkunde in der Kultur des Mittelalters* (Stuttgart, 1963): 137–38.
25. *Causae et curae* 105.
26. DOD III.10.38, PL 197: 1038a.
27. Dronke, *Women Writers* 163.
28. *Vita* 2.7, PL 197: 109d.

in delight, so in that ardor he forgets himself and cannot contain himself."[29] A woman, on the other hand, has a broader pelvis and more permeable skin, so the wind diffuses itself and burns more gently, although more often on account of her natural moisture. Thus, a woman can more easily restrain her desire—though, not satisfied with a purely medical account, Hildegard added that she does so "either from fear or from modesty," suggesting that social constraints strongly reinforce nature. Beyond these physical and emotional factors, there is also a teleological reason why female passion must be subdued:

> pleasure in woman is like the sunlight, which mildly, gently, and continuously suffuses the earth with its warmth to make it fruitful, for, if it burned more keenly in its constant blaze, it would injure the fruit instead of helping it grow. Likewise, pleasure in woman has a mild and gentle, yet continuous warmth to let her conceive and bear children.[30]

Masculine ardor and female restraint suggest several other analogies, equally expressive and morally neutral. The passionate woman, compared with her mate, is like a hearth fire compared with the blaze of a volcano, or like a boat in a light gale beside a ship caught in a mighty storm.[31] Woman no longer conceives from her husband's *sudor* in Edenic innocence.

> But the great love that was in Adam when Eve came forth from him, and the sweetness of the sleep with which he then slept, were turned in his transgression into a contrary mode of sweetness. And so, because a man still feels this great sweetness in himself, and is like a stag thirsting for the fountain, he races swiftly to the woman and she to him—she like a threshing-floor pounded by his many strokes and brought to heat when the grains are threshed inside her.[32]

29. *Causae et curae* 69.
30. *Causae et curae* 76.
31. *Causae et curae* 136, 69–70. One of the *Prose Salernitan Questions* (B.7, p. 4) uses a similar analogy to make the opposite point: a fire in moist wood, though harder to kindle, also burns more strongly once lighted.
32. *Causae et curae* 136–37, trans. Dronke, *Women Writers* 176.

This poignant erotic text raises several questions. One wonders, first of all, how Hildegard came to such an unvirginal appreciation of her subject. The lyrical style, the fresh clash of metaphors, are all her own, scarcely borrowed from standard medical tracts. Such passages bespeak a woman who, virgin though she was, had clearly come to terms with her own sensuality, and in all likelihood talked with other women about theirs. Her many visitors, we must recall, included not only priests and monastics seeking spiritual counsel but also matrons like Sibyl of Lausanne in search of what we would now call marriage counseling.[33] For all her warnings against the sins of the flesh, she was neither naive nor prudish. And when she took up the Psalmist's image of the thirsty stag (Ps. 41:2), a metaphor of the soul's deep yearning for God, she betrayed a feeling for the beauty of even passionate love, which her initial sentence would seem to deplore.[34] St. Bernard and his confreres delighted in transposing the erotic poetry of the Song of Songs to the plane of mystical love; but here Hildegard, very much in spite of herself, did the reverse. This text, like the analogy of creation and procreation in the *Scivias*, reveals a strong erotic sensitivity, which somehow managed to coexist with the ascesis of chastity and the nostalgia for Eden.

Beyond her generic ascription of the earthy and fiery complexions to men and the watery and airy to women, Hildegard offered a discussion of individual types. It was standard practice to classify personality types according to their predominant humor: sanguine, phlegmatic, choleric, or melancholic. What is unprecedented about Hildegard's characterology, as

33. Sibyl must have been unusual among these visitors in that she could read simple Latin. The majority were probably illiterate and would have had to communicate with the abbess in person or by messenger. Thus, although few letters to such women are extant, Hildegard's *Vita* and the *Acta* prepared for her canonization are rich in records of her dealings with them. This largely invisible class supplies a social context for much of the material in her medical works.

34. The metaphor of the lover as thirsty stag became a commonplace of later medieval romance. Marcelle Thiébaux, *The Stag of Love: The Chase in Medieval Literature* (Ithaca, 1974): 158–59 and 222–28.

several scholars have noted, is its emphasis on psychosexual traits, as well as the presentation of separate character sketches for women and men.[35] The sanguine woman, she observed, has "soft and delicate flesh and slender veins"; her complexion is fair; she is fertile, tender in her lovemaking, and "subtle in arts." Phlegmatic women are swarthier, inclined to be hardworking and practical; theirs is a "somewhat masculine" character and, although they can easily attract men, they can just as easily do without them. But if they remain celibate they become temperamental, and if they consort with men their lust is untrammeled. On the opposite end of the spectrum is the choleric woman: pale, discreet, and kindhearted, she earns the respect rather than the love of men, and tends to intimidate them. She is naturally chaste, yet happier married than single because she needs a man to whom she can pledge her feminine loyalty. The only woman who is better off without a husband is the melancholic—a complicated type who easily succumbs to sickness and exhaustion. Women of this type are gaunt in body and "wandering in their thoughts," and find little pleasure in sex.[36] Dronke has aptly characterized the four types as "the gentle châtelaine and the smouldering earthy working woman," "the austere headmistress," and "the neurotic—or the intellectual." It seems probable that Hildegard understood her own temperament as melancholic, on account of her unusually susceptible constitution (*diffluentis naturae*).[37]

In these character sketches Hildegard seems to have worked less from classical humoral theory, which merely provided her with a convenient framework, than from her own observations of the women around her. Like the modern typologies developed by Jung and his followers,[38] her schema

---

35. Diepgen, *Frau und Frauenheilkunde* 76; Klibansky et al., *Saturn and Melancholy* 111; Scholz, "Hildegard von Bingen" 377; Dronke, *Women Writers* 180–83.

36. *Causae et curae* 87–89.

37. Dronke, *Women Writers* 181–83.

38. The psychoanalytic use of typology, inaugurated by C. G. Jung, can be seen as a legitimate stepchild of the medieval system of temperaments. Building on Jung's schema of thinking, feeling, sensing, and intuitive types,

can be seen as a practical guide to help women understand their psychosomatic tendencies, perhaps even to choose marriage or celibacy (if they had the luxury of choice) on the basis of realistic self-knowledge. Her observations on the sexual proclivities of each type could have helped her advise prospective nuns on whether or not to take the veil. It is worth noting that, despite her high regard for virginity, she warned that it is not for all but requires a special vocation.[39] At a later stage, the character types may have served her as a tool to diagnose the ills of her sisters, for each character sketch ends by detailing the symptoms the woman can suffer at menopause.

GOD, SATAN, AND FERTILITY

In the *Causes and Cures*, Hildegard furnished several descriptions of intercourse and conception, which supplement an early passage in the *Scivias*. Her biological notions derive, loosely enough, from the Galenic tradition; she seems to have been untouched by the influence of Arabic or even Salernitan theories current in her time, nor does she appear to have known Constantine the African's treatise *On Intercourse*.[40] As she articulated her own hypotheses about the sexual act, she ranged back and forth between a neutral kind of naturalism and a strongly felt need to involve both God and Satan in the

---

his disciple Toni Wolff developed a psychosexual typology especially for women. Her four types are the mother, the hetaera, the amazon, and the medium—a category that includes "medieval mystics, seers, sibyls, and healers." "Strukturformen der weiblichen Psyche," in *Studien zu C. G. Jungs Psychologie* (Zurich, 1959): 269–83.

39. Ep. 141, PL 197: 372d: "nulla feminea forma hoc incipiat, quod Spiritus sanctus in illam non misit, ne postea vacua remaneat." Hildegard also opposed the offering of children as monastic oblates without their consent. *Scivias* II.5.45–46, pp. 213–15.

40. On Hildegard's archaism see Heinrich Schipperges, "Einflüsse arabischer Medizin auf die Mikrokosmosliteratur des 12. Jahrhunderts," in Paul Wilpert, ed., *Antike und Orient im Mittelalter*, vol. 1 of *Miscellanea Mediaevalia* (Berlin, 1962): 135; John Riddle, "Theory and Practice in Medieval Medicine," *Viator* 5 (1974): 171. Constantine's influential *De coitu*, which treats the subject from an exclusively masculine standpoint, has been translated by Paul Delany in *Chaucer Review* 4 (1970): 56–65.

process. Hence, for instance, one description begins with a schematic correlation between four human faculties and the four elements.

> Such is the beginning of every person's conception and formation (*coagulatio*). In the human being there exist will, consideration, power, and consent. Will comes first, because every person has a wish to do this thing or that. And consideration follows and examines whether the thing is fitting or unfitting, sober or unchaste. Then comes power, which has the ability to consummate the act. And there follows consent, because the act cannot be consummated unless consent approves it as worthy. These are the four forces in human conception.
>
> Then the four elements, which stir up the four humors in man, superabound in turmoil. Fire, which is dry, kindles the will beyond measure; air, which is moist, moves consideration beyond measure; water, or foam, causes power to surge beyond measure; and finally earth, which is lukewarm, makes consent boil up beyond measure. And all of these, because of their superabundance, arouse a kind of tempest and draw from the blood a poisonous foam, which is semen. When this falls into its place, the woman's blood unites itself with it and causes it to become bloody.

Thus far, intercourse and conception can be described with reference to psychosomatic forces, but, as the account continues, both divine and demonic agency are called into play.

> For human conception begins with the pleasure that the serpent breathed into the first human being in the fruit, because at that time the man's blood is agitated by pleasure. This blood ejaculates a cool foam into the woman, which is coagulated by the warmth of the mother's flesh and distended into a bloody form; and the foam, retained in that warmth, later grows from the mother's dry nourishment to the dimensions of a small human shape; until the Creator's handwriting (*scriptura*), which formed mankind, fills the whole breadth of the human shape—just as a potter fashions his chosen vessel.[41]

It would appear that the devil inspires the pleasure of intercourse; God's contribution in quickening the fetus comes

41. *Causae et curae* 59–60.

later. This supposition is borne out by another passage where, speaking of the *ventus delectationis*, Hildegard wrote:

> And this burning wind sometimes arises in an idle person busied with no cares, and it surges in the chest and makes the person glad, so it rises from the chest to the brain and fills the whole brain and its blood vessels with a burning heat, and then it also touches the lungs and the heart, and thus it descends to the genitals—in a man to the loins, in a woman to the navel. And in this way the person's knowledge falls into a slumber of ignorance. But then the devil's suggestion unites itself with these influences in a stormy tyranny, and that person blazes up in lust, forgetting shame.[42]

The demonized physiology of desire is consistent with Hildegard's assertion that the devil poisoned Adam's seed when he corrupted Eve with lust. Indeed, the semen retains its venomous quality until it is neutralized by the benign elements in the womb: "it remains a poisonous foam until fire or heat warms it, air or breath dries it, water or fluid dampens it with pure moisture, and earth or skin confines it."[43] Consciously or not, Hildegard transferred archaic taboos about the impurity of menstrual blood to the corresponding male fluid, which Galen and Constantine the African had described as "pure and warm."[44] For Hildegard, on the contrary, the semen was cold and tainted, whereas the maternal blood had a warming, wholesome influence on the fetus. As the embryo grows in the womb, it is gradually though never wholly purified of its initial taint, until in the second month the soul enters the body "like a warm, impetuous wind" and makes itself at home there "like a silkworm in its cocoon." In the first month

---

42. *Causae et curae* 140. For a similar but more precise version of this physiology, which was a medical commonplace, see Constantine, *De coitu* 56, and *Prose Salernitan Questions* B.16, p. 11. On the navel as the seat of female passion see Rabanus Maurus, *De universo* VI, PL 111: 167d.

43. *Causae et curae* 60–62.

44. On the harmful qualities of menstrual blood see Diepgen, *Frau und Frauenheilkunde* 139–43. Rabanus Maurus said that from its contamination "crops do not grow, wine turns sour, plants die, trees lose their fruit, iron rusts, copper turns black; if dogs should eat of it, they grow rabid." *De universo* VI, PL 111: 174b; cf. Isidore of Seville, *Etymologiae* XI.141, PL 82: 414b.

the budding fetal members are only separated by indenta-
tions, like clay cracked in the heat of the sun; but after quickening they begin to unfold like the petals of a flower.

In her more optimistic moods, Hildegard could leave the
devil aside and treat lovemaking as a God-given fulfillment of
Adam's prophecy that "the two shall become one flesh."
Given her conventional (ultimately Aristotelian) view of sexual secretions as concoctions from the blood,[45] she opined that
in intercourse, when, "from the powerful force of the man's
desire, his melted blood flows forth and revolves like a mill
wheel, it receives some of the woman's foamy secretion into
itself," and vice versa.[46] With this reciprocal mingling of
blood, man and woman become one flesh, and the same
"eternal energy (*vis aeternitatis*) that brings the infant from its
mother's womb" accomplishes the union. The process has no
blame attached to it here, and Hildegard stressed its mutual-
ity: both partners must cooperate actively. Unlike the devil-
ridden accounts, this one recalls a remarkable passage from
Hugh of St. Victor, in which that theologian tried to explain
how the Virgin conceived by the Holy Spirit through an analogy with the normal process. Forced unions, said Hugh, are
infertile because "nature operates in woman through love of
man and in man through love of woman"; if either is lacking,
no true mingling of flesh and therefore no conception can
occur. In the Virgin's case, the Holy Spirit not only planted
the divine Son in her womb but also elicited her own contribution of maternal flesh through her love for him, in lieu of a
man.[47]

For Hildegard as for Hugh, mutual desire was a biological
prerequisite for conception. The underlying medical notion
appears to have been the "two-seed theory" of Hippocrates

45. Cf. Aristotle, *De generatione animalium* I.19; *Prose Salernitan Questions*
B.4, p. 3: "Sperm is human seed [male or female] compounded from the
purest and most wholesome of all the members and humors, and especially
of the blood, which is the nourishment of the whole body."

46. *Causae et curae* 68.

47. Hugh of St. Victor, *On the Sacraments of the Christian Faith* II.1.8, trans.
Roy Deferrari (Cambridge, Mass., 1951): 229.

and Galen, which associates the female orgasm with the emission of seed necessary for conception. Thus, medical writers more prosaic than Hugh of St. Victor could opine that prostitutes seldom conceive because they have intercourse without pleasure, and therefore emit no seed.[48] Hildegard, however, was ambivalent about the existence of female seed;[49] the essential factor for her was the commingling of concocted blood. Incidentally, this theory furnished her with a medical argument against adultery. A married person's blood, she observed, is already commingled with that of his or her spouse; in an illegitimate union, the fetus is contaminated by the mixture of three or more alien bloodstreams.[50]

This theory bears comparison with a celebrated passage on generation in the *Scivias*. In the fourth vision of that work, Hildegard saw men and women carrying vessels of milk and making cheeses. The milk represents human seed and the cheese, the human beings formed from it.

> Some of the milk is thick and from it strong cheeses are made, because that seed in its strength, favorably and well concocted and tempered, produces energetic people endowed with a great radiance of spiritual as well as carnal gifts, like the great fathers and noblemen; so that they prosper in wisdom, discernment, and success in their achievements and flourish in the sight of both God and man, because the devil finds no place in them.[51]

Others are less fortunate. From thinner milk, which represents scanty, half-concocted, and half-tempered semen, are

48. William of Conches, *Dragmaticon*; recension in *Prose Salernitan Questions* B.10, p. 6.

49. In *Scivias* I.4.13 (p. 75) Hildegard described "tam viri quam mulieres, in corporibus suis humanum semen habentes." But in the *Causae et curae* she wrote that woman's blood does not produce semen but only a "tenuem et parvam spumam . . . sed magis sanguineam quam albam" (p. 60). For the origins of the two-seed theory see the Hippocratic work *On Intercourse and Pregnancy* I.21, trans. T. U. H. Ellinger (New York, 1952). Aristotle denied the existence of female seed in *De generatione animalium* I.19, 727a.

50. *Causae et curae* 68. Cf. *Prose Salernitan Questions* B. 46, pp. 22–23, where it is said that a bastard may resemble the cuckolded husband because the guilty lovers' spirits are so oppressed by their dread of his return that the seed is impressed with his image.

51. *Scivias* I.4.13, p. 75.

curdled mild cheeses—people who are "often stupid, luke-warm, and useless to God and the world" because they do not vigorously seek God. Finally, there are bitter cheeses cur-dled from spoiled milk. These represent the products of wrongly mingled seed (adulterous unions); they are often de-formed and suffer "bitterness, trouble, and oppression of heart," which render them incapable of raising their minds to heaven. Nevertheless, with grace and arduous effort, they can win the victory by patiently struggling against these defects of character.

With this moralizing thrust, Hildegard qualified the deter-minism that otherwise dominates her analogy. But in any case, it is a form of determinism incompatible with the texts we have just examined. In them we saw human nature corrupted en masse by "the devil's suggestion" and the inherently tainted semen, whereas here only the ill-tempered seed is tainted and the rest produces offspring in which "the devil finds no place." Nor did Hildegard explain how the favorable or unfavorable constitution of the fetus affects the soul, which is not present at conception but rather infused "at the time divinely or-dained" in the form of a fiery sphere. Given such difficulties, it is not surprising that the artist of the Rupertsberg *Scivias* simplified matters by restoring the devil to his wonted place. In the apposite miniature we see, together with a pregnant woman whose child is being quickened, a company of men and woman proffering their bowls of cheese. Slightly above and to the left, a small brown demon slyly insinuates what looks like a toadstool into one of the baskets (Fig. 5).

Aside from its intrinsic interest, Hildegard's cheese anal-ogy raises the problem of her sources in a particularly acute form. Its original "learned" source, Aristotle's *On the Genera-tion of Animals*, had not yet been translated in her day, and it is even less conceivable that she knew Avicenna's version of the analogy.[52] Perhaps her visionary imagination was simply

52. Aristotle, *De generatione animalium* II.4, 739b; Avicenna, *Canon of Med-icine* I.196, trans. O. C. Gruner (London, 1930): 230.

Fig. 5. *The quickening of the child and the tribulations of the soul.* Left: the soul, in the form of a many-eyed golden square, is infused into the embryo lying in its mother's womb; the contribution of the child's ancestors is represented by men and women with bowls of cheese. Right (bottom to top): the soul suffers many trials and assaults by demons before reaching its tabernacle in the heavenly Jerusalem. *Scivias* I.4, Eibingen ms.

elaborating on Job 10:10–11: "Did you not pour me out like milk and curdle me like cheese? You clothed me with skin and flesh, and knit me together with bones and nerves." It is also possible, however, that the Aristotelian lore appropriated by Arabic physicians had passed into (or even grown out of) the tradition of European folk medicine. A recent article by Peter Dronke cites various contemporary folk customs in which cheese and childbearing are loosely related.[53] Closer to Hildegard's time, we have an early-fourteenth-century witness from Montaillou. Béatrice de Planissoles, one of the village women questioned by the inquisitors, testified that her lover had relieved her fear of pregnancy by using a certain herbal contraceptive. Béatrice thought the herb was the same one cowherds used to hang over a caldron of milk while making cheese, to retard the curdling action of the rennet. By analogy, it could also hinder the coagulation of semen in the womb, and thus prevent conception.[54] As we have no reason to suppose that either the peasant woman or the philandering priest of Montaillou had read Aristotle, we may assume that his "cheese analogy" characterized popular as well as educated thought about the process of generation.

Aside from demonic malice and ill-tempered semen, Hildegard proposed at least two other deterministic theories to explain how conception goes wrong. One of these, among her most original contributions, appears to be a refinement of the *Scivias* vision. In the second book of the *Causes and Cures*, she returned to the subject of strong and weak semen, without reference to the devil's poison. Now, however, she maintained that if the man's semen was ample, a male child would be procreated; if it was thin, a female would be conceived. In ascribing the child's sex to the father's biological contribution, she was in rough accord with modern genetics.[55] But the

53. Peter Dronke, "Problemata Hildegardiana," *Mittellateinisches Jahrbuch* 16 (1981): 114–16.
54. Emmanuel LeRoy Ladurie, *Montaillou: The Promised Land of Error*, trans. Barbara Bray (New York, 1979): 172–73.
55. Salernitan writers, on the other hand, asserted that the child's sex might be determined by the relative preponderance of male or female seed,

child's character is here determined by an independent variable. There are still three classes of human beings—virtuous, weak, and bitter—as in the cheese analogy. Yet Hildegard now said that the child, whether male or female, would be of virtuous character if the parents cherished each other at the hour of conception *in recto amore caritatis.*[56] If such love was lacking on one side or the other, the offspring would be weak and not virtuous, and if neither the man's nor the woman's love was genuine charity, their child would inherit their bitterness. This theory, with its allowance for a factor almost universally neglected in Hildegard's time, may be the most appealing of all her hypotheses. Yet even here she did not discuss the vagaries of conjugal or parental love beyond the hour of conception, so the deterministic bias remains paramount.

Yet another theory tries to explain the strength or weakness of the semen, and thus of the child's health and character, astrologically. Hildegard's attitude toward this science too was ambivalent. While the *Scivias* contains a polemic against stargazing,[57] the *Causes and Cures* displays a firm belief in the moon's influence on bodily and spiritual states.[58] As to conception, Hildegard stated unequivocally that

> the blood in every human being increases and diminishes according to the waxing and waning of the moon. . . . When, as

---

implantation of the fetus on the right or the left side of the womb, and degree of warmth or cold during pregnancy. Claude Thomasset, "La représentation de la sexualité et de la génération dans la pensée scientifique médiévale," in Willy van Hoecke and Andries Welkenhuysen, eds., *Love and Marriage in the Twelfth Century* (Louvain, 1981): 6.

56. *Causae et curae* 35–36.

57. *Scivias* I.3.20–23, pp. 50–55.

58. *Causae et curae* 16–19. Hildegard indicated, albeit obscurely, that the lunar cycle brings about changes in atmospheric moisture, which in turn affect the flow of humors in the body, thus altering the psychosomatic states and the behavior of men and women. However, the influence also works in reverse: from another point of view, human transgressions are themselves a cause of mutability in the weather and the moon. Cutting across this reciprocal process is the assurance that "the Holy Spirit overcomes changeable human nature" and breaks through the cycle. These qualifications militate against the authenticity of a purely deterministic lunar horoscope appended

the moon waxes, the blood in human beings is increased, then both men and women are fertile for bearing fruit—for generating children—since then . . . the man's semen is powerful and robust; and in the waning of the moon, when human blood also wanes, the man's semen is feeble and without strength, like dregs. . . . If a woman conceives a child then, whether boy or girl, it will be infirm and feeble and not virtuous.[59]

Since the phase of the moon affects fertility as well as viability of offspring, it follows that "a man should take the maturity of his own body into account and seek the proper phases of the moon as zealously as one who offers his pure prayers . . . so that his children do not waste away and die."[60] In effect, Hildegard was recommending the "natural" method of family planning—except that she preferred to use it in the service of procreation rather than contraception, and that she mistakenly connected the lunar cycle with the man's rather than the woman's fertility. It is interesting, however, that ancient writers and recent studies concur in associating menstruation with the new moon for a majority of women, in whose case the full moon would be the time of ovulation and hence of peak fertility. Hildegard, unlike many medical writers, recognized this as the optimum time for conception.[61]

---

to *Causae et curae* in the Copenhagen manuscript. The horoscope, which provides detailed character sketches and predictions concerning health and longevity for boys and girls conceived on each day of the lunar cycle, has been rejected as spurious by Hans Liebeschütz (*Das allegorische Weltbild der heiligen Hildegard von Bingen* [Leipzig, 1930]: 85, n. 2), Schipperges ("Einflüsse arabischer Medizin" 134, n. 17), and Schrader and Führkötter (*Echtheit* 57), although Dronke has recently tried to reinstate it (*Women Writers* 178–79).

59. *Causae et curae* 77–78, trans. Dronke, *Women Writers* 177–78.

60. *Causae et curae* 18.

61. For menstruation at the waning moon see Aristotle, *De generatione animalium* II.4, 738a, and *Historia animalium* VII.2.1. The *Prose Salernitan Questions* B.20, p. 12, say "talis purgatio de mense in mensem in novilunio fieri debet." According to Diepgen, it was widely believed that young women menstruated with the new moon, mature women at the full moon, and older women at the waning moon. Following Aristotle and Avicenna, many writers held that the best days for conception were those immediately following the period, and the worst those after midcycle. *Frau und Frauenheilkunde* 141–42.

GYNECOLOGY

At the end of the *Causes and Cures*, Hildegard proposed a number of gynecological remedies, some of which are duplicated in her *Book of Simple Medicine*.[62] These treatments are of the kinds most commonly used by female empirics at the time: herbal concoctions, salves, potions, plasters, and baths, together with some general dietary prescriptions and a stock of charms and incantations.[63] The core of Hildegard's pharmacology can be traced back to ancient authors like Galen, Pliny, and Dioscorides, as amplified by such compilers as Isidore, Rabanus Maurus, Walafrid Strabo, and Macer Floridus.[64] But the abbess worked from her own observation as well, and her command of herbal lore extended to more than two hundred plants. In addition, she recommended some more exotic "simples" (ingredients) such as animal parts and gems, which often entailed the use of sympathetic magic. Despite her attempts to explain sexual behavior and generation scientifically, she provided no rationale for most of her therapeutic methods beyond the homeopathic principle of balancing qualities by their contraries.[65] In practice, as a recent historian of medicine has argued, such time-honored cures may have healed more patients than the increasingly complex professional medicine taught at Salerno and Montpellier, because the new theory was so far removed from fact and actual practice as to be unworkable. As early as the late tenth century, the Arabic physician Rhazes felt he had to explain "The Reason Why the Ignorant Physicians, the Common People,

62. The fifteenth-century ms entitled *Subtilitatum diversarum naturarum creaturarum libri novem* (Paris BN Cod. 6952), which Charles Daremberg and F. A. Reuss used as the basis for their edition in PL 197, differs widely from the other two surviving mss of the work, and appears to contain interpolations from the *Causae et curae*. In the absence of a critical edition, it is impossible to ascertain the original state of the text.

63. See Irmgard Müller, "Krankheit und Heilmittel im Werk Hildegards von Bingen," *Festschrift* 311–49; Muriel Hughes, *Women Healers in Medieval Life and Literature* (New York, 1943), ch. 3.

64. Jerry Stannard, "Greco-Roman Materia Medica in Medieval Germany," *Bulletin of the History of Medicine* 46 (1972): 455–68.

65. Diepgen, *Frau und Frauenheilkunde* 213.

and the Women in the Cities are More Successful than Men of Science in Treating Certain Diseases."[66]

As for "women in the cities," it is not necessary to assume that such empirics—who practiced throughout medieval Europe—limited themselves solely to female troubles. But midwifery and gynecological problems were the chief part of their stock in trade, as female patients felt a natural reluctance to consult male physicians about such difficulties.[67] This reticence seems to have persisted throughout the Middle Ages; both "Trotula" in the late twelfth century and Jacoba Felicie in the early fourteenth mentioned female modesty to justify the medical practice of women.[68] Although Hildegard, as a nun, would not have served as physician or midwife to the community at large, she was distinguished both as a medical writer and as a healer, and she may well have provided medical help within her own convent. So it is not unreasonable to compare some of her prescriptions with those of the so-called *Trotula Major* (*Diseases of Women*), which was the only gynecological text readily available in her time.[69] Modern scholars

66. Riddle, "Theory and Practice in Medieval Medicine." The epistle of Rhazes, a precursor of Avicenna, can be found in Bayard Dodge, ed. and trans., *Fihrist* (New York, 1970), II: 708.

67. The reluctance may at times have been mutual. Vern Bullough has cited several thirteenth- and fourteenth-century physicians who warn against the danger of treating female patients, as well as the ignorance of female practitioners. He concluded that "most medieval physicians dealt only minimally with women patients. . . . Often women were left to other women to oversee, while the physician himself concentrated on the more worthy sex." "Medieval Medical and Scientific Views of Women," *Viator* 4 (1973): 501.

68. "Trotula," *The Diseases of Women*, trans. Elizabeth Mason-Hohl (Los Angeles, 1940): frontispiece and p. 2: "women on account of modesty and the fragility and delicacy of the state of [their private] parts dare not reveal the difficulties of their sicknesses to a male doctor." Jacoba, a Parisian doctor tried for practicing medicine without a license in 1322, argued in her defense that "a woman before now would permit herself to die rather than reveal the secrets of her infirmity to any man, because of the honor of the female sex and the shame which she would feel." For her case see Hughes, *Women Healers* 91; documents in *Chartularium universitatis Parisiensis*, ed. Heinrich Denifle et al. (Paris, 1889–1897), II: 257–67.

69. Diepgen, *Frau und Frauenheilkunde* 81. The works ascribed to Trotula survive in nearly one hundred mss and inspired French, German, and other vernacular recensions. Soranus's *Gynecology* was little known in the Middle Ages. The only other widely used text, *De secretis mulierum* (Pseudo-Albertus), dates from the late thirteenth century.

tend to reject Trotula's authorship of that treatise, but it remains closely connected with female practitioners, appealing more than a dozen times to the authority of the *mulieres salernitanae* (presumably midwives) and once to Trotula herself.[70] The work reflects an empiricism similar to Hildegard's but with a much greater admixture of Galenic theory. For instance, the Salernitan writer discussed several maladies (suffocation of the womb, spoiled seed, "wandering womb," ulcerated or prolapsed uterus) that were familiar to ancient gynecology but unknown to Hildegard. It is not surprising that the abbess of Bingen also failed to discuss means of procuring contraception or abortion, techniques for feigning virginity, and other morally dubious questions addressed in the *Trotula* and later Latin texts.[71]

Typical of Hildegard's remedies are the four treatments she suggested for retention of menses. First, the patient can make herself a sauna bath using fresh river water, heated tiles, and a bouquet of "warm" herbs: tansy or chrysanthemum, feverfew, and mullein.[72] After entering the bath, she should place herself on a stool with the heated herbs so that they cover her private parts up to the navel. Their natural warmth should soften her flesh and womb and open the constricted veins.[73] Second, the woman can make herself a claret from fine honeyed wine seasoned with cloves and white pepper, and pre-

70. For a good summation of the controversy see Edward Tuttle, "The *Trotula* and Old Dame Trot: A Note on the Lady of Salerno," *Bulletin of the History of Medicine* 50 (1976): 61–72. More recently John Benton has argued that "Trota" or Trotula was an authentic medical writer and practitioner of the twelfth century (not the eleventh, as is usually assumed), but not, paradoxically, the author of the works ascribed to her. "Trotula, Women's Problems, and the Professionalization of Medicine in the Middle Ages," *Bulletin of the History of Medicine* 59 (1985): 30–53.

71. On these questions see John Noonan, Jr., *Contraception* (Cambridge, Mass., 1965): 200–211.

72. *Causae et curae* 185–87; abbreviated version in LSM I.111, PL 197: 1174. To translate the names of herbs I have used Peter Riethe, *Naturkunde* (Salzburg, 1959); and George Usher, *A Dictionary of Plants Used by Man* (London, 1974).

73. Cf. Hippocrates, *Aphorisms* V.28: "Aromatic vapour baths are useful in the treatment of female disorders and would often be useful for other conditions too if they did not cause headaches." *Medical Works*, trans. John Chadwick and W. N. Mann (Oxford, 1950): 166.

pared with a different selection of warm herbs—millefolium, rue, aristologia, and dittany, in specified proportions—tempered by the coolness of the berries called *rifelbere*. Again, the warmth and purity of this concoction should have a relaxing effect and dissolve the coagulated blood in the womb. An alternative beverage, cooler if less appetizing, can be made from eggs, wine, fat, and the juice of lovage, and drunk before and after meals for five days or as long as needed. In the meantime, the patient should avoid beef and other heavy foods, confining herself to a milder diet; and she should drink well water or wine rather than flowing water, which is harsher. A similar bland diet, which Hildegard believed to be generally healthy, is also recommended for patients with the opposite problem of excessive bleeding. But whereas warmth is held to provoke menstruation, cold retards it; so the woman with an overabundant flow should bind her thighs with a linen poultice dipped in cold water.[74] She can also apply ivy warmed in water; the natural coolness of the ivy will restrain the flow, while the warmth restores health to the members. Finally, she can be helped by a gentle upward massage of the trunk and limbs, intended to reverse the flow of blood through the veins.

Compared to the *Trotula*'s recipes for menstrual disorders, Hildegard's seem relatively simple, using fewer herbs and less complicated preparations; and she said nothing of the *Trotula*'s more drastic treatments, like bloodletting, vaginal pessaries, fumigation, and intercourse. For the problem of sterility, the *Trotula* suggests a variety of causes in both the female and the male, but Hildegard named only three: the man's semen is too fluid, the womb is too cold, or "it happens by the judgment of God."[75] If the cause of the problem lies in the woman, she can try eating the womb of a sexually mature but still virgin lamb or calf, prepared with lard and other fatty meats, either before or during intercourse. Apparently the treatment

---

74. *Causae et curae* 187–88; cf. LSM II.2 and I.140, PL 197: 1211cd and 1187a.

75. "Trotula," *Diseases of Women* 16–19; *Causae et curae* 182–83; LSM VII.15, PL 197: 1324d.

is to have both medical and magical effects: the succulent juices should moisten the womb, and at the same time the pure animal's fertility will be transferred to the woman, "if God would have it so." Similarly, the patient may conceive if she eats fish roe, as fish were thought to be not only fecund but also pure because they reproduce asexually.[76]

Once the woman becomes pregnant, of course, she may suffer painful and dangerous throes in childbirth. We have already seen the apocalyptic quality that Hildegard, qua theologian, ascribed to labor pangs as part of the curse of Eve. But in her other capacity she offered several remedies to ease difficult labor, of which the mildest is a moist poultice containing fennel and hazelwort.[77] Fennel was an herb traditionally used to loosen various bodily constrictions. Walafrid Strabo recommended a potion of fennel seed and goat's milk for the woman in labor; Macer Floridus thought of the herb as a diuretic and aphrodisiac; the German herbalist Hans Folcz said it increases the flow of milk.[78] Resorting to more exotic measures, the pregnant woman may have her womb anointed with a little pulverized crane's blood dissolved in water, bind the bird's right foot over her navel, and examine her face in the cup of blood as in a mirror.[79] Seeing her reflection, a typically Hildegardian touch, may have been intended to double the bird's magic power, which may be due to its rapid flight and ability to escape danger. If no crane's foot is available, the patient may substitute either the heart of a lion or the pebbles upon which a mouse has given birth.[80] And, failing even these, she could try a magic charm with the semiprecious gem called sardius (red chalcedony or carnelian). Although one lapidary vaguely recommends that women carry this gem,[81]

76. LSM IV, preface, PL 197: 1267b.

77. *Causae et curae* 188; LSM I.66, PL 197: 1157d–58a.

78. Strabo, *Hortulus* X.211–13; Macer Floridus, *De viribus herbarum* XVII.695–97; Folcz, *Confectbuch* 11.256–57. Texts in J. L. Choulant, ed., *Macer Floridus* (Leipzig, 1832): 148, 56–57, 192.

79. LSM VI.4, PL 197: 1289bc.

80. LSM VII.3 and VII.39, PL 197: 1315cd and 1335cd.

81. Damigeron (Paris BN Cod. lat. 7418), ed. Eugenius Abel, *Orphei Lithica* (Berlin, 1881): 195.

Hildegard's use of it seems to be unique. She told the woman to stroke her thighs with the gem and say, "As you, jewel, shone by the command of God in the first angel, so you, infant, come forth as a shining man abiding in God." Then the patient should hold the jewel over her vagina and recite another charm: "Be opened, passages and portal, in the name of that epiphany by which Christ appeared as God and man and opened the gates of hell; that you, infant, may go out at that portal without your own or your mother's death."[82] After this, the woman should bind the stone in a belt and gird herself with it, and safe delivery will follow.

HEALING AND MAGIC

Although it is easy to imagine Hildegard recommending herbal concoctions or baths to actual women, it is difficult to conceive that she would send them off to hunt lions or ransack mouseholes when more convenient forms of treatment were available. Such remedies do not appear in the *Causes and Cures*, and Hildegard may have included them in her encyclopedia more for completeness than for use.[83] With the lapidary charm, however, we are on different ground. For Hildegard, belief in the virtue of gems, which was universal, involved more than natural magic. Precious stones, fiery in their nature and origin, have an affinity with the fire of the Spirit and the fire in which Satan burns; Lucifer in all his glory was adorned with them, but when he fell he lost them and they remained on earth "in honor and blessing and for healing."[84] Now the devil flees from gems because they remind him of his lost beauty; and because of their innate virtue they can be used

---

82. LSM IV.7, PL 197: 1255ab.

83. Rare or even mythical ingredients do, however, appear in recipe collections that show every sign of being intended for actual use. See the strange miscellany of medical and magical texts in the twelfth-century Alsatian rotulus described by Lucille Pinto, "The Folk Practice of Gynecology and Obstetrics in the Middle Ages," *Bulletin of the History of Medicine* 47 (1973): 513–23.

84. LSM IV, preface, PL 197: 1247–50; Peter Riethe, "Die medizinische Lithologie der Hildegard von Bingen," *Festschrift* 351–70.

only for good and honorable ends, not for murderous and lascivious ones. In the sardius charm, Hildegard's incantation recalls both the primal glory of Lucifer and his defeat at the harrowing of hell. The first formula asks that, by virtue of the jewel, the newborn child may shine like the lost angel before he fell, and the second that he may escape death as Adam and Eve escaped hell at the Resurrection. This bit of applied theology compresses Hildegard's worldview into a lapidary phrase.

There are no clear lines of demarcation between medical, magical, and miraculous ways of healing; when Hildegard prescribed a similar incantation for Sibyl's hemorrhage (see Chapter 1), the charm itself was to be written on a scroll and used in lieu of a gem, which the matron probably could not afford. Conversely, a magical object could be used without the verbal formula. Hildegard's *Vita* tells how three matrons suffering in labor gave birth with the help of a girdle made from the saint's own hair, which her nuns had been saving as a relic.[85] This mode of healing is only an extension of the methods Hildegard recommended in her lifetime.

One of the abbess's favorite gems—sapphire to her, lapis lazuli to moderns—could help women in another common plight. As we have seen, the sapphire was a stone she associated with divine Wisdom; her lapidary says that it can cleanse the eyes, improve the mind, and drive away demons. According to Marbode of Rennes, the foremost authority on gems, it "makes God favorable to prayers" and "cools interior burning," but its wearer must be particularly chaste.[86] These virtues may account for its role in Hildegard's charm to rid women of unwelcome suitors. In case "the devil has incited any man to fall in love with a woman" and she does not respond in kind, she may pour wine over a sapphire three times as she asks the stone to deliver her from the man's blazing lust. Then she (or a friend, if she is wary) must have the lover drink this wine for three days in succession, and he will be

---

85. *Vita* 3.41, PL 197: 119d–20a.
86. Marbode, *De lapidibus* 5, ed. John Riddle (Wiesbaden, 1977): 41–43.

"cured."[87] Or, if the woman herself has been victimized with a love potion (*zauber amoris*), she can be purged of its poison with plantain juice or delivered from amorous madness by placing leaves of fresh betony, a most powerful herb, in her nostrils and under her tongue.[88] Mandragora is also cited as a potent antidote—this is somewhat odd, given that plant's ancient fame as an aphrodisiac and fertility charm. An aromatic steam bath or potion with wild lettuce will likewise do the trick.[89]

In fairness, it should be noted that all these remedies may be equally needed by a man who suffers from his own or some woman's unrequited love. Either sex can be victimized. Thus, our encyclopedia of medicine opens a window onto the world of Tristan and Isolde, where love philters and similar forms of enchantment are a real and potent danger. To the various sexual determinisms we have already considered, we must add manipulation of the heart by magic, which Hildegard saw as a diabolical practice wholly unlike her own beneficent charms.

The seer's *Acta* contain further instances of conflict between what would nowadays be called black and white magic. These miracle stories did not suffice to secure her canonization at Rome, so the modern reader will not be the first to take them with a grain of salt. Nevertheless, some of the alleged miracles provide a necessary supplement to Hildegard's correspondence, to the degree that they reflect her dealings with laywomen and with the lower classes of society. In what circumstances would such women be likely to seek help from the local saint or miracle worker? Aside from the expected healings and exorcisms (in which a prominent theme is restoring the insane to their right minds), three of these stories are of

---

87. LSM IV.6, PL 197: 1253–54.

88. LSM I.101, I.128, PL 197: 1169c–70a and 1182c–83a. Walafrid Strabo called this plant "all-sufficient" (*Hortulus* 20, p. 153); Macer Floridus said it is an antidote to poison (*De viribus* 11, p. 48).

89. LSM I.56, I.92, PL 197: 1151bc and 1165d–66a. For the classic use of mandragora see the story of Leah and Rachel in Gen. 30:14–17.

particular interest for the glimpses they afford of the saint's environment.

One account tells of a wretched wife whose husband did homage to the devil, promising him a sacrifice every year. After placating the fiend first with beasts and then with children, the sorcerer was at last to give him his wife; but the intended victim discovered his plans in time and fled to Hildegard in desperation. The saint gave her a lock of hair to bind into her own coiffure, so that, when the devil arrived, he found himself unable to take the wife "because of Hildegard's incantations" and broke the hapless husband's neck instead.[90]

In a more ambiguous case, a matron no more happily married is accused of murdering her husband and sentenced to purge herself by the ordeal of hot iron. This curious judicial procedure places the burden of proof on God: the accused is to carry a red-hot bar of iron for nine steps, and if it burns her hands she is guilty; if not, innocent. Seeking the miracle required for her acquittal, the widow asked Hildegard to bless the iron and then passed through the trial unharmed.[91] To be sure, the astonishment of the public reflects a certain skepticism about the judicial principle at stake: if God routinely vindicates the innocent, why does the accused need a special blessing from a saint, and if she is guilty, why does the blessing work? One thinks again of Isolde enduring the same trial, saving her honor through a clever ruse.[92]

But if Hildegard could protect the innocent, she could also reform the guilty. A third "miracle" occurred when the seer met a young girl named Berrudis, who for reasons of her own had disguised herself as a schoolboy. Hildegard immediately saw through the disguise and warned the girl to "convert to

90. *Acta* 6, PL 197: 135bc.
91. *Acta* 3, PL 197: 133bc.
92. Tried for adultery, the guilty heroine swears that she has held no man between her legs save her husband (King Mark) and the leper (actually Tristan in disguise), who has just carried her across a ford. Because her oath is literally true, she escapes unharmed.

a better state," implying that she had not long to live. Berrudis repented and resumed her feminine clothing, but she also darkened her face "lest many men fall in love with her," and shortly thereafter died.[93] Presumably, the miracle lay in Hildegard's gift of foresight, though it may be more significant that she chastised the girl for renouncing her womanhood, an act that other miracle watchers would have found meritorious.[94]

Taken together, Hildegard's medical works and her reputed miracles reveal a solicitude for all the afflictions of women— in physical and mental illness, in barrenness and childbirth, in the throes of passion and the trials of marriage. In her writings, she concerned herself no less zealously with the ills of men. Nevertheless, of the individual miracles recorded in her *Acta*, seventeen were performed for women as opposed to only six for men—and, of the latter, two are miracles of judgment. (These figures do not account for the healing of many unnamed epileptics, demoniacs, and fever patients, whose gender is not specified.) In the third book of the saint's *Vita*, the figures are more balanced: sixteen women and twelve men are numbered among her beneficiaries. Given a certain amount of repetition in the testimony, it is not always possible to determine whether various witnesses were referring to the same or different events. Hildegard's letters, on the other hand, show a preponderance of male correspondents, for the obvious reason that more men were literate; of the women, the great majority were abbesses. So we can discern two distinct subgroups of Hildegard's clientele, so to speak. While her spiritual and social prominence gave her an extraordinary freedom in the public sphere—the world of men—she also

93. *Acta* 3, PL 197: 133ab.
94. Caesarius of Heisterbach told the story of a girl named Hildegundis, who, after many adventures, disguised herself as Brother Joseph and died as a monk of Schönau in 1188. In his eyes the girl's religious life was exemplary: "Tanta est fortitudo mentis in quibusdam feminis, ut merito laudetur." *Dialogus miraculorum* I.40, ed. Joseph Strange (Cologne, 1851): 52–53.

remained the mistress of a female community, not only serving her nuns but also filling the local matrons' need for a trusted authority of their own sex whom they could seek in their distress.

Our varied sources portray Hildegard as one equally versed in ordinary and extraordinary means of healing, but, in her own eyes, such a distinction scarcely existed. Nor did she seem unduly troubled by the discrepancies in her view of sex. Behind them we glimpse a woman capable of astonishing empathy with her married sisters as well as with men, and willing to observe the sexual comedy from above, from below, and from within. If she never quite decided how much was due to God or to Satan, to human passions, natural powers, or magical interference, her very indecision kept her from false simplicities. We may conjecture that, whenever her prophetic and reforming zeal outweighed all other concerns, as in the *Scivias*, she contented herself with a forceful but conventional presentation of good and evil in which God's law and Satan's iniquity, virtue and vice, obedience and sin, are sharply delineated and opposed. When she wrote as a moralist, she aimed her challenge at the sluggish will rather than the searching mind; clarity, not subtlety, was the chief desideratum. So if she had to concern herself with sexual behavior, she remained close to the classical positions on original sin, concupiscence, fornication, and marriage, explaining how fallen sexuality must be controlled rather than how it functions in its natural (or subnatural) state.

But when she laid aside her prophetic trumpet and wrote simply as an observer of the world, she let her instinct for the unity of life lead her further and further into the seamless web of being, in which good and evil are interwoven in a psychophysical pattern so complex that each single phenomenon is overdetermined by all the rest, or, more precisely, by its place in the whole. In this vision, which informs much of the *Activity of God* and most of the *Causes and Cures*, biological and celestial forces do indeed shape human character; but the reverse is also true, so that if a man can blame his moral turpitude on the phase of the moon, it is equally plausible to blame unwholesome lunar influences on human sins. This interdependence and reciprocity of forces affects sexual behavior as well as everything else.

Hildegard's thinking about sexuality builds on two premises that are central to the late-twentieth-century feminist ideal of the self: personal moral freedom, and a holistic conception of body and spirit. But for the contemporary feminist, these tenets are both indispensable, whereas for Hildegard they were profoundly opposed. Hence it is at this point that popular presentations are most likely to distort her thought in order to recreate her as a feminist heroine. A fair study of the evidence, however, shows that Hildegard associated moral and spiritual freedom with a dualistic conception of the self: the soul makes its way toward salvation by sharply divorcing itself from the desires of the body. The holistic conception, on the other hand, is correlated with a pessimistic and even deterministic view of human life. Caught in the intricate meshes of the cosmos, beautiful yet fallen, the struggling will seems helpless to cut against the grain of the pattern. And, although that pattern is still informed by the Wisdom that shaped paradisal nature, it is also deeply tainted, and, from the standpoint of divine judgment, irremediably corrupt. Only a completely new beginning can save it, not by restoring sexuality to its Edenic state but by transcending it altogether. That new grace, the redemption of the divine pattern and the destruction of the serpent who marred it, is virginity.

In the final scene of her *Play of Virtues*, Hildegard portrayed the devil taking his last stand in a quarrel with Castitas. She boasts that in the mind of the Highest she has crushed his head through the "sweet miracle" she worked in the Virgin, by which the devil's "belly"—sexual nature in all its corruption—is confounded. Satan replies, "You know not what you worship, for your own belly is empty of the beautiful form received from man—in this you break the command that God commanded in the sweet union of the sexes, so you don't even know what you are!"[95] To give the devil his due, the form *is* beautiful and the union is sweet; Hildegard did not deny it. But Satan gets his comeuppance: the child of Chastity is fairer than all the sons of Adam, and he alone can free the daughters of Eve from their agony.

95. *Ordo virtutum* 190–91.

5

The Mother of God

"God is an intelligible sphere whose center is everywhere, whose circumference is nowhere." So runs the celebrated axiom of Hildegard's contemporary Alan of Lille.[1] The physician of Bingen had much in common with the metaphysician of France, notably the vitalist and sapiential cast of her theology, and she too liked to imagine God's essence in the form of a circle. But where Alan delighted in the mind-defying paradox, Hildegard mapped what she could see. "God remained whole like a wheel. . . . The round of the wheel is fatherhood, the fullness of the wheel is divinity. All things are in it and all stem from it, and beyond it there is no creator"—only Lucifer stretching out toward the void.[2] Within the wheel of the Godhead are time and eternity, cosmos and microcosm. This same wheel appears again in the *Activity of God*, and this time it is divided into quadrants (Fig. 6).[3] The upper-left portion is green, representing the eternal freshness of the world in the mind of God before creation; the upper-right is red, indicating the glory of the redeemed universe after the end. Pallor and darkness mingle in the bottom half of the circle, which denotes the anguish of time. Then the wheel begins to spin as the ages roll, but at its center, unmoving, is the form of a woman. She is Caritas, resting at one with the foreknowledge

---

1. Alan of Lille, *Theologicae regulae* 7, PL 210: 627a; *Sermo de sphaera intelligibili*, ed. Marie-Thérèse d'Alverny, *Alain de Lille: Textes inédits* (Paris, 1965): 297–306. The axiom has been traced to the pseudohermetic Book of the Twenty-Four Masters; see Joseph Ratzinger, *The Theology of History in St. Bonaventure*, trans. Zachary Hayes (Chicago, 1971): 144.

2. *Causae et curae* 2, emended and trans. Peter Dronke, *Women Writers of the Middle Ages* (Cambridge, 1984): 241 and 172.

3. DOD III.10.1, PL 197: 997.

Fig. 6. *Wheel of Charity*. Caritas rests in the center of the wheel of eternity and history. *De operatione Dei* III.10, Lucca, Biblioteca Statale, Cod. lat. 1942. Courtesy of Biblioteca Statale di Lucca.

of God, and before her face is a tablet that reads, "I will reveal the silver-hued shape of beauty, for great is the radiance of the Godhead, which has no beginning."

We have met Caritas before. In Hildegard's letter to Adam of Ebrach, she appeared as the Lady of the universe, with an ivory tablet displaying the sapphire form of Christ, and she spoke the words of Psalm 109: "With you is the beginning in the day of your virtue, in the splendor of the holy ones; I bore you from the womb before the morning star."[4] Mutatis mutandis, the apparition is the same: Caritas the revealer of eternal beauty is also Caritas the mother, and the Child she bore before the morning star was on earth the Son of the Virgin. So, unlike Alan's paradoxical sphere, Hildegard's wheel of divinity can be diagramed and labeled. Its circumference is the fatherhood of God, and its center, the motherhood of Mary.

With the Mother of God we come to the heart of Hildegard's theology of the feminine. She is the capstone of the arch formed by the celestial foreshadowing of Wisdom on the one side and the embodied fertility of Eve on the other. It is Mary who brings the sapiential visions to their fulfillment; she reveals the eternal counsel, predestined by Love before the world began, because through her the Incarnation is accomplished and God becomes man. Thus she unites the celestial with the earthly, the divine with flesh. At the same time, she is the new Eve, who by her virginity renews what the first mother lost by her carnality. Mary together with her Son is the supreme theophany, the revelation of God's ultimate will; she is also the exemplar of a new creation, which, unlike the one that perished, will be imbued with all virtues, strong to resist the serpent and pure in the face of his lust. In her concrete particularity, Mary is the opposite of Eve; but in the mind of God she is the archetype of Eve and therefore of womankind as such. Finally, she is the paradigm of that second virgin mother, Ecclesia. Overshadowed by the Holy Spirit, the Vir-

4. Ep. 30, PL 197: 192d.

gin Annunciate is a model for every priest at the altar, who like her brings the body of Christ into the world; and in her virginal childbearing she resembles the Church, who gives birth to children in baptism without losing the integrity of her faith. In all these ways, Mary was central for Hildegard. With her strongly incarnational view of the world and her tendency to see original sin as a fall into sexuality, Hildegard turned toward a theology of atonement in which the virgin birth is at least as important as the cross.[5]

Hildegard's hymns to the Virgin, sometimes awkward and sometimes stunningly artistic, reveal a Marian piety as distinctive as everything else in her work.[6] Yet in some ways, her Mariology is so traditional that it seems antiquated in its own age.[7] Unlike her contemporaries, including such conservative Benedictines as Rupert of Deutz and Honorius of Regensburg, Hildegard ignored the new currents of Marian devotion fostered by St. Anselm and St. Bernard. She saw no visions of Mary, recounted no miracles of the Virgin, and ignored apocryphal legends of her birth and childhood. Nor did she have any affective devotion to the maiden suckling her child or the mater dolorosa weeping by the cross. Doctrinally, she ignored current debates over the Immaculate Conception and the Assumption. Mary in her roles as bride of God, mother of Christians, and queen of heaven seldom appears in Hildegard's writings. All these omissions, startling in a writer

5. In the concordance published with the CCCM *Scivias*, the most doctrinal of all Hildegard's works, the words *crux*, *passio*, and *sacrificium* together occupy about a column and a half, while *virgo* and *virginitas* take up nearly three columns. The two approaches to the atonement are not mutually exclusive, but Hildegard's emphasis is clear.

6. The songs have been discussed by Peter Walter, "*Virgo filium dei portasti*. Maria in den Gesängen der hl. Hildegard von Bingen," *Archiv für mittelrheinische Kirchengeschichte* 29 (1977): 75–96; and Barbara Grant, "Five Liturgical Songs by Hildegard von Bingen," *Signs* 5 (1980): 557–67.

7. On contemporary Marian doctrine see Jean Leclercq, "Dévotion et théologie mariales dans le monachisme bénédictin," in *Maria* 2: 547–78; Walter Delius, *Geschichte der Marienverehrung* (Munich, 1963); Hilda Graef, *Mary: A History of Doctrine and Devotion* 1 (New York, 1963).

whose range is so broad, serve to accentuate her intense focus on the Incarnation itself.[8] There is a strikingly impersonal quality in her lyrics: she cared as little for the "personality" of Mary as she cared for the psychology of Eve. Both women are larger than life, not individuals but cosmic theophanies of the feminine; and the purpose of the feminine is to manifest God in the world.

MARY AND THE ANCIENT COUNSEL

Hildegard's sapiential Mariology has its roots in the Carolingian period, in the gradual development of Marian liturgy and iconography. As early as the mid–seventh century, when the feast of Mary's Assumption was introduced in Rome, the epistle chosen for the Mass was taken from the great aretalogy of Wisdom in Ecclus. 24:11–20.[9] By the late tenth century, liturgical manuscripts include a regular Saturday Mass in honor of the Blessed Virgin, containing a lesson that begins with the verse "From the beginning and before the world was I created, and unto the world to come I shall not cease to be" (Ecclus. 24:14).[10] Thus, the liturgy itself forges a bond, if not an identity, between the Mother of God and eternal Wisdom, hinting at a special predestination of Mary.

Theologians readily took up the theme. In the eleventh century St. Peter Damian, an ardent devotee of Mary, hailed her as the woman "chosen and elect before the foundation of

8. The close link between Marian piety and the central dogma is characteristic of earlier medieval devotion, and of the Eastern Church to this day. Ilene Forsyth has observed that the Romanesque Madonna synthesizes, whereas Gothic Madonnas diversify and isolate aspects of the Marian mystery. *The Throne of Wisdom: Wood Sculptures of the Madonna in Romanesque France* (Princeton, 1972): 29.

9. Attested in lectionaries of Corbie and Mürbach (eighth century). Georges Frénaud, "Le Culte de Notre Dame dans l'ancienne liturgie latine," *Maria* 6: 175; Étienne Catta, "*Sedes Sapientiae*," *Maria* 6: 693–94.

10. Norcia Missal, Rome, Vallicellana B.8 (late tenth century); MS. Vat. Pal. lat. 510; also attested in two eleventh-century lectionaries from Besançon and Trier. Frénaud, "Le Culte de Notre Dame" 188–90; Catta, "*Sedes Sapientiae*" 695–96.

the world in the counsel of eternal Wisdom."[11] By the high Romanesque period, the doctrine was very widely diffused. St. Bernard taught it in one of his influential homilies "super Missus est," calling Mary the one "in and through whom God our King decided before the ages to work salvation in the midst of the earth."[12] Likewise, Godfrey of Admont (d. 1165), a Benedictine abbot who reformed many houses in southern Germany, carried this sapiential Mariology to great lengths. Affirming the Immaculate Conception, he presented Mary as God's predestined bride and "helpmeet": "Ardently thirsting for man's salvation from the beginning, for this he created her, his beloved, preserving her sinless in the realm of sin . . . that he might have a companion in his desire and a helper to fulfill what he desired at the opportune time."[13] In the *Mirror of Virgins*, the author called Mary the Wisdom that God possessed "in the beginning of his ways" (Prov. 8:22), and a reference to her predestination crowns a dialogue on metaphysics: "How could the Mother ordained from of old, from eternity, not be present with her Son in a mysterious unity? For did not the primal origin of all divine works lie hidden in them invisibly, with the perfect fullness of the eternal will and the supreme goodness, to be unfolded at the foreordained time?"[14] The doctrine of the absolute predestination of Christ has its corollary in the special predestination of the Virgin. Mother and Son together, hidden in the mind of God from eternity, disclose the secret for which the world was made.

It is in this sense that Hildegard envisioned Mary as the centerpiece of God's eternal plan, his beloved from before all time. In the Dendermonde manuscript of her *Symphonia*, which in all likelihood was produced under the abbess's own supervision, the liturgical pieces are arranged in precise hierarchical order, with one significant exception. Two antiphons to God the Father are followed by no fewer than twelve

11. Peter Damian, *Sermo 45 in Nativitate S. Mariae*, CCCM 57: 273.
12. Bernard of Clairvaux, *Homilia super Missus est* 4.8, *Opera* 4: 54.
13. Godfrey of Admont, *Homilia 31 in Annunciatione*, PL 174: 770bc.
14. *Speculum virginum*, London BL Arundel 44, fol. 41ʳ.

songs to the Virgin. Of the next five pieces, three honor the
Holy Spirit and one each is directed to Caritas and to the Trinity.[15] No lyric in the manuscript is addressed directly to Christ.
So the Mother of God appears in the position that belongs to
her Son, between the first and the third persons of the Trinity;
only through her can Christ and then the Spirit be revealed.
As the vessel of the Incarnation, she takes her place not
among creatures but in the heart of God, where all creatures
are predestined. She is the verdure and the flower hidden in
the very seeds of being.

> O branch, God foresaw your
>   flowering
> on the first day of his creation.[16]
> You are the shining lily,
> the point before all creation
> where God fixed his gaze.[17]

The Incarnation can even be conceived as a divine romance:
like Zeus or Apollo, God beheld the beauty of a maiden and
determined to unite himself with her.

> O what a mighty wonder!
> God gazed on his fairest daughter
> as an eagle sets its eye upon the sun
> when the supernal Father saw the Virgin's splendor
> and wished his Word to take flesh in her.[18]

Changing the metaphor, Mary is the one who restores the
fallen substance of the world. In the beginning, God created

---

15. Peter Dronke, "The Composition of Hildegard of Bingen's *Symphonia*,"
Sacris Erudiri 19 (1969–70): 381–93. The later "Riesenkodex," prepared at the
Rupertsberg after Hildegard's death, contains four additional Marian pieces
either composed at a later date or lost from the earlier ms, which is incomplete. In the Riesenkodex, the songs have also been rearranged to correct the
seeming anomaly in the position of Mary.

16. *Lieder* no. 13: 224; for the *virgo/virga* see Num. 17:8 and Isa. 11:1.

17. *Lieder* no. 12: 222.

18. *Lieder* no. 14: 226–28. For the eagle as symbol of the contemplative,
cf. DOD III.9.10, PL 197: 993–94; Ep. 29, 190c; *Vita* 1.27, 110ab. Hildegard
was reversing the usual application of the image, making Mary rather than
God the object of the gaze.

the primordial matter of the universe through his Word, but the woman who was supposed to manifest his glory instead brought chaos out of order. Through Mary, this *materia* itself is renewed when the Word becomes flesh, so that in her the whole cosmos can become luminous and charged with divine energies (*virtutes*).[19] Thus, the antiphon "O splendidissima gemma" presents Mary as recreatrix of the world.

> O resplendent jewel and unclouded brightness
> of the sunlight streaming through you—
> a fountain leaping from the Father's heart—
> his own and only Word
> through which he created
> the world's first matrix,
> which Eve threw into chaos:
> for you the Father
> fashioned this Word as man,
> so you are that luminous matrix
> through which the same Word
> breathed forth all virtues,
> as in the primal matrix
> it brought forth all creatures.[20]

This lyric typifies Hildegard's idiosyncratic art at its best, with its economy of language and saturation of thought and image. The antiphon forms a single complex sentence; through an intricate sequence of relative clauses and appositions, Hildegard let the focus of meditation shift from Mary herself (jewel and brightness) to Christ (sunlight, fountain, and Word) to the Father, and thence to creation and its undoing through Eve. Only then did Hildegard resume her address to Mary, which is not a plea but a doctrinal assertion. The repetition of *materia*, with its implicit play on *mater*, cre-

---

19. On *materia* see ch. 2, nn. 53 and 55. Godfrey of Admont called the Virgin "perpetuae salutis materia" and "humanae redemptionis singularis materia" (PL 174: 769b and 964a). A twelfth-century litany from Mainz addresses her as "mater et materia nostre salutis." G. G. Meersseman, *Der Hymnos Akathistos im Abendland* (Freiburg, 1960), II: 252.

20. Appendix B, no. 2; *Scivias* III.13.1, p. 615. Pudentiana Barth and M.-I. Ritscher have translated "Pater" in line 9 as a vocative, but surely this would be out of place in an antiphon addressed to Mary.

ates both an antithesis and a parallelism like that of the
Psalms. Mary, the serene and sunlit morning, scatters the
clouds with which Eve overshadowed (*turbavit*) the original
day. Her maternity brings forth a new creation, which is like
the first, only better: in the primal matrix the Word created
physical being, but in the luminous matrix he sent the Spirit
(*exspiravit*) to fill the world with divine being.

A second parallel connects the eternal generation of the
Word "from the Father's heart" with his temporal generation
from Mary. The unifying figure is the fountain of light (Ps.
35:10). Christ is eternally born of God like radiance from the
sun, in keeping with one of the most ancient Trinitarian metaphors; he is also living water—a fountain welling from the
Father and streaming into the Mother, making her pregnant.
The image of the gem evokes Mary's virginity *in partu*. Medieval paintings of the Annunciation frequently show a ray of
sunlight passing through a glass window to indicate that
Mary's virginity was no more violated by the conception and
birth of Christ than glass is shattered by the light. The
preacher Hildebert of Lavardin, in a homily close to the sense
of Hildegard's poem, compared the Mother of God to a crystal. If this stone is immersed in water and then set in blazing
sunlight, it is known to emit sparks, and, as its integrity is
unharmed by its resplendence, so Mary's virginity is untouched by the birth of her Son.[21]

In "O splendidissima gemma," the celebration of Mary as
recreatrix stops just short of affirming that Eve's fall was fortunate. This patristic doctrine does not logically follow from
the absolute predestination of Christ, for if the Incarnation
lay in God's eternal counsel regardless of sin, it is not necessary to praise that "fortunate fall, which merited so great a
Redeemer."[22] Nevertheless, Hildegard shared with most of
her contemporaries the view that creation attained a greater

21. Hildebert of Lavardin, *Sermo 142 in Adventu Domini*, PL 171: 933–34.
22. From the Exsultet sung at the Paschal Vigil: O certe necessarium Adae
peccatum, quod Christi morte deletum est! O felix culpa, quae talem ac tan-
tum meruit habere Redemptorem!

glory through the childbearing of Mary than it had lost in the fall of Eve. "The Virgin, in the sunlight of the ancient counsel, changed the fall of the woman into a good, and God did this to confound the devil who had deceived the woman."[23] So while the fall itself must be lamented, lamentation is swallowed up in thanksgiving at the thought of the new Eve. The predestination of Mary and this *felix culpa* motif merge in the quasi-poetic text "O vita, quae surrexisti."

> O life—you who arose in the dawn
> when the high King in mercy made
>   known
> the wisdom of the wise man of old—
> since through the old destroyer's doorway
> a woman entered death:
> O grief, O sorrow, O the woe
> that were built in the woman!
>
> O dawn, you washed them away
> in a woman who was clean.
> O form of woman, sister of Wisdom,
> how great is your glory!
> For in you there rose a life unquenchable
> that death shall never stifle.
> Wisdom exalted you to make
> all creatures fairer in your beauty
> than they were when the world was
>   born.[24]

This prose poem occurs in Hildegard's epilogue to the *Life of St. Rupert*, which takes the form of a letter to her spiritual sisters. It is here alone that she used her unique Marian title "sister of Wisdom" (*soror Sapientiae*), recalling Prov. 7:4: "Say to Wisdom, You are my sister, and call insight your intimate friend." The book of Proverbs was one of four writings ascribed to King Solomon, who is probably the "wise man of old" mentioned in the first stanza. Solomon was also reputed to be the author of the Song of Songs, and, as we have seen, Hildegard identified the sister-bride in that royal love song

23. *Prooemium Vitae S. Disibodi* 3, Pitra 353.
24. *Ad Vitam S. Ruperti Epilogus* 6, Pitra 364.

with Sapientia. If Wisdom was the consort of Solomon, who composed the marriage song of Christ and the Church, the "sister of Wisdom" is Mary, mother and consort of the "true Solomon," Christ.

Hildegard's lyric is the verbal equivalent of a Romanesque Madonna, the so-called Throne of Wisdom type, in which the hieratic Christ Child sits in the lap of Mary like a king upon his throne, alluding typologically to Solomon and Sapientia.[25] Hildegard would undoubtedly have seen such sculptures, which were ubiquitous in her day. Majestic and impersonal as her songs, these austerely impressive works sometimes bear the inscription "In gremio Matris residet Sapientia Patris" (In the bosom of the Mother rests the Wisdom of the Father).[26] Another rhyming epigram that occurs in this context, and that belongs to the same constellation of sapiential motifs, is "Stella maris solem fert virgo puerpera prolem" (The star of the sea brings the sun; the childbearing Virgin a Son). Mary is the morning star who heralds the dawning sun of justice; Hildegard called her the aurora.[27] Liturgically, the dawn of redemption is associated with both Mary and Sapientia in an antiphon for the Assumption: "Virgin most prudent, whither are you going, glowing brightly as the dawn?"[28] Behind this, in turn, we find the wise virgins of the parable as well as the

25. Forsyth, *Throne of Wisdom* 22–30. The throne of Solomon iconography derives from I Kings 10:18 as interpreted, for example, by Guibert of Nogent: "The Wisdom of God the Father . . . is that Solomon who makes himself a throne of ivory when he comes to dwell in the Virgin, than whom no one was ever more chaste." *De laude S. Mariae,* PL 156: 543.

26. See for instance the Majestas of Beaucaire (Forsyth, *Throne of Wisdom,* pl. 2); the adoration of the Magi at Arezzo (p. 26, n. 5); miniature from the Stuttgart *Passionale* in Hanns Swarzenski, *Vorgotische Miniaturen* (Königstein, 1927): 43.

27. Cf. Pseudo-Damian: "When the Virgin was born the day broke; for Mary, herald of the true light, brightened the sky with the glory of dawn by her birth. She is the morning star in the midst of the cloud that, gleaming with great splendor in the height of heaven, colors the world below with more splendid rays. She is the dawn that precedes, or rather gives birth to, the sun of justice, yielding to it alone in brightness." *Sermo 41 in Assumptione,* PL 144: 719d.

28. Virgo prudentissima, quo progrederis, quasi aurora valde rutilans? Antiphon for Magnificat, First Vespers; quoted in *Scivias* II.3.9, p. 140, and II.5.5, p. 180.

Song of Songs: "Who is she that comes forth as the rising dawn, fair as the moon, bright as the sun?" (6:9). The dawn is Mary's particular sign in heaven; the image links her in one way with Christ the sun and Ecclesia the moon, and in another with Hildegard's Eve, the shining but fatally darkened cloud.

EVE AND MARY

No theme of Mariology is older or more universal than the contrast of Eve and Mary, a topos that dates back to the second century.[29] Irenaeus, one of the first theologians to develop this theme, observed that "the former was beguiled into fleeing God, the latter was persuaded to obey God, that the Virgin Mary might become an advocate for the virgin Eve. Through a virgin, mankind came under the bondage of death; so also through a Virgin the bonds were loosed, and virginal disobedience was balanced by a Virgin's obedience."[30] For the Greek father, the contrast between the two virgins had as yet no sexual connotations. But the Augustinian ethos, linking original sin with concupiscence, led to a practical redefinition of "obedience" and "disobedience" in terms of chastity and lust. And, as the theory and practice of virginity came to play an increasingly major role in Christian life, Irenaeus's comparison of the two virgins gave way to a contrast between the sinful *mulier* and the saintly *virgo*. St. Ambrose set the tone for the new antithesis: "Through a woman came folly, through a virgin wisdom."[31] The contrast was strengthened by the apocryphal tradition that Mary was the first woman to take a vow of virginity.[32]

29. See Hugo Koch, *Virgo Eva—Virgo Maria* (Berlin, 1937); Ernst Guldan, *Eva und Maria* (Graz and Cologne, 1966); and the works cited in n. 7.

30. Irenaeus, *Adversus Haereses* V.19.1, PG 7: 1175–76. This text is a lesson for the Saturday office in the Roman breviary.

31. Ambrose, *In Lucam* IV.7, CCSL 14: 108.

32. *Gospel of Pseudo-Matthew* 8, ed. B. H. Cowper, *The Apocryphal Gospels*, 5th ed. (London, 1881): 34–64. This tradition was adopted by Augustine, *Sermo 291 in Nativitate S. Joannis Baptistae* 5, PL 38: 1319, and made its way into the common stock of medieval lore.

In a remarkable vision of the *Scivias,* Hildegard alluded to
both contrasts—the seduced woman with the Virgin, the
rebel with the obedient handmaid—by using a single evocative symbol for both chastity and obedience. This vision represents the fall not from the standpoint of Satan and Eve, like
Scivias I.2, but from that of God and Adam, with a veiled reference to Mary. The seer first witnessed God creating the
world and quickening man with the breath of life. Next the
Holy Trinity (symbolized by fire, flame, and a blast of wind)
offers Adam a flower, which he sniffs but refuses to pluck
(Fig. 7).

> By means of the flame, burning keenly with a gentle blast, that
> luminous fire offered the man a shining white flower, hanging
> upon the flame like a dewdrop upon a blade of grass. The man
> scented its fragrance with his nostrils, but did not taste it with
> his mouth or touch it with his hands. So, turning away, he fell
> into thick darkness from which he was unable to rise.[33]

This flower, according to the gloss of the vision, represents
"the sweet commandment of shining obedience, clinging to
the Word in moist, verdant fruitfulness."[34] Through obedience
to the fiery Word and the dewy, life-giving Spirit, Adam could
have borne much fruit if he had plucked this flower. But why
should Hildegard have altered the legend to replace the sin
of taking a forbidden fruit with the failure to take a mandatory
flower? The substitution is a stroke of brilliance. In the first
place, it illustrates Hildegard's positive conception of the Virtues by making Adam's disobedience a sin of omission, not
of commission. But, more to the point, the "shining white
flower" can only be the lily of the Annunciation, just as the
artist has represented it in the miniature. Its twin image, the
dewdrop on the blade of grass, is also one of Hildegard's favorite metaphors for the conception of Christ.[35] So Adam's act

---

33. *Scivias* II.1, p. 110.
34. *Scivias* II.1.8, p. 116.
35. DOD III.7.13, PL 197: 974d; III.9.3, 986c; Ep. 47, 231c; *Lieder* nos. 12
and 71. Cf. the antiphon for the Benedictus at Lauds of Christmas Eve: "Orie-
tur sicut sol Salvator mundi: et descendet in uterum Virginis, sicut imber
super gramen."

p tduu iaceus refurrexit. ⁊ homi

Fig. 7. *Adam created, fallen, and redeemed.* Upper register: the sphere of the Trinity, and Adam sniffing but failing to pluck the flower of obedience. Center: the six days of creation, surrounded by the night of the fallen world. Lower register: Christ rising to redeem the Old Adam. *Scivias* II.1, Eibingen ms.

of sin forms an iconographic counterpart to Mary's act of obedience. Adam rejects the dew, the verdure, the blossom, and the light; but in Mary the "verdant fruitfulness" is once again released into the world.

> Your womb held joy like the grass
> when the dew falls, when heaven

> freshens its green—
> even as it did in you,
> O mother of all gladness.[36]

Notice, too, the synesthetic character of Hildegard's vision: the proffered flower at once glimmers with light, exudes moisture, breathes fragrance. And, as in a montage, one image is superimposed on another: the heavenly flame bears an earthly flower and, from another perspective, celestial dew falls on a terrestrial blade of grass. Both images evoke the meeting of the worlds in the Incarnation, and both look forward to Mary's inversion of Adam's fall. The same vision can be read in reverse, so to speak, as the luminous fire reddens into a dawn still framing the virginal lily.

> O how precious
> is the integrity of this Virgin,
> she whose portal is closed
> and whose body the Holy One
> flooded with his warmth
> until a flower sprang in her
> and the Son of God came forth
> from her secret chamber like the dawn.
>
> Thence the tender shoot,
> her Son, opened Paradise
> through the cloister of her womb
> and the Son of God came forth
> from her secret chamber like the dawn.[37]

Mary's "enclosure," her seal of maidenhood, is the key that opens the sealed garden of Eden.

> Today the closed portal
> has opened to us the door
> the serpent slammed on the woman:
> the flower of the maiden Mary
> gleams in the dawn.[38]

---

36. *Lieder* no. 12: 224.
37. Appendix B, no. 3.
38. *Lieder* no. 6: 218.

In Paradise there was as yet no generation: Adam was created from the virgin earth, and Eve from the virgin Adam. When the serpent confounded them through lust, fruitful virginity perished until the advent of Mary. Giving birth "not from virile seed, but by mystic inspiration," in the words of an Ambrosian hymn,[39] she at last is able to generate purely and so to defeat the ancient foe. "As Adam arose from the inviolate earth, so also Christ was born of the inviolate Mary, and he was holy."[40] Again, "just as Eve was taken from her sleeping husband, who was not wounded but looked upon her with joy, so the unique Virgin clasped her Son in her bosom with joy."[41] In another passage Hildegard called Mary the "sleeping earth," combining these figures: she is the earth from which the new Adam is taken, and she sleeps in a dreamlike idyll as Adam did at the birth of Eve. When the Virgin receives the angelic greeting, she nods her assent by looking at the earth from which she was taken—a gesture that expresses both her humility and her significance as the "new earth" of Paradise.[42] Had Christ not been born of a virgin, he could not have been paradisal man.

ATONEMENT THROUGH
THE VIRGIN BIRTH

Mary's virginity is more than a new beginning, a poetic reminiscence of the garden; it is also a necessary condition for the purity of Christ. St. Bernard argued that Mary herself could not have been conceived in holiness, "for how could there be holiness without the sanctifying Spirit, or how could the Holy Spirit have fellowship with sin? And indeed, how could sin

39. Veni Redemptor Gentium: Non ex virili semine/ Sed mystico spiramine,/ Verbum Dei factum est caro/ Fructusque ventris floruit.

40. In festo Purificationis, *Expositio Evangeliorum* 9, Pitra 267. For the same comparison see Honorius, *Speculum Ecclesiae*, PL 172: 849b; and Godfrey of Admont, *Homilia 27 in Annunciatione*, PL 174: 748d. It is first recorded in Irenaeus, *Adversus Haereses* III.21.10, PG 7: 954.

41. DOD III.7.13, PL 197: 974d.

42. DOD I.1.17, PL 197: 750cd.

have been absent where lust was not lacking?"[43] This is the standard Augustinian line, and Hildegard, for all her naturalism, agreed. In a sermon on the Christmas gospel, John 1:14 ("And the Word became flesh and dwelt among us"), she clearly correlated holiness with virginal birth and sin with sexual generation. The atonement begins with—and could not have begun without—the purity of Mary.

> "And the Word became flesh." This means that the same Word that had fashioned flesh from the earth with the breath of life himself put on a garment of pure flesh and slept, just as Adam had slept without sin when a part of his flesh was made into a woman. Thus the Word became flesh and grew to be a man, and dwelt among us like the Adam [*sic*] before their sin, when they were still immutable and whole as God had created them, and no evil had yet entered into them. In this way the Word dwells among us, loving people in goodness and truth.
>
> But when the serpent's cunning assaulted the Adam, their blood was poisoned and sin began teeming from the blood, from the desire of the flesh, and from the desire of man (John 1:13). Then they despoiled and destroyed themselves, so that afterward no flesh could become righteous or just except the Child the Virgin conceived from the heavenly wind that came upon her, and from which he grew and waxed strong. For this reason, in him there was no anger, or swelling of wicked desire (*malae voluntatis*), or taste of virility (*virilis sudoris*), or any evil.
>
> And this pure, chaste little girl, unshaken by the storms of desire, was clean flesh: therefore the Word entered into her and grew into a man.[44]

To accentuate Mary's purity Hildegard presented her as a mere child (*puellula*), not a woman. (According to the revelations of Elisabeth of Schönau, the Virgin was only fifteen at the time of the Annunciation.)[45] Her designation as "pure

43. Bernard of Clairvaux, Ep. 174.7, *Opera* 7: 391. On the Immaculate Conception see Kari Børresen, *Anthropologie médiévale et théologie mariale* (Oslo, 1971).

44. In Nativitate Domini, *Expositio Evangeliorum*, Pitra 251. The curious use of "Adam" as a collective noun may echo the archaic usage of Gen. 5:2, "Et vocavit nomen eorum Adam," or it may be due to a faulty transcript of the homily made by Hildegard's auditors and subsequently copied.

45. Elisabeth of Schönau, *Liber visionum* II.32, in F. W. E. Roth, ed., *Die Visionen der heiligen Elisabeth und die Schriften der Abte Ekbert und Emecho von Schönau* (Brünn, 1884): 5.

flesh" in this text probably implies that she was exempt from menstruation, the curse of Eve. In the *Book of Life's Merits* Christ declares, "I was incarnate of her flesh, which had never secreted any filth, pure as the flesh of Adam in the beginning."[46] Because the Virgin is exempt from fallen sexuality, it does not even matter whether she is likened to Adam, Eve, or the sexless fecundity of the earth. Although she embodies the primordial feminine, by the standards of this fallen world she is "neither male nor female."

According to a very ancient doctrine, Mary's virginal motherhood was a stratagem God used to conceal the birth of his Son from the devil. Ignatius of Antioch, in his second-century letter to the Ephesians, had spoken of "three mysteries" concealed from the evil one: "Mary's virginity was hidden from the prince of this world; so was her child-bearing, and so was the death of the Lord. All these three trumpet-tongued secrets were brought to pass in the deep silence of God."[47] The virginal birth of Christ, no less than his sacrificial death, was necessary to God's "plan for the utter destruction of death." Thus Hildegard:

> There could not, indeed there must not, be any carnal pollution in the mind of the Virgin. For the destructive and lethal death of mankind was deceived, unknowing as if asleep, when the Son of God came in great silence in the dawn, in a humble maiden. Death went forth as if secure, not knowing the life that sweet Virgin carried, for her virginity was concealed from it.[48]

The same theme is expressed poetically in the antiphon "O tu illustrata," which contrasts Mary's radiant purity with the corruption of Eve. The first stanza links the Virgin in turn

---

46. LVM VI.53, Pitra 238. On this question see Charles Wood, "The Doctor's Dilemma: Sin, Salvation, and the Menstrual Cycle in Medieval Thought," *Speculum* 56 (1981): 710–27.

47. Ignatius of Antioch, Ep. ad Ephesos 19, trans. Maxwell Staniforth, *Early Christian Writings* (Harmondsworth, 1968): 81.

48. *Scivias* III.1, p. 330. Cf. the Christmas Alleluia verse based on Wisdom 18:15: Dum medium silentium tenerent omnia, et nox in suo cursu medium iter perageret, omnipotens Sermo tuus, Domine, a regalibus sedibus venit, Alleluia.

with each person of the Trinity, particularly with the Spirit, whose inbreathing counteracts what the devil belched into Eve. In the second stanza, Hildegard admired the hiddenness of the eternal counsel that restored wholeness, repealing Eve's artificial "laws" of carnality and death.

> Pierced by the light of God,
> O shining maid Mary,
> flooded with the Word of God,
> your body blossomed
> from the entering Spirit of God,
> who breathed on you and purged you
> of the poison that Eve took
> in the breach of purity—
> when she caught the infection
> from the devil's suggestion.
>
> Wondrously you hid within you
> undefiled flesh
> by the counsel of God
> when God's Son blossomed in your body
> and the Holy One brought him
> to birth, against the laws
> of flesh that Eve built—
> coupled to wholeness
> in the seedbed of holiness.[49]

Although the conception of Mary herself was not an issue for Hildegard, her personal freedom from lust and her perpetual virginity were crucial. Because every child is generated from the blood of its mother, it was imperative not only that Christ himself should be born without intercourse but that Mary's own blood should not once have been tainted by the stirrings of desire. This is a recurrent theme in the *Scivias*. The Virgin's flesh "never burned in the sweetness of lust, nor was it ever touched"; she "could have no stain in her virginity whence it might be weakened"; her beauty shone "without

49. Appendix B, no. 4. Unfortunately, the corruption of Eve seems to have infected the text. Lines 6–9 are problematic. The literal meaning appears to be: "[the Spirit] who breathed upon you and, within you, sucked out that which Eve carried away in the rending of purity."

spot of sin or fluid of human filth, and without longing for the deed done in sinful desires."[50] Just as the flowering branch of Aaron was cut off from its tree, "man was cut off from her mind so that she was never touched by the delight of intercourse."[51] Nevertheless, she required yet further purification in order to conceive Christ.[52] At the Annunciation, "the power of the Most High overshadowed her, for he so caressed her in his warmth that . . . he utterly cleansed her from all the heat of sin."[53] The cooling shelter of the Spirit, like a sunshade, tempers the powerful blaze of divinity and filters out the fire of passion.[54] This overshadowing, however, the reversal of Eve's, brings not darkness but light. There is an unlike likeness between fallen intercourse, with its ardor and moisture, and virginal union with the Spirit, which is an antithetical burning fountain.[55] The dew from on high cools the fires of lust, while the flame from on high dries up the humors of lust.

Like Hugh of St. Victor, Hildegard described Mary's conception as normal except that the Holy Spirit took the place of a man.

> The warmth of a man kindles a woman to conceive. Therefore, the warmth of the living and unquenchable fire came to kindle the Virgin and made her fertile, and cleansed the foam of human pleasure from her blood. From this utterly pure and

50. *Scivias* II.6.14, p. 243; III.1, p. 330; III.1.8, p. 336.
51. DOD III.7.3, PL 197: 963c.
52. The doctrine of the Immaculate Conception was not yet established, and many theologians believed that the Virgin was partially sanctified in her mother's womb and totally purified at the Annunciation. See for instance Paschasius Radbertus, *De partu virginis* 1, CCCM 56c: 53–54; Bernard of Clairvaux, *Sermo 2 in Assumptione* 2, *Opera* 5: 232; Godfrey of Admont, *Homilia 27 in Annunciatione*, PL 174: 756c.
53. Ep. 43, PL 197: 213a.
54. Cf. Radbertus, *De partu virginis* 1, CCCM 56c: 48; Godfrey, *Homilia 23 in Annunciatione*, PL 174: 762–63.
55. "God is an unquenchable fire and a living fountain. . . . Whence he consumed all carnal desire in the Virgin Mary so that, without fire of sin, his Son put on his humanity from her. For the Holy Spirit, who is a living fountain, suffused her with his gentle moisture as dew descends upon the grain." Ep. 47, PL 197: 231bc.

> chaste blood it caused a small clot to coagulate . . . and this coagulum became flesh in the form of an infant, and in this way the infant grew until birth.[56]

Christ extended his unique purity to all when he "plunged into the waters" of baptism and thus "purified the virile seed, as fire casts out water."[57] In the New Testament (Rom. 6:3–4), to be baptized is to participate in Christ's death and burial; but Hildegard imagined it as a vicarious sharing in his birth, whereby the waters in which he has immersed himself wash away the taint of conception. Likewise, the rite of circumcision, which is normally understood as a prefiguration of baptism, anticipates the virginity of Mary because it is a sign of sexual discipline. When Abraham circumcised himself, he "wounded the neck of the ancient serpent"—an allusion at once to the circumcised member and to Mary's triumph over Satan (Gen. 3:15 Vg).[58]

We have seen that Eve, in the unfallen world of Hildegard's speculation, was meant to give birth "painlessly from her side," as she herself had been brought from Adam's side. In Mary this promise is fulfilled.

> When the blessed Virgin was a little weakened, as if drowsy with sleep, the infant came forth from her side—not from the opening of the womb—without her knowledge and without pain, corruption, or filth, just as Eve emerged from the side of Adam. He did not enter through the vagina, for if he had come out that way there would have been corruption; but since the mother was intact in that place, the infant did not emerge there. And no placenta covered the infant in the Virgin Mother's womb, in the manner of other infants, because he was not conceived from virile seed.[59]

Hildegard went on to relate legends about the childhood of Christ, indicating the apocryphal provenance of this doctrine.

---

56. Fragment IV.6–7, p. 68.
57. LVM VI.54, Pitra 239. More explicitly still, Christ "cleansed the deadly conception of man when he was conceived and born of the Holy Spirit from the Virgin Mary, with no sin [contracted from] masculine nature." Ep. 47, PL 197: 231a.
58. *Prooemium Vitae S. Disibodi* 2, Pitra 353.
59. Fragment IV.7, p. 68.

Like many of her legends about Adam and Eve, it can be traced back ultimately to Jewish sources. As Edouard Cothenet has shown, the motif of Mary's painless childbearing derives from rabbinic legends about the birth of Moses. Josephus claimed that the mother of Moses gave birth to her son without pain; according to Jewish tradition, she enjoyed this privilege because "holy women do not share the fate of Eve."[60] In Jewish-Christian circles such legends were transferred to Mary. The idea that the Virgin not only conceived but also gave birth by a miracle is first attested in the *Ascension of Isaiah*, a late-first-century Judeo-Christian apocalypse, which asserts that after two months of pregnancy "Mary straightway looked with her eyes and saw a small babe, and she was astonished."[61]

In later Christian centuries, despite wide belief in Mary's virginity *in partu*, the idea of her childbearing *clauso utero* was understandably suspected of docetism. St. Ambrose had to defend the notion against Jovinian, and St. Jerome against Helvidius. Ratramnus, in the ninth century, countered a German "heresy" which maintained that "the infant Christ was not truly born in a human way through the opening of the virginal womb, but monstrously passed from the womb into the light of day by an unknown path—which is not birth, but eruption!"[62] But this "heresy" would become the later orthodoxy. Ratramnus's opponent, Radbertus, prevailed via his polemic *On the Childbearing of the Virgin*, in which he argued that perpetual virginity logically entailed childbirth without labor pangs, afterbirth, or the opening of the womb.[63] This peculiar interpretation of virginity *in partu*, docetic or not, had estab-

---

60. Josephus, *Antiquitates* II.9.4; cited in Louis Ginzberg, *The Legends of the Jews*, trans. Henrietta Szold (Philadelphia, 1954), V: 397, n. 41. See also Edouard Cothenet, "Marie dans les Apocryphes," *Maria* 6: 81–82.

61. *Ascension of Isaiah* XI.8, trans. R. H. Charles (London, 1900): 76. Childbirth without pain is listed as one of the messianic promises in the Syriac *Apocalypse of Baruch* 73.7, ed. R. H. Charles, *Apocrypha and Pseudepigrapha of the Old Testament* (Oxford, 1913), II: 518.

62. Ratramnus, "De eo quod Christus ex virgine natus est" 1, PL 121: 83a.

63. Radbertus, *De partu virginis* 1, CCCM 56c: 56–58.

lished itself so firmly by the twelfth century that Abelard once tarred a theologian with heresy for asserting the contrary.[64]

While this teaching may appear to proclaim a grace that denies rather than perfecting nature, for Hildegard it was quite the opposite: the so-called "law of nature" is really the false law of death imposed on Eve by the serpent. Mary, on the other hand, gives birth to Christ in a way that both restores and surpasses the law of Paradise, which would have obtained before the fall. Eve, the victimized mother, had in turn victimized her children; but Mary is the pure mother who purifies them. Thus, in the responsory "O vis eternitatis," Hildegard took up the theme of Adam's defiled "garment of skin," the flesh, which Mary cleanses by clothing Christ in it.

> O strength of the Everlasting!
> In your heart you set all in order,
> all things created through your Word,
> even as you willed;
> and your Word himself put on flesh
> in that form that was drawn out of Adam
> and thus the great pain was washed from his garments.[65]

It is striking that Hildegard wrote as if Mary herself had been "drawn out of Adam": the archetypal unity of Woman, the *feminea forma*, here embraces both poles of the antithesis. On the other hand, the responsory "O clarissima Mater," which salutes Mary as the great physician, lets the polarity emerge more starkly.

> O shining Mother of sacred healing,
> through your holy Son you poured balm
> on the sobbing wounds
> of death that Eve built
> in the torment of souls.
> You have overthrown death,
> building up life.[66]

64. Abelard, *Introductio ad Theologiam* II.6, PL 178: 1056c.
65. *Lieder* no. 58: 276.
66. *Lieder* no. 4: 216.

Not only human beings but the very elements rejoice at the purity that comes through Mary. Hildegard saw the fall in cosmic terms: after the sin of Eve the elements, once pristine and immutable, were whirled into corruption and decay, the universe lost its godlike fixity, and ever since "the whole creation has been groaning in travail" (Rom. 8:22).[67] Because of the inseparable bond of macrocosm and microcosm, only the Savior's birth in the flesh and the consequent purification of human seed could rescue the universe itself from a decay like that of mankind. In the elliptical antiphon "Cum processit factura," Hildegard envisioned the glum state of fallen humanity, doomed to be born "of mingled blood" and no longer purely, now illumined by a dawn that cleansed the whole fabric of creation.

> While the work of God's finger,
> formed in God's image,
> was born of mingled blood,
> exiled because Adam fell—
> the elements, excellent Mary,
> received joy in you:
> at daybreak the heavens blaze
> and ring with praise.[68]

For Hildegard the composer, music was the supreme embodiment of joy. Adam's voice in Eden, she believed, rang with such resonance that mere mortals could not have endured the sound; but, after Eve gave birth in travail, the wailing of the infant taught humankind to lament: "For Eve had conceived all weeping in pain; but in Mary joy resounded with the music of the lyre, with the harmony of song."[69] *Sym-*

---

67. For the immutability of the world before the fall and after the last judgment see *Scivias* III.12.15, p. 613; *Causae et curae* 10.

68. Appendix B, no. 5. The antiphon is difficult. I take the first four lines to refer to the fallen state, and the last four to describe the world's response to the Incarnation. This event cannot be the subject of lines 1–4, because Christ was emphatically not born "in ortu mixti sanguinis."

69. *Ad Vitam S. Ruperti Epilogus* 1, Pitra 360. On Adam cf. Ep. 47, PL 197: 220c; LSM VII.3, 1315ab.

phonia, the harmonious blending of instruments and voices, rightly celebrates the one who harmonized the worlds.

In the office for the Nativity of the Virgin, Mary is honored as the new Miriam, sister of Moses, leading the redeemed people of God out of exile with timbrels and dancing (Exod. 15:20). A sermon of Ambrosius Autpertus, included in the office of the feast, gives classic expression to the motif.

> Eve sorrowed, but Mary exulted; Eve carried weeping in her womb, but Mary carried joy, for Eve brought forth a sinner, but Mary innocence itself. . . . Mary may now play on her instruments, the Mother strike the cymbals with swift fingers. The joyful choruses may sound out and songs alternate with sweet harmonies. Hear, then, how she sings, she who leads our chorus. For she says, "My soul magnifies the Lord." . . . The new childbearing of Mary vanquishes the childbearing of Eve, and Mary's song puts an end to Eve's lamentation.[70]

Hildegard's "symphony of Mary" is a song of the elements, of the angels, of the Church.

> Your womb held joy when all heaven's
> harmony rang from you,
> for virgin, you bore the Son of God
> when in God your chastity blazed.
> . . . .
> Let the whole Church flush with rapture
> and resound with song
> for the sake of sweet Mary,
> the maiden all-praised,
> the Mother of God.[71]

So the Incarnation is the embodiment of music itself: Mary bears not only the Word but the Song of God in her flesh. Hildegard introduced her "Symphony of Virgins," a lyrical prayer for her community, with a haunting invocation to Christ placed on the lips of Mary.

---

70. Pseudo-Augustine, *Sermo* 194.1–2, PL 39: 2105; translation adapted from the Breviary.

71. *Lieder* no. 12: 224.

O Son beloved,
whom I bore in my womb
by the might of the circling
wheel of the holy
God who created me
and formed my whole frame
and set in my womb
all manner of music
in all blossoms of melody:
now a throng of virgins
follows me and you.
Deign to save them,
O Son most lovely![72]

Music, like fragrance, is immaterial substance; arising on earth it ascends to heaven, filling the air with its presence and luring the soul to praise. This lyric is almost an invitation to the dance: Mary precedes the choir of virgins, who follow the music she herself has become. While abiding like Caritas at the center of the circling wheel—its form mirrored by the prayer itself—like Sapientia she "plays before God at all times, playing in the sphere of the earth" (Prov. 8:30).

MARY AS THE FEMININE IDEAL

As the sister of Wisdom, Mary is the fulfillment of all that Eve was meant to be; as the second Eve, she is the polar opposite of the first. But what of her relation to the daughters of Eve? Recent critiques of Mariology, notably Marina Warner's *Alone of All Her Sex*, have attacked the medieval cult of the Virgin for promoting misogyny by setting up an unattainable standard that makes all actual women fall short.[73] Obviously, no woman can hope to be both mother and virgin. Hildegard, for her part, proposed no concrete imitation of Mary; although she advocated virginity, she did not exhort virgins to

---

72. *Ad Vitam S. Ruperti Epilogus* 2, Pitra 360.
73. Marina Warner, *Alone of All Her Sex: The Myth and the Cult of the Virgin Mary* (New York, 1976). The title—and thesis—of this useful study is taken from a hymn verse by Sedulius Scotus: "sola sine exemplo placuisti femina Christo."

"conceive Christ in the spirit as Mary conceived him in the flesh," a doctrine central to the *Mirror of Virgins* and other works of its kind.[74] She did, however, universalize Mary's womanhood in certain characteristic ways.

Most important is her cherished theme of power perfected in weakness.

> From the warmth of God the Virgin's flesh, like a tabernacle, blazed so that a man was born of her in more splendid faith and more ardent love than when God married Eve to Adam before the fall. God himself had created the man strong and the woman weak, and her weakness gave birth to the world. Likewise, divinity is strong but the flesh of the Son of God is weak—and through it the world is restored to its original life.[75]

This passage from the *Book of Life's Merits* reinforces the connection between woman's fertility and her frailty. But, more significant, this feminine frailty corresponds to the divine humanity in which God wrought salvation by the power of weakness. Hildegard's thought here is the same as Elisabeth's in the vision where she saw Ecclesia strengthened by Christ's fragile feet of clay. The Incarnation, like the marriage of Adam and Eve, is a deliberate wedding of strength and weakness; both are as necessary in redemption as in creation. Because "woman signifies the humanity of the Son of God,"[76] not only Mary but feminine weakness per se is exalted when Christ is born of a woman.

The text also implies a feminizing of Jesus himself. Godfrey of Admont remarked, in a commentary on Psalm 18, that "in that bridal chamber, the womb of the most blessed Virgin, the

74. "The Church, in which virgins are allotted the finest place, is incorrupt like Mary, in that she daily conceives and continually gives birth. . . . It is greater, I say, to conceive and bear Christ spiritually than to procreate carnally children who are bound to die. . . . So if you conceive by the Holy Spirit, . . . what you bear in the womb of your mind is a child of freedom, not a burden; a child of light, not of heaviness." *Speculum virginum*, London BL Arundel 44, fols. 10ᵛ, 20ʳ, 71ʳ.

75. LVM IV.32, Pitra 158, as emended by Heinrich Schipperges. Pitra's text has *mendum* for *mundum* in the second sentence.

76. DOD I.4.100, PL 197: 885c.

Son of God became alike bridegroom and bride: bridegroom in his divinity, bride in his humanity."[77] The "feminine" aspect of Christ tends to be assimilated to the femininity of Mary, and through her to femininity at large. We can see this process taking place in a text from the *Scivias*, where Hildegard meditated on the Marian title of *Mater misericordiae*. Mercy, like almost all the Virtues, appears in the form of a woman, but in this case Hildegard provided specific reasons for her gender. Christ of course is the true Mercy, but he had been eternally "overshadowed" in God, like the Virgin Annunciate, until the Father chose to manifest the Son through Mary.[78] Thus Mercy itself takes on a feminine character. Moreover, merciful behavior is more becoming to a woman than to a man: "For as a woman veils her head, so mercy subdues the death of souls. And as a woman is gentler than a man, so mercy is gentler than the raging fury of crimes in a sinner's madness, before his heart has been visited by God." In this complex of associations, the figure of Mary establishes a link between the femininity of God and the kind of virtuous attitude the seer viewed as typically female. One can only hope that she did not, by analogy, view the "raging fury of crimes" as typically male.

Along with generic frailty and mercy, Mary personifies the virtue of humility. This in itself is commonplace; in the literature on virginity, nuns are continually advised that their chastity without humility is of little worth.[79] Nuns eschew marriage, however, and Mary was betrothed. Hildegard explained that even her miraculous conception did not make her independent of man. Perfect humility required obedient sub-

77. Godfrey of Admont, *Homilia 28 in Annunciatione*, PL 174: 760b.

78. *Scivias* III.3.8, p. 380. In LVM I.17, Pitra 13, Misericordia alludes to the Annunciation when she proclaims, "I was present in that fiat by which all creatures came into being."

79. For example Bernard of Clairvaux, *Homilia super Missus est* 1.8, *Opera* 4: 20; Rupert of Deutz, *Comment. in Apocalypsim* 2.3, PL 169: 900d; further references in Matthäus Bernards, *Speculum Virginum. Geistigkeit und Seelenleben der Frau im Hochmittelalter* (Cologne and Graz, 1955): 51.

mission to Joseph as well as God, in conventional marriage as well as virginity.[80]

> When Mary the mother of Jesus was betrothed to Joseph, God respected the justice of the original order in which he had married Adam and Eve. And he wanted the Mother of his Son to be betrothed to a man so that he could guard and care for her faithfully, and she could be subject to him. For every woman with child ought to have a husband to look after her. And in this is justice, that humility follows in submission. For if Mary had had no one to care for her, pride would easily have snatched her, as if she had not needed a husband to provide for her.[81]

By submitting humbly to Joseph, the Virgin Mary becomes, in yet another sense, "an advocate for the virgin Eve," who dominated her husband. Proud Eve is brought low, humble Mary is exalted, thus paradoxically validating the old order of creation and at the same time inaugurating a new order that transcends it. But despite the reversed hierarchy of redemption, in which God acts through the weaker woman rather than the stronger man, the social implications remain conservative. God has elected the weak to confound the strong, yet in mundane existence the "strong" male is still dominant. Mary is an exception who proves the rule that she breaks— much like Hildegard herself, who in spite of her divine election always remained the "poor little female."

In her antiphon "O quam magnum miraculum," Hildegard exalted the submissiveness of Mary and at the same time universalized her as the quintessential woman, once again conflating Mary with Eve.

> O what a miracle!
> Into the submissive form of a woman
> entered the King.

---

80. The holy family occupied an important place in medieval doctrine and canon law regarding marriage. Penny Schine Gold, "The Marriage of Mary and Joseph in the Twelfth-Century Ideology of Marriage," in Vern Bullough and James Brundage, eds., *Sexual Practices and the Medieval Church* (Buffalo, 1982): 102–17.

81. In Vigilia Nativitatis Domini, *Expositio Evangeliorum* 1, Pitra 245.

> This is what God did
> because humility mounts above all.
> And O what felicity
> dwells in this form:
> for malice, which flowed from woman—
> woman has now demolished!
> She has enhanced the sweet fragrance
> of all the virtues
> and graced the heavens
> more than she once disgraced the earth.[82]

Grammatically, only one woman figures in the poem; in the last line Hildegard surprisingly chose the adverb *prius* instead of the expected *prima*, so that instead of contrasting Eve's action with Mary's, she made "the Woman" at once the scourge of earth and the ornament of heaven. The *feminea forma* appears under both aspects, ruining and restoring—but she has graced heaven *more* than she once disgraced the earth, so the net result is an exaltation of Woman as such. This is also the message of the antiphon "Quia ergo femina."

> Because a woman built the house of death
> a shining maid tore it down:
> so the sublimest blessing
> comes in the form of a woman
> surpassing all creation,
> for God became man in a maid
> most tender and blessed.[83]

But the fullest expression of this theme comes in Hildegard's sequence "O virga ac diadema," the most polished and comprehensive of all her Marian lyrics. She herself was particularly fond of this sequence; long after her death, her nuns recalled how she used to walk about the cloister chanting it to herself with a special radiance about her.[84] The sequence combines all the Marian motifs we have considered: the predestination of the Virgin, her purity and newness of life, verdure and sunrise, cosmic harmony and joy. Because of its

---

82. Appendix B, no. 6.
83. *Lieder* no. 7: 218.
84. *Acta* 4, PL 197: 133c.

length, it also possesses a more carefully wrought and revealing structure than most of Hildegard's lyrics. Leaving
aside the initial salutation and the closing prayer, the sequence can be divided into three sections, each containing
two strophic pairs. In the first section (1a–2b), Mary's "blossoming" is contrasted with natural generation and in particular with Adam's; in the third section (5a–6b), her motherhood is compared with Eve's. These two complementary
antitheses frame a central section, which is sapiential rather
than dialectical. In strophe 3, Mary appears as the final cause
and matrix (*materia*) of the world; in 4b she is seen as the beloved of God and the joy of the redeemed creation. Strophe
4a, at the center of the sequence, alludes once more to Adam
and Eve, but the context is no longer one of antithesis. As in
the responsory "O vis aeternitatis" and the antiphons we
have just examined, Mary *is* Eve: there is only one Woman,
she who was born of Adam in order to be, like Sapientia, the
mirror of God's beauty and "the embrace of his whole creation." This distinctive affirmation, set midway between the
two more predictable contrasts, typifies the place of Hildegard's sapiential and unitive vision as it uneasily but triumphantly prevails amid a world of dualities.

> 1a. O scepter and crown of royal purple,
> secure in your fastness as a breastplate:
>
> 1b. Verdant, you bloomed in a fresh way—
> not the way Adam sired all our race.
>
> 2a. Hail, all hail!
> from your womb came a fresh life—
> a life that Adam stripped from his sons.
>
> 2b. You did not spring from the dew,
> O blossom, nor from the rain—
> that was no wind that swept over you—
> but the brightness of God made you spring
> from a branch most noble.
>
> 3a. O branch, God foresaw your flowering
> on the first day of his creation.
>
> 3b. And he made you as a golden matrix,
> O all-praised maid, for his Word.

4a. What strength dwells in the side of man
from which God made the form of woman
to be the mirror of all his beauty,
the embrace of his whole creation.

4b. Thence the celestial organs chime
and the whole earth marvels,
Mary all-praised,
for God has deeply loved you.

5a. How we must mourn, how we must weep
because a guilty sadness
flowed through a serpent's cunning
into a woman.

5b. For she that God meant to be mother of all
tore her own womb with the wounds
of ignorance, and gave birth to grief,
consummate grief for her kind.

6a. But from your womb, O dawn,
arose a new sun
that burnt the whole of Eve's guilt away
and through you brought a blessing greater
than the harm that Eve did.

6b. Saving Lady, who bore the new light
for humankind:
gather the members of your Son
into the harmony on high.[85]

"O virga ac diadema" is but the most elaborate expression of themes that pervade all Hildegard's writing about the Virgin. If we step back for a moment from the details, what seems most distinctive about this body of prose and song is the near-total absence of Mary as a person. She is rather a state of existence, an embodied Eden. Her flesh is the garden where God dwells; everything about her is joy, innocence, asexual eros. Her beauty is not that of a human form but that of intangible essences—light and fragrance and song. It is surely significant that the visionary who had such a gift for graphic description, and who wrote sixteen songs in Mary's honor, almost never claimed to have seen her face or heard her voice. Nor does Mary have personal feelings or a personal

85. Appendix B, no. 7.

history: aside from the moment of the Incarnation, her life does not matter.

The ideal she personifies is Virginity, but it is not the monastic virginity purchased by fallen humanity at the price of renunciation, discipline, and suffering. Hence she is no model for direct imitation. Hers is rather the virginity of Paradise. It is an aesthetic rather than ascetic state; there is no hint of strain about her. Unlike most hymnodists, Hildegard did not even stress the paradox that Mary is both virgin and mother; in fact, she seems scarcely to have perceived that it *was* a paradox. For her, virginity and maternity were not mutually exclusive terms but aspects of the unique feminine birthright that Eve unfortunately spoiled. Mary is supreme because she at last enters into the inheritance, bearing a child without the tragic fall into sexuality. She both embodies the lost Paradise in her own person and provides access to it through her Son.

MARY, THE CHURCH, AND
THE PRIESTHOOD

In the last strophe of "O virga ac diadema," as Barbara Grant has remarked, "Mary is, Isis-like, re-membering the mystical body of Christ."[86] In this role she figures as gracious mother and even savior (*salvatrix*) of the Church. But it is more significant that Mary is the type or prefiguration of Ecclesia, just as Eve was the type of Mary and Sapientia the archetype of Eve. In patristic theology, the symbol of Ecclesia as virgin mother, in the likeness of Mary, is no less ancient than Irenaeus's contrast between the old and the new Eve.[87] St. Cyprian, who was particularly fond of this theme, described the Church as Christ's pure and fruitful bride; no one can have

86. Grant, "Five Liturgical Songs" 564.
87. See Joseph Plumpe, *Mater Ecclesia: An Inquiry into the Concept of the Church as Mother in Early Christianity* (Washington, 1943): Hervé Coathalem, *Le parallelisme entre la Sainte Vierge et l'Église dans la tradition latine jusqu'à la fin du XII*e *siècle* (Rome, 1954).

God for his Father unless he has the Church for his Mother.[88] Augustine frequently pointed out parallels between Mater Ecclesia and the Mother of God. The Church is a mother in charity and a virgin in integrity; she bears the members of Christ as Mary bore the head; to both his mother and his bride, Christ grants the gift of fertility without harming virginity.[89] Leo the Great stressed the Spirit's role: "The very one who was born of a virgin mother by the Holy Spirit makes his undefiled Church fruitful by the same inspiration, that through the childbirth of baptism a countless throng of God's children may be born."[90] Caesarius of Arles preached:

> In the figure of Mary can we not see a type of the holy Church? To the Church indeed the Holy Spirit descended, the power of the Most High overshadowed her, and from her Christ goes forth mighty in power. She is undefiled in intercourse, fertile in childbirth, virgin in chastity; she conceives not of man, but of the Spirit.[91]

The "womb" of the Church is the baptismal font, fertilized and sanctified by the Spirit—an act dramatically symbolized at the consecration of the font, when the paschal candle is plunged into the water.[92] So it was to baptism that Hildegard referred when, in a wholly traditional way, she compared Ecclesia's childbearing to Mary's.

> The Church is the virginal mother of all Christians, for in the mystery of the Holy Spirit she conceives and bears them. . . . And as the Holy Spirit overshadowed the blessed Mother so that, without pain, she wonderfully conceived and bore the Son of God yet remained a virgin, so also the Holy Spirit illumines the Church, the happy mother of believers. . . . As balm exudes from a tree, as potent medicines pour from a vase of onyx, as radiant splendor flashes from a dia-

---

88. Cyprian, Ep. 74.6, CSEL 3²: 804.
89. Augustine, *Sermones* 191.3, 192.2, 213.7, 341.5, in PL 38: 1010, 1012–13, 1064 and PL 39: 1496; *De sancta virginitate* 2, PL 40: 397.
90. Leo, *Sermo* 63.6, PL 54: 356bc.
91. Pseudo-Augustine, *Sermo* 121.5, PL 39: 1989.
92. See F. J. Dölger, "*Aqua ignita: Wärmung und Weihe des Taufwassers*," *Antike und Christentum* 5 (1936): 175–83.

mond without hindrance—so the Son of God was born of the Virgin with no barrier of corruption. And so too the Church, his bride, bears her children with no opposition from error, yet remains a virgin in the integrity of faith.[93]

Aside from some distinctive metaphors, which recall the imagery of "O clarissima Mater" and "O splendidissima gemma," this analogy is commonplace, for baptism is the Church's maternal act par excellence. Less familiar, but no less important for Hildegard, is the analogy between Mary's "overshadowing" and the other great sacrament. In a discussion of the Eucharist, she commented that "that same power of the Most High which formed flesh in the Virgin's womb changes the oblation of bread and wine on the altar into the sacrament of flesh and blood, brooding over it with his power, at the words of the priest."[94] The word *brooding* (*fovens*) was chosen advisedly; rich in connotations, it suggests first of all the Spirit of God "brooding over the waters" like a mother bird, warming creation into life (Gen. 1;2).[95] In the Hebrew and Syriac tradition, the Holy Spirit (*ruach*) is feminine, and, as early as the second century, a Judeo-Christian poet saw fit to compare the teeming waters of Genesis, warmed by this great maternal presence, with the womb of Mary.[96] Even though the Vulgate version of Genesis eliminates the image of the bird, the variant reading remained familiar enough, and in the twelfth century certain theologians revived the ancient notion of the Annunciation as a second genesis. Thus Rupert of Deutz: "The Holy Spirit, who in the beginning was borne over the waters, came upon the blessed Virgin and ineffably

93. *Scivias* II.3.12–13, pp. 142–43.
94. Ep. 43, PL 197: 213a.
95. In the Vulgate Gen. 1:2 reads "Spiritus Dei ferebatur super aquas," but Ambrose introduced a more accurate translation, which, following the Hebrew and Syriac, has *fovebat* instead of *ferebatur*. *Hexaemeron* I.8.29, CSEL 32¹: 28–29; Marie-Thérèse d'Alverny, "Le cosmos symbolique du douzième siècle," *Archives d'histoire doctrinale et littéraire du moyen âge* 28 (1953): 71, n. 1.
96. *Odes of Solomon* 19: "The Spirit spread its wings over the Virgin's womb,/ she conceived and bore a child,/ and she became Mother, the Virgin,/ with great mercy." Cited in Jean Daniélou, *Théologie du Judéo-Christianisme* (Tournai, 1958): 43.

overshadowed her womb, like a bird warming an egg beneath with its longed-for brooding."[97] And Hildegard: "the Virgin bore a Son by the warmth of the Holy Spirit brooding over her; and as a chick would never hatch from an egg without the warmth of the hen, so the Virgin would never have borne a Son without the warmth of the Holy Spirit."[98]

Again, Mary renews the *prima materia*; she experiences a potency like the surge of divine energy that the cosmic waters knew in the beginning, because through her pregnancy the Spirit is re-creating the world. But the Christ whom Mary bore once is born daily in the Church, not only in baptism but whenever his body is confected in the Eucharist. So the same analogy will serve for each consecration: the Holy Spirit descends like a mother bird spreading its wings over the egg until the chick hatches and flies to heaven, leaving only a shell (the visible forms of bread and wine) beneath.[99] This is an essentially Eastern theology of the Eucharist, sacramental rather than sacrificial in its emphasis. Once again not the cross but the Incarnation provides the focal point of devotion.[100]

To combat the perennial emergence of eucharistic heresies, orthodox theologians continually maintained that Christ's eucharistic body was the very same flesh that was born of Mary. Radbertus, the ninth-century champion of Mary's virginity *in partu*, successfully defended this position as well in a contest with his sparring partner, Ratramnus.[101] Two centuries later

---

97. Rupert of Deutz, *De glorificatione Trinitatis* IX.6, PL 169: 186d. Gerhoch of Reichersberg also used the image in the *Comment. in Psalmos*, PL 193: 639b. A thirteenth-century window at Auxerre represents the visual equivalent: it shows the dove that denotes the Creator Spirit not "borne over the waters" but enclosed in a womblike aureole with waters on every side.

98. Ep. 47, PL 197: 238b.

99. *Scivias* II.6.36, pp. 264–65.

100. Some of the closest parallels to Hildegard's eucharistic teaching can be found in the medieval Syriac tradition. See Sebastian Brock, "Mary and the Eucharist: An Oriental Perspective," *Sobornost* 1:2 (1979): 50–59.

101. "It is no marvel if the Holy Spirit, who created the man Christ in the Virgin's womb without seed, daily forms the flesh and blood of Christ by invisible power from the substance of bread and wine." Radbertus, *De corpore et sanguine Domini* 3, CCCM 16: 27.

Peter Damian asserted graphically that "that body of Christ which the most blessed Virgin bore, fondled in her lap, wrapped in swaddling bands, nursed with maternal care—that very body, I say, and no other, we now beyond any doubt receive from the holy altar."[102] Certain missals contain a eucharistic prayer, inspired by Byzantine sources, which asks that the Holy Spirit, "who filled the womb of blessed Mary with the truth of his splendor, may graciously assume the gifts set forth on [this] altar."[103] It is probably to safeguard the true, fleshly reality of the eucharistic body, as much as to exalt the honor of Mary, that Godfrey of Admont called her the "singular matter of all the sacraments."[104]

Hildegard approached this same doctrine in a more oblique and symbolic fashion. I have noted her special predilection for natural images—branch, foliage, and flower—suggested by the standard play on *virgo* and *virga*. In her fertility, the Virgin is assimilated to the many trees of life in Scripture: the branch from the root of Jesse (Isa. 11:1), the tree of Wisdom (Ecclus. 24), the tree "planted by streams of water" in Psalm 1, and so forth. But, because of her virginity, she is still more like the dry yet supernaturally blooming branch of Aaron (Num. 17:1–11).[105] This paradox of arid *viriditas*, or fertility without sexuality, is what Hildegard connected with the Eucharist. In the *Scivias* she explained that for the sacrament of the altar, only wheat bread is used because wheat is the purest of grains: it flourishes without pith or sap, just as the body of Christ grew from a virgin without the noxious seed of man. The analogy harks back, once again, to her doctrine of redemption through sexual purity.

> Wheat is the strongest and finest of all crops because it has no sap or pith in its stalk like other trees. . . . For as a stalk of

102. Peter Damian, *Sermo 45 in Nativitate S. Mariae,* CCCM 57: 267.

103. Bobbio Missal 127; Gelasian Sacramentary II.14.3. Cited in Frénaud, "Le Culte de Notre Dame" 162–63.

104. Godfrey of Admont, *Homilia in festum Assumptionis,* PL 174: 974b.

105. Cf. the exquisite strophe from a sequence of Notker: Te virga/ arida Aaron/ flore speciosa/ te figurat,/ Maria,/ sine viri semine/ nato floridam. *Analecta hymnica* 53¹: 1911.

wheat, flourishing without pith, yields dry grain in its pure ear, so the blessed Virgin, conceiving without virile potency, brought forth her most holy Son in simple innocence. He did not draw the sap of sin from his Mother because she conceived him without the pith of man, as the blade of wheat yields no sap to the grain. For its vigor and verdure come not from a pithy stem but from the sun, the rain, and the gentle breeze.[106]

So the pure grain, untainted by any sexual fluids, becomes the eucharistic body of the Virgin's Son. This theme is developed more subtly in one of Hildegard's maturest songs, "O viridissima virga."

> Hail, branch most verdant,
> born in the spirited blast of the quest
> of the saints.
>
> When the time came
> for your boughs to blossom—
> O hail, hail to you!—
> the warm sun distilled in you
> a perfume like balsam.
>
> For in you bloomed the fair flower
> that made all the spices fragrant,
> dry though they were,
> and they all burst into verdure.
>
> So the heavens rained dew upon the grass
> and the whole earth exulted,
> for her womb brought forth wheat,
> for the birds of heaven made their nests in it.
>
> Then a meal was made ready,
> great joy for the keepers of the feast.
> So in you, sweet maid,
> no gladness is lacking.
>
> Eve despised all of this!
> Now praise be to God Most High.[107]

When the Spirit comes upon the Virgin, the heavens rain dew from above and the earth brings forth a Savior (Isa. 45:8), who is both the messianic feast and the great tree of the Kingdom,

---

106. *Scivias* II.6.26, p. 255.
107. Appendix B, no. 8.

in whose branches the birds of the air build their nests (Matt.
13:32). Christ, who made a virgin fertile, also makes the desert bloom. The spices that offer him their foliage and fragrance are those extolled in the Song of Songs; for the Bride
comes up from the desert "like a column of smoke perfumed
with myrrh and frankincense, with all the fragrant powders
of the merchant" (3:6).[108] In Hildegard's lexicon of symbols,
the word *pigmentarius* (spice merchant or herbalist) means
"priest."[109] As Honorius explained, Christ himself is "the true
herbalist, that is, the physician of souls. His collection of
herbs is the congregation of the righteous, for all of whom the
Virgin was a seasoning of virtues, like a precious powder of
spices."[110]

Mary is not only the source of the eucharistic body, the
pure wheat or blossoming branch. In a more personal way,
she is also the paradigm of every priest who confects that
body. At the Annunciation, Mary welcomed the overshadowing Spirit with her words of humble assent, thus making
the Incarnation possible. So at the Eucharist the priest must
invoke the same life-giving Spirit with words of obedience.
Just as the Virgin pronounced her fiat and then conceived, so
"the priest, faithfully believing in God and offering him a pure
oblation with a devout heart, will utter the words of salvation
in humble service."[111] Thereupon the miracle of transforma-
tion will occur. The analogy is threefold: the brooding Spirit
together with the uttered Word accomplishes creation, Incarnation, and consecration. As Mary's fiat in response to Ga-
briel echoed the primeval *fiat lux*, every priest now echoes her.

> When the priest repeats the words of God, the body of the
> incarnate Word of God is again confected. Through the Word
> all creatures, which had not yet been manifested, came into

108. This verse is used as a responsory for Matins on the feast of the
Assumption.
109. *Scivias* II.5.1, p. 177 (title): "Quod apostoli et pigmentarii sequaces
eorum   videlicet   sacerdotes   Ecclesiam   doctrina   sua   splendidissime
circumdant."
110. Honorius, *Sigillum beatae Mariae*, PL 172: 504d.
111. *Scivias* II.6.15, p. 244.

being; and the same Word was incarnate of the Virgin Mary as in the twinkling of an eye, when she said with humility, "Behold the handmaid of the Lord."[112]

Hildegard addressed these remarks to the prelates of Mainz in an admonitory letter, and it seems likely that she intended a moral as well as a metaphysical analogy. Because the priest who makes Christ present has taken the place of Mary, he must remember to act in the spirit of Mary—with faith, devotion, obedience, and humility. Unlike Elisabeth of Schönau, Hildegard never saw Mary herself as a priest; instead she taught that a priest is—and therefore should be—like Mary. By overshadowing the Virgin, the Holy Spirit first brought Christ into the world, and now brings him continually to his own by overshadowing the baptismal waters and the eucharistic bread. Therefore the Church, virgin mother of the faithful, does well to imitate Mary, Virgin Mother of God; this means that she and all her priests must let themselves be overshadowed continually by the Highest. To shame them into this attitude, as embodied in her own "poor little feminine form," was no small part of Hildegard's prophetic mission.

112. Ep. 47, PL 197: 225b.

6

The Bride of Christ

No fewer than five visions in the *Scivias* portray the exalted feminine figure named Ecclesia: bride of Christ, inviolate virgin, mother of the faithful. In preference to other familiar images of the Church—body of Christ, ark of salvation, and so forth—Hildegard turned repeatedly to this consummate form of Woman, who embodies the whole of redeemed humanity in union with God.[1] She is the final epiphany of the feminine, and historically the last manifestation of the eternal counsel.

Beyond time, Caritas and Sapientia reveal the Incarnation as God's changeless purpose, the final cause of his creation. Eve, at the dawn of time, is both the shining promise and the tragic betrayal of that purpose. In Mary, the new and immaculate beginning, the eternal counsel is fulfilled and made known to the world; and in Ecclesia it follows its painful but triumphant course through history to a consummation at the end of time. From the perspective of salvation history, Mary giving birth to her Son occupies the central moment, "the fullness of time." On either side of her are ranged Eve as a proleptic figure and Ecclesia as an eschatological figure. Viewed synchronically, or as Hildegard would say, "symphonically," these three theophanies of the feminine in history reveal the three human faces of the feminine divine.

Typologically, both Eve and Mary are recapitulated in Ecclesia. Like Mary, the Church can be envisaged as a second

1. On her ecclesiology in general see Giovanna della Croce, "Ildegarda di Bingen e il mistero della Chiesa," *Ephemerides carmeliticae* 17 (1966): 158–73; Margot Schmidt, "Die Kirche—'Eine Erde der Lebendigen.' Zum Kirchenbild bei Hildegard von Bingen" (Mainz, 1980): Bischöflichen Ordinariat, aktuelle information, no. 16.

Eve, for as the first woman was formed from the side of her sleeping husband, so the Church was "born" of the second Adam when his side was pierced on the cross, that she might become his bride. In her fruitful virginity, Ecclesia is also comparable to Mary. But Mary alone is mother and virgin in her unique personal being; Ecclesia, like Eve, is a corporate and in that sense a fictive person. Insofar as Eve represents woman as such, all mothers are her daughters in the order of generation, sharing in her fruitfulness as well as her sin. And, in the order of regeneration, all consecrated virgins are the daughters of Ecclesia. So it is the personified Church, together with Mary, who provides a role model for nuns and virginal saints. But unlike Mary, Ecclesia also shares in the victimization of Eve. The devil could not harm the Mother of God, but he continually assaults the bride of Christ. In her role as virgin, the Church can be ravished by rapacious clergy and, ultimately, by the Antichrist himself; in her role as mother, she can be bereft of her children through schism and heresy. Thus the pure virgin who comes down from heaven to marry Christ on the cross, who shares his wedding feast at the Eucharist and bears his children in baptism, also appears in history as the beleaguered bride and the *mater dolorosa*. In these epiphanies, Ecclesia serves as the mouthpiece for Hildegard's strongest critique of contemporary churchmen. Much of her apocalyptic preaching is constellated by the vision of Ecclesia in extremis, just as Ecclesia in grandeur provides a focal point for teaching on the sacraments, virginity, and pastoral care.

At the same time, however, this *figura* is used in various incidental ways to reinforce Hildegard's conservative views on the subordination of women. A woman, for instance, is explicitly barred from the priesthood; she is forbidden to enter the church for a time after her virginity is taken; and, metaphorically, she is made to represent the most flagrant vices that the seer castigated in the churchmen of her day. So, while the ideas outlined in this chapter constitute the fullest flowering of Hildegard's theology of the feminine, they also accentuate the rift between symbolic exaltation and pragmatic subjection.

THE CHURCH ETERNAL IN HEAVEN

As the reader will expect, Ecclesia has an important sapiential dimension. Hildegard's treatment of the concrete historical Church makes sense only in light of her belief in an ideal, timeless, and preexistent Church in the heavens. Theologically, this notion is of a piece with the absolute predestination of Christ and the special predestination of Mary, and it has more explicit support in the New Testament than either of these doctrines.[2] Paul spoke of the elect chosen by God "before the foundation of the world . . . according to his purpose which he set forth in Christ, as a plan for the fullness of time" (Eph. 1:4–10; cf. II Tim. 1:9). The epistle to the Hebrews describes a heavenly Jerusalem, "the Church of the first-born who are enrolled in heaven" together with the angels (Heb. 12:22–23); and this Jerusalem, according to Paul, "is our mother" (Gal. 4:26). Allegorically, she corresponds to Abraham's free wife, Sarah, as opposed to his slave girl, Hagar.

The Apostle's typology laid the groundwork for a fundamental aspect of early Christian ecclesiology. In the *Shepherd*, a visionary work of the late first or second century, the seer Hermas beholds Ecclesia in the form of an aged woman, and an angel explains that she appears thus "because she was created before all things . . . and for her sake the world was framed."[3] According to II Clement, "the Church is not limited to the present, but existed from the beginning. For it was spiritual, as was our Jesus, and was made manifest in the last days . . . in the flesh of Christ." Clement was also aware of Ecclesia's gender: "The male is Christ; the female is the Church."[4] Irenaeus, Tertullian, Clement of Alexandria, Ori-

---

2. See Johannes Beumer, "Die altchristliche Idee einer präexistierenden Kirche und ihre theologische Auswertung," *Wissenschaft und Weisheit* 9 (1942): 13–22.

3. *Der Hirt des Hermas* II.4, ed. Molly Whittaker, in *Griechische christliche Schriftsteller* (Berlin, 1956), 48: 7; trans. J. B. Lightfoot in *Excluded Books of the New Testament* (London, 1927): 264.

4. II Clement 14, ed. Karl Bihlmeyer in *Die apostolischen Väter* I (Tübingen, 1924); trans. Cyril Richardson in *Early Christian Fathers* (New York, 1970): 199.

gen, Ambrose, and Leo all bore witness to this doctrine of the preexistent bride of Christ.

The teaching survived into the Middle Ages, linking the doctrine of Christ's absolute predestination with the allegorical figure of Ecclesia. Once again, it is this distinctive bond between the feminine figure and the doctrine of preexistence that characterizes the sapiential strain in twelfth-century thought. St. Bernard remarked, "According to predestination, there was never a time when the Church of the elect was not with God . . . never was she not beloved."[5] For Rupert of Deutz, "our Mother is the one harmonious and beloved City of God and of all his blessed angels. From her womb we were aborted and cast out when, in the person of our forefather who lost the peace of Paradise because of sin, we were banished and fell into this exile."[6] In this view, the appearance of the Church on earth was not a historical novelty but the revelation of a formerly hidden truth, or the restoration of a lost original grace. Gerhoch of Reichersberg saw the building of Ecclesia as the inmost meaning of creation, the consummate work of the Trinity.

> Glory be to the Father, who created her matter from nothing through the Word; and to the Son, who together with the Father built her from the foreordained matter; and to the Holy Spirit, who has already consecrated her foundations and in the end will yet consecrate her whole structure.[7]

Gerhoch's metaphors of *materia* and *aedificatio* evoke the concrete image of the Church as building, the temple made from living stones (I Pet. 2:5), alongside a more abstract notion of the Church as prime matter, the substrate of the world, which God created out of nothing. *Materia* is also a rich concept for Hildegard: we have already seen Caritas as the *materia*

---

5. Bernard of Clairvaux, *Sermo super Cantica* 78.3, *Opera* 2:268; Yves Congar, "L'ecclésiologie de S. Bernard," *Analecta sacri ordinis Cisterciensis* 9 (1953): 151, n. 5.

6. Rupert of Deutz, *In Iohannem* 3.5, CCCM 9: 139.

7. Gerhoch of Reichersberg, *Comment. in Psalmos* 29, PL 193: 1285a.

of creation and Mary as the luminous and golden *materia* of re-creation. So also Ecclesia.

> The heavenly Jerusalem, who was to be adorned by the supreme architect, almighty God, appeared in his presence as the matrix (*materia*) of all things before the creation of the world. . . . For God wished Jerusalem, which is built from the holy works of human beings and appears as a bride adorned for her husband, to exist for the praise of his humanity, even as he created the angels for the praise and honor of his divinity.[8]

Ecclesia is both bride and city (Apoc. 21:2); she is to know God intimately as a single soul, yet also collectively as his people. Only through the complementary figure of the city can the bride's character as a "corporate person" be brought to the fore. It is noteworthy that, while Hildegard applied the imagery of Paradise to the Virgin, she preferred that of the apocalyptic city for the Church. Thus, although both the garden and the city have strong associations with the feminine, they indicate different phases in its fulfillment. Mary and Ecclesia are the Alpha and Omega of redemption, the first and the last. Mary is a builder, but the Church is a building, a collective entity constructed "from the holy works of human beings." Her nature mirrors the paradoxical "already" and "not yet" of the Kingdom of God, for although the Church is in one sense the building material of the world, in another sense she has yet to be raised. The female *Virtutes* will construct her, in token of that synergy which is one of the primary meanings of the feminine divine.[9] As city and bride of Christ,

8. Ep. 47, PL 197: 227d–28a.
9. "You see all the Virtues of God descending and ascending, going to their work weighed down with stones. For in the Only-Begotten of God, the luminous Virtues descend as it were through his humanity and tend upward through his divinity. They also descend through him to the hearts of the faithful, who, renouncing their own will with a good heart, make themselves flexible for righteous works, like a workman who bends down to lift a stone that he carries to the building. And they rise upward in him when they thankfully offer the heavenly works accomplished among men and women to God, that the body of Christ may be brought nearer to completion in its faithful members." *Scivias* III.8.13, p. 495.

Ecclesia is said "to exist for the praise of his humanity," as an earthly counterpart of the angels who praise his divinity. Once again, "the woman signifies the humanity of the Son of God."

In Hildegard's letters, one of her favorite closing benedictions is the prayer "may you become a living stone in the celestial Jerusalem."[10] Ecclesia-as-building is a phenomenon in which all may participate, both as God's co-workers and as his workmanship (I Cor. 3:9).[11] The temple that the saints build, and themselves are, is also the house of Wisdom (Prov. 9:1). In a sequence honoring St. Maximinus, whose cult flourished in Trier, Hildegard saluted this missionary as at once builder and wall of the temple of Wisdom, whom he embraces in the midst of the Church.

> Lucent among you
> is this architect, wall of the temple, he who longed
> for an eagle's wings as he kissed
> his foster-mother, Wisdom, in Ekklesia's glorious fecundity.[12]

The precise relationship of Sapientia *nutrix* to the Church is hard to specify; here, as elsewhere, the seer's highly compressed imagery tends to conflate concepts that a more analytical theology would distinguish. But conflation seems to be precisely Hildegard's point: the architect becomes one with the wall he builds, in a complete fusion of worker and work, and the divine Sapientia merges with the human Ecclesia so that, under the sign of her sacred maternity, God's fruitfulness can no longer be distinguished from man's.

But what of woman's? In the *Book of Life's Merits*, Hildegard presented a very different picture of the house that Wisdom

---

10. Cf. Epp. 47, 77, 86, 116, 137, and 140 in Pitra.

11. Heinrich Schipperges, introduction to *Welt und Mensch: Das Buch "De Operatione Dei"* (Salzburg, 1965).

12. *Lieder* no. 76: 296; trans. Peter Dronke in *The Medieval Lyric* (London, 1968): 76–77. For "gloriosa fecunditas" cf. Cyprian, *De habitu virginum* 3, CSEL 3[1]: 189: "The glorious fecundity of Mother Ecclesia rejoices and blossoms abundantly in [virgins], and the more that rich virginity adds to its number, the more the mother's joy increases." This text is read in the Common of Virgins, Second Nocturn, Fourth Lesson.

built. Apropos of Ecclus. 1:16, "The fear of the Lord is the beginning of wisdom . . . and it is observed among chosen women,"[13] she remarked:

> God designed woman so that she would fear him and fear her husband as well. So it is right for a woman to be fearful (*timida*) at all times. For she is the house of wisdom, as it were, because things earthly and heavenly are perfected in her. On the one hand man is born of her, and, on the other, good works are revealed in her together with chaste modesty. . . . A God-fearing (*timorata*) woman gathers all the riches of good works and holy virtues into her bosom and never ceases, until she has accomplished much good.[14]

The text is strikingly ambivalent about the status of women, or so it appears by modern standards. For Hildegard every woman could be what Ecclesia is, a house of wisdom, either through motherhood (bearing the children of wisdom in her body) or through virginity (collecting the works of wisdom in her heart). Because of this great dignity, it befits her to be humble and reverent—like Mary in the house of Joseph. For woman there is to be no soaring on eagle's wings, only discreet feminine modesty. So in spite of, if not because of, her exalted spiritual status, her social inferiority is again reinforced. In effect, Hildegard was confounding a Biblical virtue, "fear of the Lord," with that gender-specific fearfulness for which, in the early days of her mission, she had bitterly reproached herself.[15] There is no allowance here for conflict between the fear of God and the fear of men, which she herself had often experienced. Whatever the abbess might say, however, she could always make an exception for herself. The more vehemently she prophesied to the Ecclesia on earth, the less she felt obliged to show herself "timid at all times."

---

13. Verse 1:16b reads "cum electis feminis graditur" in the Clementine revised Vulgate (Rome, 1592), and "cum electis seminis creditur" in the Stuttgart *Biblia Sacra* (1969). Hildegard's reading is "cum electis feminis creditur."

14. LVM I.96, Pitra 44.

15. In her earliest letter she wrote to St. Bernard, "Two years ago I saw you in this vision as a man gazing on the sun, and not fearful but greatly daring; and I wept because I only blush and am timid (*inaudax*)." Ep. 29, PL 197: 190ab.

A more forceful vision governs Hildegard's antiphon "O orzchis Ecclesia," composed for the dedication of a church.[16] In this bizarre lyric, a synesthetic tour de force rendered still more obscure by the presence of five words from her secret language, the composer presented Ecclesia as a kind of warrior maiden and, at the same time, "city of the sciences" (*urbs scientiarum*).

> O boundless Ecclesia,
> girded with the arms of God
> and arrayed in hyacinth,
> you are the fragrance
> of the wounds of nations,
> the City of Knowledge!
> Amid lofty music
> you have been anointed,
> O glistening gem![17]

This Ecclesia is dressed for the battlefield rather than the nuptial feast, as in the contemporary *Play of Antichrist*, where Ecclesia comes onstage "in feminine dress, wearing a breastplate and crowned."[18] Still militant on earth, the conquering Church bears the wounds of battle even in victory. Hildegard's enigmatic figure of fragrant wounds can be clarified by a passage in her *Play of Virtues*: at the end of that drama, Christ bares his wounds to the Father as he prays for the Church, asking that the wounds in his body may be converted to gems.[19] In medieval exegesis, wounds are a stock metaphor for sins: the wounds of the penitent soul are anointed with the oil of forgiveness and cleansed by the wounds (*stigmata*) of Christ.[20] Through this transfiguring grace, the festering wounds of nations heal to become the fragrant wounds of the Church.

16. The antiphon is entitled "Cantus ad Romam" in the Zwiefalten MS. (Stuttgart, Landesbibliothek Cod. Theol. Phil. 4° 253, fol. 28ʳ), which gives a slightly different text.

17. Appendix B, no. 9.

18. Gerhard Günther, ed., *Der Antichrist, Der staufische Ludus de Antichristo* (Hamburg, 1970): 92; trans. John Wright, *The Play of Antichrist* (Toronto, 1967).

19. *Ordo virtutum* 192; cf. DOD III.10.8, PL 197: 1005d–6a.

20. Cf. Bernard of Clairvaux, *Sermo super Cantica* 10.5–6, *Opera* 1:50–51.

The transition between this image and the next is unusually abrupt, even for Hildegard. Perhaps she knew Hugh of St. Victor's conception of the arts and sciences as remedies for the wounds of original sin,[21] or Honorius's allegory *On the Exile and Homeland of the Soul*. In that treatise the soul travels from her place of exile, Ignorantia, through ten cities representing the liberal arts and other disciplines, until she finally arrives at her homeland, Sapientia.[22] But from a prophet like Hildegard, who on principle rejected all human teaching, *urbs scientiarum* is an unexpectedly humanistic title for the New Jerusalem. It would appear that human knowledge, despite its inadequacy, can be incorporated into the temple of wisdom by a divine transmutation, just as the wounds of sin can be transformed into perfumes or jewels. The sciences, like the saints, can become building blocks of Ecclesia.

SYNAGOGUE AND CHURCH

Hildegard's doctrine of a "church before the Church" has a second major aspect: alongside the notion of her preexistence in heaven, many fathers had argued for Ecclesia's ancient and continuous presence in history. Augustine and Gregory the Great believed that the earthly Church, or City of God, numbered its generations at least from Abel if not from Adam.[23] As the Nicene fathers had said of the Logos, "There never was when he was not," their medieval successors said in a different sense of the Church. The Lamb of God was slain from the beginning of the world, Hugh of St. Victor maintained, "because from the beginning of the world there were those for whom he was slain at the end of the world."[24] Similarly, Godfrey of Admont claimed that "never from the foun-

---

21. Hugh of St. Victor, *Didascalicon de studio legendi* I.5 and VI.14, trans. Jerome Taylor (New York, 1961): 52, 152.

22. Honorius, *De animae exsilio et patria*, PL 172: 1241–46.

23. Yves Congar, "Ecclesia ab Abel," in Marcel Reding, ed., *Abhandlungen über Theologie und Kirche. Festschrift für Karl Adam* (Düsseldorf, 1952): 79–108.

24. Hugh of St. Victor, *De arca Noe morali* 1.4, PL 176: 631a.

the world was there a time in which God had no one belonging to his Church."[25]

In practical terms, this church before the Church normally meant the people of Israel, who like Ecclesia could be personified in the form of a woman, Synagoga.[26] Despite the prevalence of anti-Judaism, theologians in the Augustinian tradition held a fairly liberal view of the Synagogue as not merely the enemy but also the type and "mother" of Ecclesia.[27] Honorius, in his commentary on the Song of Songs, observed that Christ calls the Church his sister (4:9) because both have God for their Father and the Synagogue (*primitiva Ecclesia*) for their mother. The Jewish nation could be called "mother and nurse" of the infant Church, "for from her were born the Apostles, who begot the Church through the Gospel and nourished her through the teaching of the Law."[28] Gerhoch of Reichersberg could refer to the Synagogue as the "ancient church of the fathers" and to the Gentile church as "synagogue of the nations."[29] And Rupert of Deutz carried the identification further, claiming that it was Ecclesia who conceived Christ through Abraham's faith, bore him in her womb during the age of patriarchs and prophets, travailed in his passion, and rejoiced at his birth in the resurrection.[30]

Of course the antagonism between Christians and Jews also affected the symbol, creating a more complex relationship than simple typology or simple antithesis. According to Peter

25. Godfrey of Admont, *Homilia* 77, PL 174: 1014d.

26. Friedrich Ohly, "Synagoge und Ecclesia. Typologisches in mittelalterlicher Dichtung," in Paul Wilpert, ed., *Judentum im Mittelalter*, vol. 4 of *Miscellanea Mediaevalia* (Berlin, 1966): 350–69; Wolfgang Seiferth, *Synagogue and Church in the Middle Ages: Two Symbols in Art and Literature*, trans. Lee Chadeayne and Paul Gottwald (New York, 1970).

27. Wolfgang Beinert, *Die Kirche—Gottes Heil in der Welt. Die Lehre von der Kirche nach den Schriften des Rupert von Deutz, Honorius Augustodunensis und Gerhoch von Reichersberg* (Münster, 1973): 356–68.

28. Honorius, *Expositio in Cantica* IV.8, PL 172: 475bc.

29. Gerhoch of Reichersberg, *De investigatione Antichristi* 35, ed. Friedrich Scheibelberger, *Gerhohi Reichersbergensis praepositi opera hactenus inedita* (Linz, 1875): 267; *Comment. in Psalmos* 7, PL 193: 730a.

30. Rupert of Deutz, *In Iohannis Evangelium* 12, CCCM 9: 684; *Comment. in Naum* 1, PL 168: 531–32.

Chrysologus, Synagoga gave birth to Christ in the flesh and later became the hostile mother-in-law of his bride, Ecclesia of the Gentiles.[31] Unfortunately, the rivalry of the two women lent itself more readily to popular thought and visual art than did their continuity. Among the most frequent typological motifs in art, from the ninth century onward, is the Crucifixion shown with two symbolic figures, Ecclesia on Christ's right side and Synagoga on his left.[32] The one, open-eyed and regal, presents a chalice to catch the precious blood and flaunts a banner to mark her victory. The other, blindfolded and humbled, turns away her face; sometimes she holds a broken staff to show that her dominion has ended. This iconographic formula tersely conveys the Pauline theology of election, as interpreted by the mainstream of medieval exegesis. Because the Jews rejected Christ, their minds were veiled so they could not understand the Scriptures (II Cor. 3:14–15), and God elected the Gentiles instead, "to make Israel jealous" (Rom. 11:11). The Church of the Gentiles, formerly barren and desolate, could now rejoice because her children outnumbered those of God's first bride, Israel (Gal. 4:27). In less sophisticated milieus, this antithesis could degenerate into a mere opposition between faith and unbelief, insight and blindness, freedom and bondage, Christian charity and Jewish infamy.

In short, the double vision of Synagoga as precursor and opposite of Ecclesia places the two women in a relationship analogous to that of Eve and Mary. Hildegard, as usual, developed both aspects of the ambivalence, bringing out the full play of identity and difference. Here is her first vision of Ecclesia:

> I saw the image of a woman as tall as a great city, radiant from heaven to earth: her head was crowned with a marvelous

31. Peter Chrysologus, *Sermo* 164, PL 52: 632–33. Further references in Sebastien Tromp, "Ecclesia Sponsa Virgo Mater," *Gregorianum* 18 (1937): 12.
32. Alfred Raddatz, "Ecclesia und Synagoge. Geschichtliche Hintergründe und Bedeutung der Entstehung eines mittelalterlichen Bildmotivs," in *Judentum im Mittelalter, Katalog für die Ausstellung im Schloss Halbturm* (Burgenland, 1978): 109–11.

diadem, and her arms were draped with splendor as with sleeves. . . . Standing before the altar in the sight of God, she embraced it with outspread arms; and her eyes pierced keenly throughout all heaven. But I could not perceive any of her garments, except that she was all aglow with luminous brightness, and clothed in great splendor. In her breast appeared the dawn.[33] (Fig. 8, upper right)

And Synagoga:

I saw the image of a certain woman, pale from the head down to the navel and black from the navel to the feet, which were bloody. Around her feet was a pure and shining white cloud. But she had no eyes. With her hands folded beneath her armpits, she stood by the altar in the sight of God but did not touch it. And in her heart stood Abraham, and in her breast Moses, and in her womb the rest of the prophets, all displaying their signs and admiring the beauty of Ecclesia. The woman was as tall as a tower of some city; and around her head was a circlet like the dawn.[34] (Fig. 9)

Synagoga, like Rupert's Old Testament Church, is "pregnant" with Christ through the expectant prophets, who therefore appear in her womb. Her great magnitude prefigures the City of God and the towering might of Ecclesia. But where Synagoga is blind, Ecclesia has eyes that pierce heaven; the one folds her arms in inertia, the other lifts hers in prayer and embraces the altar of God. Ecclesia is "clothed in splendor" (which the Rupertsberg artist interpreted with gold leaf), but Synagoga is pale because she knows the mysteries of God only in overshadowing. As Rita Otto has observed, the artist appropriately turned this pallor into a faded purple, emblematic of lapsed royalty and priesthood.[35] But iconographic convention demands that the figure by "read" from the top down, as her several colors denote successive periods of history. So,

33. *Scivias* II.3, pp. 134–35.
34. *Scivias* I.5, p. 93.
35. Rita Otto, "Zu einigen Miniaturen einer *Scivias*handschrift des 12. Jahrhunderts," *Mainzer Zeitschriften* 67–68 (1972–73): 132. See also Charles Singer, "Allegorical Representation of the Synagogue in a Twelfth Century Illuminated Manuscript of Hildegard of Bingen," *Jewish Quarterly Review*, n.s. 5 (1915): 267–88.

Fig. 8. *The womb of the Church as net of Christ*. Top right: Ecclesia embracing the altar of Christ. Top left: Mother Ecclesia with her children making melody. Bottom right: baptism through invocation of the Trinity; catechumens are reborn in the womb of Ecclesia, which is also the net of Christ. Bottom left: Christ instructs the faithful in the two ways of salvation and perdition. *Scivias* II.3, Eibingen ms.

Fig. 9. *Synagoga as Mother of the Incarnation*. Moses sits in her bosom and the expectant prophets in her womb. *Scivias* I.5, Eibingen ms.

pale at first in expectancy, the Synagogue becomes black through carnality and sin, and blood-red in the end through the murder of Christ. Yet the radiance of dawn about her forehead and the luminous cloud around her feet signify, respectively, the Incarnation and the faith of the Church. The shining cloud, symbol of Eve, fittingly swirls around these feet stained with the blood of Christ because Ecclesia, the new Eve, was born of Christ's wounded flesh. Likewise, the dawn, symbol of the election of Mary, crowns Synagoga's head because Israel was predestined to be "Mother of the Incarnation."

Viewed from another perspective, the somber yet majestic figure of Synagoga rises up between the emblems of Eve at her feet and Mary at her head, for she holds an intermediate place between the fallen mother of all living and the Mother of God. The pallor of her *obumbratio*, which signifies the obscurity of prophetic knowledge,[36] also represents an "overshadowing" midway between Eve's and Mary's, because she has been doubly touched by the grace of God and the devil's deception. Visually, the subtle interplay of Hildegard's signs places this image in its proper context within the intricate symbol system of her *Scivias*. In the vision of Adam's fall (II.1, Fig. 7), the prophets shine like stars through the night of sin while a darkened Adam refuses to pluck the flower of obedience, just as blind Synagoga ignores the prophets' vision and refuses to touch the spiritual altar. The emblem of stars for prophets sheds light in turn upon the vision of Eve (*Scivias* I.2, Fig. 2), who like Synagoga is pregnant with salvation despite the darkening of her own mind. Both Eve and Synagoga are to be "saved by their childbearing" (I Tim. 2:15). As Eve unexpectedly becomes the apocalyptic woman clothed with the sun, so in the last days, Hildegard prophesied, "Synagoga will faithfully transform herself into Ecclesia."[37] This pro-

---

36. *Scivias* III.11.27, p. 592: "mortal eyes cannot see me, but I show my miracles to those whom I will in overshadowing."

37. *Scivias* I.5.6, p. 97; cf. DOD III.10.18, PL 197: 1021b. Belief in the ultimate conversion of the Jews was widespread; see Bernard of Clairvaux,

foundly symbolic materfamilias, reminiscent of Eve, Mary, and Ecclesia at once, embodies the whole drama of blind, faithless, yet expectant humanity, crowned with the eternal counsel of a grace that could be obscured but not finally vanquished by human sin.

THE WEDDING ON CALVARY

After dealing with Synagoga on her own terms, Hildegard could reduce the symbolic Crucifixion iconography to the figures of Christ and Ecclesia alone. The motif of Christ's marriage to the Church on the cross, as shaped by the new Eve typology, is even older than the pictorial contrast of Synagoga and Ecclesia.[38] Its elements derive from a potpourri of Biblical texts. Ecclesia, like Eve, was created from the side of her sleeping bridegroom (Gen. 2:21–23) to be united with him in a spotless marriage (Eph. 5:25–27); her "dowry" is the blood and water, representing baptism and the Eucharist, which flowed from Christ's side on the cross (John 19:34); and their sacramental union, the "marriage of the Lamb," is reenacted in every communion of the faithful (Apoc. 19:7–9). This complex of ideas, patient of endless elaboration, can be found in virtually all the Eastern and Western fathers, though perhaps the most concise version is that of the late-third- or fourth-century *Symposium of Virgins* by Methodius of Patara:

> Out of His bones and flesh the Church was born; . . . indeed for her sake the Logos left His Father in heaven and came down, to cleave to His Wife; and . . . He slept in the ecstasy of His passion, choosing to die for her "that He Himself might cleanse her in the bath and present her to Himself a Church

---

Sermo super Cantica 79.5, *Opera* 2: 275; Honorius, *Sigillum beatae Mariae*, PL 172: 514–15. In the *Play of Antichrist* the converted Jews win the crown of martyrdom while the entire Gentile Church is falling to Antichrist.

38. Sebastien Tromp, "De nativitate Ecclesiae ex corde Iesu in cruce," *Gregorianum* 13 (1932): 489–527; Odo Casel, "Die Kirche als Braut Christi nach Schrift, Väterlehre und Liturgie," *Theologie der Zeit* 1 (1936): 91–111; Claude Chavasse, *The Bride of Christ: An Enquiry into the Nuptial Element in Early Christianity* (London, 1940).

glorious and without blemish," prepared to receive the spiritual and blessed seed which He Himself sows.[39]

In the *Scivias*, Hildegard likewise interpreted the Crucifixion as Ecclesia's wedding, but, rather than speaking of the Church's "birth," she altered the topos to show the bride descending from heaven in accord with the doctrine of her preexistence. As usual, this notion inspires a certain lofty optimism; there is little in the text to indicate that Christ's passion entailed suffering or pain.

> I saw that, while the Son of God was hanging on the cross, the image of the aforesaid woman [Ecclesia] came hastening down from the ancient counsel like a shining splendor. By divine power she was led to him, and, suffused with the blood that flowed from his side, she rose up and was joined to him by the heavenly Father's will in happy betrothal, with the noble dowry of his flesh and blood.
>
> And I heard a voice from heaven saying to him, "Let her be a bride to you, Son, for the restoration of my people whose mother she will be, regenerating souls through the saving mystery of water and the Spirit."[40]

The Rupertsberg miniature of this vision (Fig. 10) accentuates the unity of Christ's passion and the Eucharist, understood as a wedding feast, by depicting the Crucifixion in the upper register and the Mass in the lower, with the golden figure of Ecclesia linking the two scenes. Above, the bride catches some of the streaming blood in her chalice while the rest illumines her eyes—an allusion to the legend of Longinus, the blind centurion healed by Christ's blood.[41] Below,

39. Methodius of Patara, *Symposium* 3.8, ed. Herbert Musurillo, *Sources chrétiennes* 95: 106; trans. in Joseph Plumpe, *Mater Ecclesia: An Inquiry into the Concept of the Church as Mother in Early Christianity* (Washington, 1943): 112.

40. *Scivias* II.6, pp. 229–30. Cf. Ep. 47, PL 197: 227–28: "The heavenly Jerusalem . . . was renewed in all beauty through the shedding of his blood. For when the elements lay wrapped in darkness, she descended with the banner of victory to the cross on which the Son of God was hanging, and received that dowry from him who was conceived and born in virginity so that she too, as a virgin, might bear children by spiritual generation."

41. Knut Berg, "Une iconographie peu connue du crucifiement," *Cahiers archéologiques* 9 (1957): 319–28.

Fig. 10. *Ecclesia as bride of Christ: The wedding on Calvary.* Upper register: Ecclesia catches the blood of Christ in her chalice. Lower register: Ecclesia as priestess; the medallions represent Christ's death and resurrection as commemorated in the Canon of the Mass. *Scivias* II.6, Eibingen ms.

Ecclesia raises her eyes and hands to heaven in a priestly gesture as she offers the Eucharist, which is at once her dowry
and her marriage feast. No other priest is in evidence; only
the light pouring down on the altar designates the divine,
consecrating power. The image of Ecclesia herself as priestess
of course recalls Hildegard's analogy between the priest and
the Virgin Mary, and, more distantly, the vision of Pura Scientia in episcopal vesture. The seer clarified her use of such feminine iconography for the priesthood with the remark that,
although women cannot actually serve at the altar, yet a consecrated virgin possesses "the priesthood and the whole ministry of the altar" through her bridegroom, as if by right of
marriage.[42] A fortiori, this privilege belongs to the bride of
Christ herself.

But once again, convention divides the symbol from its apparent meaning. To explain why no actual woman can serve
at the altar, Hildegard said that woman is a "weak and infirm
habitation" who can no more consecrate the body of Christ
than she can beget her own child; and, what is more, she lacks
the beard, in other words, the visible masculinity, which is
required of a priest. But the married woman—if she is properly "fearful"—can imitate Ecclesia in a more discreet way. By
an ingenious if farfetched analogy, Hildegard compared the
modesty of Christ's bride to that of a newlywed wife. Between
her marriage on Calvary and the beginning of her mission on
Pentecost, the Church bashfully hid herself from the world
before she dared to preach openly. Following her example, a
newly married woman should stay out of church, as canon
law requires, until the "wound" of her deflowering is healed.[43]
This prosaic application of the nuptial symbolism shows the
degree to which Hildegard could relate her sublime visionary
forms to the everyday lives of women; but it also shows how,
even if she could except herself from the general laws incum-

42. *Scivias* II.6.76, p. 290.
43. *Scivias* I.2.21, p. 28. Gratian's *Decretum* I.5.1–2 refers only to the
churching of women after childbirth, not to newlyweds.

bent on feminine frailty, she was neither willing nor able to challenge the laws themselves.

Ecclesia's marriage feast—her emergence into the light—is the subject of a second antiphon for the dedication of a church. "O choruscans lux stellarum" is a companion piece to "O orzchis Ecclesia," but it celebrates the regal bride in a more straightforward and Biblical idiom.

> O glistening starlight,
> O elect, resplendent,
> and royal bride,
> O sparkling gem:
> you are arrayed as a noble dame
> without spot or wrinkle,
> you are a companion of angels,
> a fellow citizen with saints.
> Flee, flee the ancient destroyer's
> cave and come—
> come into the palace of the King![44]

This epithalamium, distantly inspired by Psalm 44, leads the bride from the serpent's lair where Eve was seduced to the royal palace. The "city of sciences" has now become the "city of the living God" described in Hebrews 12, where the spirits of the just feast with the angels. Hildegard again characterized the Church with two of her favorite images for created glory. Like the Mother of God, Ecclesia possesses a gemlike translucency to the Christ within her, and the glistening stars evoke the multitude of saints who constitute the Church, recalling the vision of mother Eve as a star-spangled cloud (Fig. 2). In Ecclesia, Eve's children emerge from the cloud to shine forth in their glory.

While the Church is allegorically the bride of Christ, she is "wedded" in a different sense to the Holy Spirit, who makes her fruitful. Vision II.4 of the *Scivias*, which deals with the sacrament of confirmation, shows the Spirit in the form of a tower literally "confirming" or upholding the woman Ecclesia

---

44. Appendix B, no. 10.

to keep her from falling (Fig. 11). But at the same time the tower is said to represent "the measureless sweetness of the Holy Spirit," pouring forth rivers of holiness and kindling fiery virtues in the Church. The image is suggestive.

> And then I saw a great round tower consisting wholly of a single white stone, with three windows in its summit. From them shone a light so intense that even the roof of this tower, which was raised in the form of a cone, could be plainly seen in the brightness of this light. These windows were decorated with beautiful emeralds. And the tower was set in the middle of [Ecclesia's] back, like a tower in a city wall, so that because of its strength the woman could by no means fall. And I saw those children who had passed through the woman's womb . . . shining with great brightness.[45]

The constellation of woman, tower, and baptismal womb points again to the *Shepherd* of Hermas, a work that Hildegard must certainly have known.[46] In Hermas's third vision, Lady Church shows the seer "a great tower being builded upon the waters" by angels, archangels, and virgins representing the virtues. Questioned by Hermas, she explains that the tower represents herself, the Church, built on the waters of baptism. Although it is being constructed from living blocks, when complete it will appear as a single stone hewn from the rock of Christ. In the *Shepherd*, the old woman who grows younger and the unfinished tower both represent the mysterious history of the Church, eternal in the heavens yet still incomplete on earth. But Hermas made no clear distinctions between Christ, the Church, and the Spirit, whereas Hildegard was obliged to be dogmatically correct.[47] For her, only the woman Ecclesia is incomplete (her legs and feet are hidden from view); the tower that designates the Spirit is already

45. *Scivias* II.4, pp. 159–60.
46. Hans Liebeschütz, *Das allegorische Weltbild der heiligen Hildegard von Bingen* (Leipzig, 1930): 53–55; Peter Dronke, "*Arbor Caritatis*," in P. L. Heyworth, ed., *Medieval Studies for J. A. W. Bennett* (Oxford, 1981): 231, n. 48.
47. At one point the "shepherd," or angel of repentance, tells Hermas: "I wish to show thee all things that the Holy Spirit, which spake with thee in the form of the Church, showed unto thee. For that Spirit is the Son of God." Similitude IX.1, trans. Lightfoot, *Excluded Books* 360.

Fig. 11. *Tower of the Church*. Ecclesia sustained by the Holy Spirit, which kindles fiery virtues. Some of her children remain faithful, while others attack her. *Scivias* II.4, Eibingen ms.

whole and perfect. Woman and tower, therefore, are no longer interchangeable symbols representing the same concept. Instead, their proximity now suggests the bride "conceiving by the Holy Spirit" in a vivid, if understated, sexual image.

CHRIST'S VIRGINS AND
THE VIRGIN CHURCH

There is nothing understated, however, in the seer's treatment of Ecclesia's virginity. Another of the *Scivias* visions (II.5) presents the bride as a queen clothed in many colors, each hue representing a different order within the Church. Ecclesia's head gleams with a snowy, crystalline whiteness (the priesthood); her bosom glows like the dawn (virginity); her waist is girded with royal purple (monasticism); and below the navel she shines like a brilliant cloud (marriage). To illustrate this vision, the Rupertsberg artist departed more than usual from the text, but the composition still renders the seer's meaning clearly (Fig. 12). The austere, almost wooden figure of Ecclesia lifts her richly vested arms toward heaven as an *orans*, in accord with an ancient iconographic type of the Church.[48] From her virginal breast flames of love surge up to heaven, and in her heart stands the scarlet figure of Virginitas with a throng of male and female virgins. She too stands with outstretched arms, imitating her mother, for in the order of virgins Hildegard saw an epitome of the whole Church.

> And where [the splendor of the Church] glowed like the dawn, its brightness rose up to the hidden mysteries of heaven. In this splendor there appeared the image of a beautiful girl, bareheaded, with dark hair, wearing a red tunic that flowed down about her feet. And I heard a voice from heaven saying, "This is the flower that blooms in the Zion above: mother and rose and lily of the valley. O flower, you will marry

---

48. Wolfgang Greisenegger, "Ecclesia," *Lexikon der christlichen Ikonographie* I: 562–69; Anton Mayer, *Das Bild der Kirche. Hauptmotive der Ecclesia im Wandel der abendländischen Kunst* (Regensburg, 1962).

Fig. 12. *Ecclesia with Virginitas and her companions.* Monks and virgins occupy the place of honor in Ecclesia's flaming heart. *Scivias* II.5, Eibingen ms.

the Son of the most mighty King and bear him offspring of supreme renown, when in your time you are comforted."

And around this girl I saw standing a great throng of people shining brighter than the sun, who were all wonderfully arrayed in gold and jewels. . . . And again I heard the voice from on high, saying, "These are the daughters of Zion, and with them are minstrels making music on the lyre and every kind of instrument, and the voice of all mirth, and the joy of joys."[49]

This lyrical vision surrounds Virginitas with the emblems of Mary—music, flowers, the blush of dawn—and it echoes a responsory for the Assumption: "Like the days of spring, roses and lilies of the valley lay around her."[50] Monks and virgins are said to imitate Mary through chastity, love, and freedom; they are like roses and lilies because, just as these flowers grow without cultivation, they choose the ascetic life freely, without constraint.[51] Like the Mother of God, the figure of Virginitas stands symbolically at the heart of the Church. Nevertheless, imitation of Mary plays a relatively minor role in Hildegard's doctrine of virginity. More often she envisioned the virginal life, especially that of nuns, as a privileged *imitatio Ecclesiae*.[52] Through the Son of Mary, the Church arose as a "new race" whose sign and glory is virginity. This newness belongs mystically to the entire Church, but literally only to virgins, who are "a living fragrance vowing the way of secret rebirth."[53] "When God was born, Ecclesia's eyes were opened in virginal nature . . . and there appeared a new, different human race that had not existed before [Christ's] nativity."[54] Hildegard did not alter the ancient doctrine of virginity as a *vita angelica*, a grace restoring the life of Paradise and antici-

---

49. *Scivias* II.5, p. 175.

50. "Et sicut dies verni circumdabant eam flores rosarum et lilia convallium." First Nocturn, Matins of the Assumption.

51. *Scivias* II.5.13, p. 187.

52. See Matthäus Bernards, *Speculum Virginum. Geistigkeit und Seelenleben der Frau im Hochmittelalter* (Cologne and Graz, 1955), and John Bugge, *Virginitas: An Essay in the History of a Medieval Ideal* (The Hague, 1975).

53. *Scivias* II.5.13, pp. 186–87. The alliterative Latin phrase is one of Hildegard's leitmotivs: "vivens odor vovens iter secretae regenerationis."

54. Ep. 101, Pitra 551.

pating the life of heaven.[55] But when she personified this "alien life" in the clear-eyed, girlish figure of Virginitas, she established a concrete and intimate bond between individual consecrated virgins and the virgin Ecclesia.

In a visionary letter to Pope Eugenius III, the seer described two symbolic buildings representing the secular and spiritual estates in the Church. The second building, which resembles the fiery tower of *Scivias* II.4, houses the monastic and clerical elite who have chosen the better part "as a star multiplies its splendor in a cloud, and as a feminine form is crowned in virginity."[56] In the ceremony for the coronation of virgins, Hildegard saw a ritual mimesis of Ecclesia's adornment,[57] and at her own monastery she went even further.

Abbess Tengswich of Andernach—the same who objected to the seer's policy of admitting only highborn nuns—marveled that the Rupertsberg virgins were rumored to attend church on feast days wearing white veils, rings on their fingers, and crowns decorated with an image of the Lamb in front and angels on the sides.[58] Rather testily, the mistress of Andernach quoted the Apostle's precept that devout women should adorn themselves modestly, not in pearls or precious attire (I Tim. 2:9). Hildegard, undaunted, replied that these strictures apply only to wives, who must submit to their husbands' "masculine power" on account of Eve's lewdness.

> These things do not apply to the virgin, however. She stands in the simplicity and the wholeness of a beautiful paradise that will never fade but remain forever green and ripe as a branch in blossom. . . . Virgins are wedded in the Holy Spirit to holiness and the dawn of virginity; therefore, it befits them to

55. Tertullian, *Ad uxorem* 1.4, CSEL 70: 102; Cyprian, *De habitu virginum* 22, CSEL 3: 203; Ambrose, *De virginitate* 1.3.11, Florilegium Patristicum 31:39; Jerome, Ep. 22.20.3, CSEL 54: 171; Augustine, Ep. 150, CSEL 44: 381.

56. Ep. 1, PL 197: 149a.

57. On this rite see Philippus Oppenheim, *Die* consecratio virginum *als geistesgeschichtliches Problem* (Rome, 1943); René Metz, *La consécration des vierges dans l'église romaine* (Paris, 1954).

58. For Tengswich's letter and Hildegard's reply see Ep. 116, PL 197: 336–38; text emended from the ms.

come to the High Priest as a whole burnt offering consecrated to God.

White garments are appropriate for the brides of Christ, Hildegard added, and they bear the image of the Lamb because they follow him wherever he goes (Apoc. 14:4). Married women are bound to veil their *viriditas*, their long hair, just as winter throws its veil over the green earth. But a virgin is free in her paradisal springtime; she veils herself only in humility, lest the hawk of pride ravage her spiritual beauty. So every nun, for the visionary abbess, became a figure of the unique virgin bride and a remembrance of Eve in the garden—in short, an epiphany of the original *feminea forma*. Hildegard's reply to the abbess of Andernach rests, finally, on a ringing appeal to the eternal Feminine: "The form of Woman flashed forth its radiance in the primal origin, where was fashioned [the womb] in which all creation lies hidden. How could this be? In two ways: by the handiwork of God's finger and by supernal beauty." One would dearly like to know what Tengswich made of this cryptic answer.

The correspondence between Tengswich and Hildegard affords another glimpse of the seer translating her visions into everyday practice, for the real veils and crowns described in Tengswich's letter are identical with the headgear of the choir of virgins in *Scivias* II.5. Thus, when Hildegard explained that her nuns wear these crowns "through a revelation in the mystic inspiration of God's finger," we know precisely which revelation she meant. It is even possible to identify the nun whom the abbess imagined as Virginitas herself. In 1151, soon after Hildegard had completed the *Scivias*, her beloved secretary Richardis von Stade was elected abbess of Birsim (now Bassum) through the influence of her brother, Archbishop Hartwig of Bremen.[59] Hildegard contested this election and

---

59. On the relations of Hildegard, Richardis, and Hartwig see Ep. 10, PL 197: 161–63; Epp. 10 and 42 in Francis Haug, ed., "Epistolae S. Hildegardis secundum codicem Stuttgartensem" *Revue bénédictine* 43 (1931): 59–71; *Echtheit* 131–41; Peter Dronke, *Women Writers of the Middle Ages* (Cambridge, 1984): 154–59.

tried by all possible means to prevent her favorite nun's departure. Nonetheless, Richardis accepted the office and left the Rupertsberg for Birsim, where she fell ill and died less than a year later. After her death, Hildegard wrote Hartwig to console him for their mutual loss. Although the world loved this flower of virginity, she declared, God loved her more and took her soul to keep it undefiled by earthly glory. She added that, while Richardis was still alive, she had seen her in a vision and heard a voice saying, "O Virginity, you stand in the royal bridal chamber!"[60]

These same words open the first speech of Castitas in the *Play of Virtues*. It is possible that Richardis played, or was meant to play, the role of this Virtue in the original performance. But the play was probably completed after Richardis's death, and this speech does not occur in the draft version that concludes the *Scivias*. It is more likely that Hildegard composed the speech and its choral response in memory of her departed daughter.

CASTITAS: O Virginity, you stand in the royal bridal chamber.
O how tenderly you burn in the King's embraces when the sun shines through you so that your noble flower shall never wilt.
O noble virgin, no shade will ever find your flower drooping!

VIRTUTES: The flower of the field falls before the wind, the rain scatters its petals.
O Virginity, you abide forever in the chorus of the company of heaven!
Hence you are a tender flower that shall never fade.[61]

The correspondence is complete. On the plane of allegory we see the stark, imposing figure of Mater Ecclesia sheltering a throng of virgins in her bosom, with the Virgin Mary at her heart. But the historical record shows us Hildegard, mother

60. Ep. 10, PL 197: 163b.
61. *Ordo virtutum* 185.

to her own flock of virgins decked in their bridal veils, with her favorite daughter in the midst of them.

Even the celestial music has its counterpart in Hildegard's "Symphony of Virgins," composed for her nuns to sing as they followed the Virgin and her Son.

> O tenderest lover,
> O giver of tenderest embraces,
> help us keep our virginity.
> We were born in dust, alas!
> and in the guilt of Adam.
> Hard it is to resist
> what tastes of the apple:
> raise us up, O Savior Christ!
> . . . .
> In your blood we were wed to you
> with the pledge of betrothal,
> renouncing man and choosing you,
> the Son of God.
> O fairest form, O sweetest fragrance
> of the delights we long for:
> Always we sigh for you with tears, in exile.
> When may we see you,
> abide with you?[62]

In this ardent love song, the daughters of Jerusalem imitate their mother, longing for Ecclesia's bridegroom, whose embrace does not destroy but confers true virginity.[63] The first stanza alludes lightly to the Song of Songs (8:5 Vg), where the bridegroom reminds the bride of Eve's fall: "Under the apple tree I raised you up; there your mother was corrupted, there she who bore you was defiled." With Christ's help, these daughters of Eve seek to emulate the new Eve, recalling her "dowry" of precious blood and the wedding at the cross. This prayer, perhaps more than any other text of Hildegard's, belongs to the emotional ambience of St. Bernard's sermons on the Song. Even this, however, is not the cry of one impas-

---

62. *Lieder* no. 40: 258–60.

63. Cf. Augustine: "A great and singular honor belongs to the bride-groom: he found [Ecclesia] a harlot and made her a virgin." *Sermo* I.8, ed. Germain Morin in *Miscellanea Agostiniana* (Rome, 1930), I: 447.

sioned soul, but a *symphonia*. Only in their unity and harmony do Christ's virgins, as a chorus, represent the virgin Ecclesia.

Of all the saints in the calendar, none appealed to Hildegard more than the legendary Ursula, who supposedly led a troupe of eleven thousand virgins to martyrdom at Cologne. This saint enjoyed great prestige after the martyrs' "relics" were fortuitously discovered in 1106, when Henry IV was enlarging the walls of Cologne and his workmen stumbled on an old Roman cemetery near the church of St. Ursula. The apparently inexhaustible supply of bones led the faithful to believe that the virgins' burial site had been discovered, and the ensuing trade in relics continued for centuries. The discoveries also aroused a new interest in Ursula's legend, fostered largely by Hildegard's protégée, Elisabeth of Schönau.[64]

The abbess's own sequence "On the Eleven Thousand Virgins" ("O Ecclesia") is roughly contemporary with Elisabeth's revelations; but, despite their friendship, in this case neither visionary influenced the other. In contrast to Elisabeth and her clients, Hildegard took no interest in the individual virgins and their fantastic histories. Instead, she treated Ursula and her companions just as she treated Richardis and her own nuns, or Mary and the throng of virgins in the bosom of Ecclesia. Ursula, too, became for her a figure of Virginitas, a type of the Church longing for her bridegroom and united with him in a death like his. This typology is clear from the first line of the sequence, which invokes not Ursula but Ecclesia. Like *Scivias* II.5, the poem opens with a colossal vision of the Church, focuses more sharply on the figura who represents her (now clad in the scarlet of her own blood), and then widens out once more to embrace the heavens.

> O Ecclesia, your eyes are like sapphire,
> your ears like Mount Bethel,

64. *Liber revelationum Elisabeth de sacro exercitu virginum Coloniensium*, ed. F. W. E. Roth in *Die Visionen der heiligen Elisabeth und die Schriften der Äbte Ekbert und Emecho von Schönau* (Brünn, 1884): 123–38; Guy de Tervarent, *La légende de Ste. Ursule dans la littérature et l'art du Moyen-âge* (Paris, 1931).

your nose like a mountain of incense and myrrh,
your mouth like the sound of many waters.

In a vision of true faith
Ursula fell in love with the Son of God
and renounced man with this world
and looked into the sun
and called to the loveliest youth, saying:

"In great desire I have desired
to come to you and sit with you
at the heavenly marriage feast,
flying to you by a strange path
as a cloud flits through purest sapphire air."

And after Ursula had spoken,
this report spread throughout all nations.
And they said,
"How naive the girl is!
She does not know what she says."

And they began to mock her
in a mighty chorus—
until the fiery burden fell upon her.

Thence all people learned
that scorn for the world is like Mount Bethel,
and they also came to know
the sweetest fragrance of incense and myrrh,
for scorn for the world mounts above all.

Then the devil rushed into his members
and in those bodies they slew
all that was noblest.

And all the elements heard it
and cried aloud before the throne of God:
"Wach! The scarlet blood of the innocent lamb
is poured out at her wedding."

Let all the heavens hear this
and praise God's Lamb in lofty chorus—
for the neck of the ancient serpent
is choked by these pearls
strung upon the Word of God.[65]

The sequence is a study in passion, an amalgam of one
girl's desire and death with the passion and marriage feast of

---

65. Appendix B, no. 11.

the Lamb. Its images bind the Apocalypse to the Song of Songs, resolving contrasts of scale in a dramatic fusion of the intimate and personal with the cosmic and elemental. Behind the figure of Ursula, apparently so ludicrous and slight, stands the bride of the Lamb with the strength of mountains, which are the refuge and the horizon of embattled Virginitas. The sapphire of Ecclesia's eyes becomes the heaven through which Ursula—her own eyes fixed like an eagle's on the sun— streams "by a strange path" toward her beloved. Ecclesia's voice, "like the sound of many waters," echoes the prophetic vision of the Son of Man (Apoc. 1:15) because, through her preaching, the bride is already at one with her bridegroom. Her nose, organ of discernment, is fragrant with the sacrifice of Christ, which will be wafted abroad by the virgin's heroic *contemptus mundi*. Ursula's cry of desire, like Ecclesia's re- sounding voice, answers and perpetuates Christ's own call. In fact, her declaration of love echoes his invitation to the Last Supper: "With desire I have desired to eat this passover with you before I suffer" (Luke 22:15). This reference to Christ's passion unites his longing and suffering with the virgin's, transforming her martyrdom into a Eucharist. "The bride of Christ goes forth not to rest but to battle"—says the *Mirror of Virgins*—"when she has preferred the Lord's chalice to the golden chalice of Babylon, offering herself and her own to God: dead to the world, a living sacrifice to God."[66]

After the eucharistic allusion, the history of Ursula's pas- sion unfolds amid the apocalyptic war between Christ and Satan, in a symmetrical array matching the *symphonia* of scof- fers against the symphony of angels, the body of Christ against the devil's body.[67] The taunt of Ursula's tormentors, "she does not know what she says," recalls the devil's mock- ery in the *Play of Virtues*, where he accuses his foes of a like

---

66. *Speculum virginum*, London BL Arundel 44, fol. 94^r.

67. The idea of the *corpus diaboli*, one of Tychonius's exegetical rules adopted by Augustine in *De doctrina christiana* III.55, was current in twelfth- century ecclesiology. Cf. Rupert of Deutz, *In Libros Regum* 2.38, CCCM 22: 1291; Honorius, *Comment. in Psalmos* 1, PL 172: 274; Gerhoch of Reichersberg, *Comment. in Psalmos* 17, PL 193: 883.

naïveté: "you know not what you are . . . you know not what you worship."[68] Neither the world nor the devil can understand the "alien life" of virginity: perhaps Hildegard was quoting some of her own less comprehending neighbors. In any case, the taunt cannot be answered directly; Ursula replies only by demonstrating her invincible contempt for the world. Through her courage, the celestial Ecclesia "descends to earth" again, as it were, and even the devil's members momentarily recognize the bride of Christ in the virgins they are about to slaughter. As the martyrs' blood cries out to heaven like Abel's, the elements invoke the blood of the Lamb shed in his—and the virgins'—betrothal. The ambiguous cry not only recalls the sacrifice of Christ, it also implies that even now his blood is pouring from the wounds of his bride in their eucharistic marriage. The nuptials are at once consummated in heaven, where, in a startling metamorphosis, the virgin and her companions become a necklace of pearls, not to adorn the bride but to choke the devil. Thus the sequence ends triumphantly, albeit surprisingly, with a memorable image of Virginitas crushing the serpent's head (Gen. 3:15).[69]

MOTHER CHURCH AND
THE MOTHERHOOD OF GOD

The virginity of Ecclesia, then, is associated with the archetypal beauty of Woman, of paradisal Eve and of Mary, but also with a painful and ascetic love that leads even to martyrdom. In each case, the symbol bears directly on the lives and deaths of actual women who choose to follow the virginal path. Ecclesia's motherhood, however, has no such significance for living mothers. On the contrary, it is a symbol that relates primarily to the tasks and qualities of male clergy. Mater Ecclesia's childbearing refers to baptism; her nursing to prophetic teaching and preaching; her maternal tenderness to the

68. *Ordo virtutum* 183–84.
69. Peter Dronke has discussed this sequence in *Poetic Individuality in the Middle Ages* (Oxford, 1970): 160–64.

sacrament of penance; and her cries of bereavement and outrage to the depredations of unworthy priests. Even when Ecclesia's maternal functions led Hildegard to reflect on the maternal bounty of God, she was honoring the feminine divine and not the motherhood of women, which remains untouched by the charm of virginity and therefore unhallowed. So what we see throughout the abbess's treatment of Mother Church is a consistent feminizing of ecclesial and clerical acts, sharpened by the willing exclusion of nonvirginal maternity and femininity from the sacred sphere.

Hildegard's iconography of baptism, which is unique, blends elements of the maternal and the masculine with that visionary syncretism that is her hallmark. In her first vision of Ecclesia (Fig. 8, lower right), she saw the figure's womb divided into many compartments, like a fishnet.

> Then I saw black infants moving across the earth through the air, like fish in water, and entering the womb of the image where it was divided into compartments. But she sighed, drawing them up to her head, whence they issued forth at her mouth, while she remained inviolate. And behold! again there appeared to me that shining light, and in it the figure of a man all ablaze with glowing fire, as in the vision I had seen before [of the Trinity, *Scivias* II.2]. And he removed a black skin from each of them and, casting those skins away, clothed each one in a pure white garment and revealed the shining light to them, saying to each one, "Put off the old garment of injustice, put on the new robe of holiness; for the gate of your inheritance has been opened to you."[70]

The vision is a collage of baptismal symbols, which together form a coherent doctrine if not a coherent image. The black infants are catechumens, stained with original sin, who rush to Mother Church in search of salvation and "enter her womb" by preparing for baptism (John 3:4). She sighs, invoking the Trinity (Matt. 28:19) and drawing her children to Christ, her head (Eph. 5:23). With this invocation she gives birth through the Word and the Spirit—or, pictorially,

70. *Scivias* II.3, p. 135.

through the mouth. Meanwhile her virginity, the pure Catholic faith, remains intact. The Son of God removes the garment of sin, the old Adam, and clothes the neophytes in the light of Christ (Gal. 3:27, Col. 3:9–10). In a novel composition faithful to Hildegard's text, the artist combined three ancient baptismal motifs: the womb of Mother Church, the invocation of the Trinity (represented by a tricolored sphere), and the garment of immortality.

The fourth motif is more problematic. Hildegard compared the catechumens to fish and the womb of Ecclesia to a fishnet, which is presumably the net of Peter, the fisher of men (Matt. 4:19). In the primitive Church, the cryptic anagram of Christ as Fish (ΙΧΘΥΣ) had inspired a whole complex of related symbolism: the baptismal font is a fish pond (*piscina*), neophytes are Peter's miraculous catch of fish (Luke 5:1–11), the Apostles' preaching is Christ's net, and the world or the Church a sea.[71] In his treatise *On Baptism*, Tertullian claimed that "according to the example of Jesus Christ, our Fish, we little fish are born in water, nor are we saved unless we remain in water."[72] Ambrose said that "the apostolic fishing gear is indeed a net that does not destroy the fish captured but preserves them and draws them up from the depth into the light."[73] But this patristic symbolism had fallen out of use by Hildegard's day, and the story of Peter's miraculous fishing served medieval exegetes mainly as a proof text for the primacy of Rome.[74] When Hildegard bound image to image, superimposing the net of Peter on the womb of Ecclesia, she revived an ancient tradition but she also feminized it, for she omitted all mention of the Apostles and spoke only of Mother Church. Ecclesia's womb is the font, the font is the great sea in which Christ the bridegroom—not Peter—casts his net,

71. Franz Dölger, ΙΧΘΥΣ. *Das Fisch-Symbol in Frühchristlicher Zeit*, 2nd ed. (Münster, 1928), I: 68–87; Hugo Rahner, *Symbole der Kirche. Die Ekklesiologie der Väter* (Salzburg, 1964): 475–90. The Greek letters stand for the words "Jesus Christ, Son of God, Savior."

72. Tertullian, *De baptismate* 1, CSEL 20: 201.

73. Ambrose, *Expositio in Lucam* IV.72, CSEL 32⁴: 176.

74. Rahner, *Symbole der Kirche* 491–503.

and the fish race to the net like children to their mother. Ardent papalist though she was, Hildegard once addressed the pope himself as the *"materia* of all spiritual offices."[75]

This idiosyncratic title is but one of many allusions to pastoral care as a kind of mothering. Hildegard used such imagery most often when writing to bishops or monastic superiors, either asking some favor or reproaching them for dereliction of duty. The letter just cited was written in 1173–74 to secure the intercession of Alexander III in her quarrel with the monks of St. Disibod. In a letter to Eugenius III in 1153, Hildegard pleaded for her patron, Archbishop Heinrich of Mainz, who had lost Barbarossa's favor and was soon to be deposed on charges of incompetence. Speaking in God's name, the abbess impugned the motives of Heinrich's enemies and asked the pontiff to judge the case "according to the motherly heart of God's mercy."[76] Although she admitted Heinrich's guilt, she reminded Eugenius that "God desires mercy rather than sacrifice," implying that leniency would lead the erring prelate more quickly to repentance. Penance is indeed "a most tender mother," she told a contrite sister abbess.[77] In the *Activity of God*, she wrote that the Creator established male and female in the soul as well as the body: strength, fortitude, and justice are masculine qualities, while mercy, compassion, and repentance are feminine.[78] She advised Alardus, abbot of St. Martin in Cologne, to teach his monks "in maternal tenderness" and not with "strident words," that they might open their mouths to receive bread instead of thistles.[79] On another occasion, she rebuked an unidentified pastor for letting his charges grow spiritually weak because they had no "breasts of motherly compassion" to suckle.[80]

75. Ep. 4, PL 197: 154d.
76. Ep. 1, PL 197: 148b. For the history of this affair see *Echtheit* 114–16 and Adelgundis Führkötter, trans., *Briefwechsel* (Salzburg, 1965): 35–36.
77. Ep. 106, PL 197: 328b.
78. DOD II.5.46, PL 197: 952a.
79. Ep. 41, PL 197: 208d.
80. Ep. 83, ed. Haug, "Epistolae S. Hildegardis" 67.

Such tropes are not peculiar to Hildegard or to the twelfth century. Like the image of Ecclesia as bride, they derive from metaphors in the Pauline epistles. The Apostle called the Corinthians "babes in Christ," whom he had to feed with milk, not solid food (I Cor. 3:1–2; cf. Heb. 5:13–14, I Pet. 2:2), and the Galatians "little children" with whom he was in travail until Christ was formed in them (Gal. 4:19). Early fathers like Clement and Origen differentiated between the "simple," or spiritual children, and the "perfect," or mothers in Christ, a distinction that was to enjoy wide currency in spiritual writings.[81] According to a well-known homily of Gregory the Great, "anyone who is Christ's brother and sister by believing becomes his mother by preaching; he gives birth to the Lord, as it were, whom he pours into the hearer's heart."[82]

In the twelfth century, the theme of spiritual motherhood enjoyed a renascence, particularly in the Song of Songs tradition.[83] Nursing, as well as childbirth, could symbolize preaching and pastoral care; according to Honorius's longer commentary on the Song, Ecclesia's breasts, which are "sweeter than wine," denote "those who are learned in both [the Old and New Testaments], who pour out the milk of teaching pressed from the two laws for little children in Christ."[84] St. Bernard interpreted the breasts of the bride as the love, sympathy, and instruction offered by Mother Church—in particular by abbots and prelates—to her children. In a classic comparison of the active and contemplative lives, he contrasted the "breasts"—the public ministry of

81. Cf. Methodius: "those who are still imperfect and only beginners are borne to the salvation of knowledge and formed as by mothers in travail, by those who are more perfect, until they are brought forth and regenerated unto the greatness and beauty of virtue; and when these by the progress of their growth in their turn have become the Church, they, too, cooperate in the birth and nurture of other children." *Symposium* III.8.74, trans. Plumpe, *Mater Ecclesia* 115. See also Rahner, *Symbole der Kirche* 13–87.

82. Gregory the Great, *Homilia 3 in Evangelia*, PL 76: 1086d.

83. Friedrich Ohly, *Hohelied-Studien. Grundzüge einer Geschichte der Hoheliedauslegung des Abendlandes bis um 1200* (Wiesbaden, 1958).

84. Honorius, *Expositio in Cantica* II.4, PL 172: 414b.

preaching and pastoral care—with the "kisses" of solitary prayer.[85]

In a recent study of maternal imagery among the Cistercians, Caroline Bynum has observed that this symbolism conveys two basic notions: paternal authority sweetened by motherly affection, and childlike dependence on God or his representative, the abbot.[86] This long, lively tradition of associating prelates with spiritual motherhood indicates that Hildegard's use of the imagery is far from typically "feminine." But neither is her usage identical with that of the Cistercians. Unlike Bernard, for example, Hildegard never exaggerated the nursing image in the direction of sentimentality, and although she spoke often of maternity, she said little of spiritual childhood. Although "nursing" frequently suggested tenderness and leniency to her, it could also refer to the vehemence and cosmic force of Ecclesia's preaching. In praise of the missionary St. Eucharius, the abbess wrote:

> In your teaching Ecclesia
> argued with such power
> that her call rang out above the mountains,
> that the hills and the woods might bow
> to suck her breasts.[87]

The triumphant boldness of this image recalls Second Isaiah promising great things to Jerusalem: "You shall suck the milk of nations, and be nursed at the breast of kings" (Isa. 60:16). In a similar text Hildegard invoked the irresistible power of Ecclesia's voice: "Who can strive against that voice that thundered, mounting up on wings, and vanquished the abyss, resounding under cover of maternal vigor?"[88] The voice

---

85. Bernard of Clairvaux, *Sermones super Cantica* 9.8–9, 10.1, 41.5, in *Opera* 1: 47–49 and 2: 31.

86. Caroline Bynum, "Jesus as Mother and Abbot as Mother: Some Themes in Twelfth-Century Cistercian Writing," in her *Jesus as Mother: Studies in the Spirituality of the High Middle Ages* (Berkeley, 1982): 110–69. See especially 154–66.

87. *Lieder* no. 75: 294.

88. Ep. 34, Pitra 520.

speaks for the prophetic Spirit, but the *materna viriditas* through which it sounds is, in this case, Hildegard herself thundering against the cardinals who deposed Heinrich of Mainz. Mater Ecclesia here presented, and represented, by the abbess of Bingen is a *mulier* without *mollities*.

A scathing public sermon that she preached at Cologne around 1163 charges all the clerics of that city with negligence: Woe to those who are given a voice and will not shout, who have breasts and will not nurse God's children![89] Hildegard reproached the clergy for neglecting doctrine and obedience, failing to discipline their subordinates, and, above all, offering no resistance to the Cathars. While priests were playing the soldier or the minstrel, seductive heretics were leading Christ's flock astray. The negligent clerics protested that no one would heed them, but Hildegard reminded them sharply that for the sake of obedience Abel braved his brother's hatred, Noah endured his neighbors' scorn, Abraham bound his son for a holocaust, and Moses suffered the reproach of his people. It is particularly striking that in this case the seer used this image of nursing not to urge mercy but to encourage stronger discipline and fearless preaching against heresy. She was no longer thinking of feminine tenderness but of members fulfilling their proper functions in the body of Christ. If preachers were silent and "the breasts of the Church" would not suckle, she averred, the whole body would suffer as catastrophe shattered the system of universal harmonies.

Like the white monks, Hildegard sometimes characterized God with feminine images transposed from the sphere of Mother Church, although their devotion to Jesus as mother was foreign to her.[90] When she applied maternal imagery to

---

89. Ep. 48, PL 197: 249b. This passage from Hildegard's sermon appears in the Riesenkodex but not in the earlier Vienna Codex 881. As the text of Ep. 48 is a transcription of Hildegard's preaching at Cologne, the passages inserted later may represent excerpts from her preaching on a similar occasion. See *Echtheit* 169–70.

90. Given Hildegard's view that woman signifies the humanity of Christ, it may be significant that she virtually never used his human name, Jesus, except in phrases like "Filius Dei Jesus Christus," preferring instead the divine and masculine titles like Son of God, Savior, Judge.

God, apart from her sapiential visions, the seer looked not to Jesus the man but to the divine nature, *divinitas*, experienced as the author of physical and spiritual life. For instance, in the *Activity of God* she expounded a verse from the Song of Songs (1:3) in which the maidens extol the breasts of the bridegroom and the bride above wine. Her gloss refers not to Christ or the Church but to *sancta divinitas*, which sustains all the just with the sweetness of virtues poured like wine into a vessel.

> Therefore the faithful . . . thirst for the justice of God and suck holiness from his breasts, nor could they ever have surfeit; but they shall delight forever in the contemplation of divinity, because holiness surpasses all human understanding. For when a person receives righteousness, he abandons himself and tastes and drinks virtues, and is strengthened by them as the veins of a drinker are filled with wine.[91]

So the milk of mother love becomes the intoxicating wine of ecstasy.

Another verse from the Song—"Who shall give you to me for my brother, sucking the breasts of my mother?" (8:1)—inspired a similar exegesis. The wretched soul wishes to call Christ her brother so she can nurse at his divine mother's breasts.

> On account of your Incarnation I call you my brother, sucking [the milk of] mercy and truth. These are the foods with which people are nourished by the Holy One, who is my mother because she created me and gives me life through the bounty of nature (*cum educatione vegetationis*). This means that the food of the Church also is full of your grace, because you grant her rich nourishment in the sacrament of your body and blood: you, the living bread and the fountain of living water.[92]

This passage from the *Scivias* illustrates the way Hildegard saw Ecclesia's motherhood as an extension of God's. Like several of the sapiential visions, the text begins with the order of creation and then correlates it with the order of redemption.

91. DOD I.2.19, PL 197: 765a.
92. *Scivias* II.6.35, p. 263.

Avoiding direct feminine imagery for Christ, it leads from God the creatrix to the figure of Mater Ecclesia, evoking the Virgin obliquely with the phrase *plena gratia*. In these two passages the divine fecundity, *ubertas*, comes to encompass all four levels of meaning: literally it is the bounty of nature, allegorically the Eucharist, morally the gift of virtue and justice, and anagogically the joy of the beatific vision.

But the divine motherhood also has a dark, sorrowful aspect. The twelfth century witnessed the beginnings of that devotion to Mary as *mater dolorosa*, the grieving mother, which would so flourish in the late Middle Ages. It is a mark of Hildegard's conservatism that for her not Mary but Ecclesia played this role; it is the Church who mourns over the sins and sufferings of her children. Ever since the time of Irenaeus, theologians had appealed to the grieving Mater Ecclesia as an indirect way of expressing God's grief over sin as well as his incomparable patience. Rupert of Deutz compared the Church, praying for the conversion of sinners, to the widow of Sarephta, who begged Elijah to resurrect her son (I Kings 17:17–24).[93] For Honorius, Mater Ecclesia was the woman of the Gospel who gives birth in sorrow, but at the end of the world she will forget her pain for joy that her child is born (John 16:21).[94] Hildegard let Mother Church exclaim:

> I conceive and bear many who weary and oppress me, their mother, with diverse troubles: heretics, schismatics, men who fight needless battles, robbers, murderers, adulterers, fornicators, and others who err like these assault me. But many of them rise again in true repentance unto eternal life, and many fall in mistaken stubbornness to eternal death.[95]

Some of these rebels, "forsaking the maternal bosom and the sweet nourishments of the Church," attack her openly. In Fig. 11 they are seen assaulting her with the sword, but they prove powerless against her might. The sorrowing mother prays God to spare such children for his Son's sake, "until the full

93. Rupert of Deutz, *In Libros Regum* 5.8, CCCM 22: 1418–19.
94. Honorius, *Speculum Ecclesiae*, PL 172: 954–55.
95. *Scivias* II.3, p. 136.

number of her children have come into the tabernacle of the heavenly city."[96]

In time of schism, the theme of Mater Ecclesia's sorrow could lend itself to pleas for unity. In the tradition of St. Cyprian, who had appealed constantly to the sufferings of Mother Church during the Novatianist schism,[97] Hildegard raised a cry of mourning in her antiphon "O virgo Ecclesia":

> O virgin Church, we must mourn,
> for the savage wolf has snatched
> your children from your side.
> O woe to the cunning serpent![98]

But the next antiphon in the *Symphonia*, "Nunc gaudeant," celebrates the lost children's return.

> Now let Ecclesia's mother-heart rejoice,
> for in harmony on high
> her children are gathered into her bosom.
> So you, shameful serpent, are disgraced,
> for those whom your jealousy held in your maw
> now gleam in the blood of God's Son.
> Praise to you, King most high! Alleluia.[99]

Concrete but rhetorically veiled events very often underlie Hildegard's grandiose images.[100] While she was composing the *Symphonia* (1151–1158), the most cataclysmic event to shake the Church was the revolt of Arnold of Brescia, a fiery populist reformer who called for radical disendowment of pope and clergy, drove Eugenius III out of Rome, and provoked the angry fulminations of St. Bernard. In 1155 the new English pope, Adrian IV, finally overthew Arnold by laying an interdict on the people of Rome during Holy Week, not to be lifted until they expelled the reformer from the city and submitted to papal rule. Arnold may well be the "savage wolf" of the first antiphon; the Age of the Wolf in Hildegard's

---

96. *Scivias* II.4.11–13, pp. 168–70.
97. Plumpe, *Mater Ecclesia* 81–108.
98. *Lieder* no. 56: 274.
99. Appendix B, no. 12.
100. *Echtheit* 116.

apocalyptic signifies an era of violence and usurpation.[101] In a letter to Adrian IV, Hildegard also alluded in very cryptic terms to his battles with wild beasts.[102] A heretic would naturally affront Ecclesia's virginity—her inviolate faith—as well as her motherly affection. If the second antiphon celebrates Arnold's downfall, the references to Christ's blood could allude to the lifting of the interdict on Rome. The sentiments of "Nunc gaudeant" echo Cyprian's impassioned prayer in the tract *On Church Unity*, "that rejoicing our Mother may receive in her bosom one body of a people united in one mind."[103]

"AN EFFEMINATE AGE"

Like any living metaphors, Hildegard's tropes are patient of inversion. This is particularly true of Ecclesia's femininity, which makes her not only virginal and fertile but also highly vulnerable to corruption. Despite the tower of the Spirit, which is her eternal security, the joyful mother can become a sorrowful mother in history, and the virgin bride can be ravished. Her purity is soiled, paradoxically, whenever the male clerics who should guard her lose their virility and turn to effeminate ways. Instead of being "motherly" in a good sense—compassionate, nurturing, and watchful in the care of their children—they become merely "womanish." It was to chastise the clergy that Hildegard denounced her own period of history as an "effeminate age" (*muliebre tempus*), inferior to both the paradisal age of "virginal nature" and the apostolic age of "masculine strength." After the Holy Spirit descended at Pentecost, she wrote, the Apostles established their doctrine as firmly as steel in a masculine age; but, in these latter days, the Church and all virtue had degenerated into feminine weakness.[104]

101. *Scivias* III.11.6, p. 579; cf. II.5, p. 176.
102. Ep. 3, PL 197: 154bc; *Echtheit* 120.
103. Cyprian, *De Ecclesiae Unitate* 23, CSEL 3¹: 230; trans. Plumpe, *Mater Ecclesia* 91.
104. DOD III.10.7, PL 197: 1005ab.

As early as 1150 or 1151, she had prophesied to Conrad III that the present "feminine"—in other words, fickle and contentious—times would cede to an era still worse.[105] Somewhat later she complained to Hillinus, archbishop of Trier (1152–1169), that "this age is neither cold nor hot, but squalid" (cf. Apoc. 3:16). It is a "time of the female form" like the time when Eve deceived Adam.[106] (It may be significant that in the same letter Hildegard extolled woman as a fount of wisdom, as if to offset this negative view of the feminine.) The prelates of Trier received a similar prophetic message, as Hildegard thundered against the feminine age that began with a certain unnamed tyrant (probably Henry IV).[107] In her *Vita* she dated the beginning of this age to circa 1100, around the time of her own birth.[108]

What exactly did Hildegard mean by the *muliebre tempus*? When she used the word *effeminate* in a pejorative sense, she did not refer simply to the appearance of feminine traits in men; these, as we have seen, may be either good or bad. It is more likely that the tag denoted what is left of the feminine when its two positive attributes—virginity and maternity—have been stripped away, leaving only the generic "feminine frailty." In the *Book of Life's Merits*, three vices are singled out for their negative femininity: Despair, Greed, and Worldly Sadness.[109] Among their qualities are weakness, cowardice, vanity, folly, and concupiscence. Even Hildegard's *Unknown Language* gives womanhood a bad name by rendering *femina* as *vanix*, with an unmistakable echo of *vanitas*.[110]

In her vehement denunciations of the effeminate age, Hildegard condemned a Church whose vain, pleasure-loving prelates had lost all manly fortitude and zeal for the Word of

---

105. Ep. 26, PL 197: 185c.
106. Ep. 13, PL 197: 167b.
107. Ep. 49, PL 197: 254cd. Cf. Fragment IV.28, p. 71: "The fifth age . . . turned to feminine levity from the time of Emperor Henry [IV]; and therefore to the scandal of men, women now prophesy."
108. *Vita* 2.16, PL 197: 102cd.
109. LVM III.50, IV.45, V. 48 in Pitra 125, 165, 202.
110. *Lingua ignota*, Pitra 497.

God in their craving for worldly honor, soft living, and wealth. Ironically, these effeminate priests are the very same she attacked elsewhere for their lack of motherly care: "they have breasts and will not nurse." Where they ought to be bold and manly, they display nothing but feminine softness; where they should be maternal and tender, they reveal only their hardness of heart; where they should imitate the virginity of Christ and the Church, they pollute themselves in fornication. In short, they possess the virtues of neither sex and the vices of both. As they are not virgins themselves, neither can they guard the virginity of the Church; her pure faith suffers defilement from the menace of the Cathars. In the face of this danger, Hildegard arose as a *virgo* and *virago*: a weak woman exalted by God to shame the effeminate. "Even though you are trampled underfoot by man because of Eve's transgression, yet proclaim the fiery work that is shown you."[111]

In some of her best-known prophetic writings, Hildegard castigated the powerful on behalf of the abused virgin Ecclesia. *On the Activity of God* identifies the Church under a certain aspect with the virtue of Justice, who proclaims that "the Church was born of me through regeneration by water and the Spirit; and we are one just as God and man are one."[112] Iustitia here, like Caritas and Sapientia elsewhere, takes on the heavenly aspect of that divine and human synergy which is the Church, the ongoing Incarnation. As Caritas mourns for her separated children, as Sapientia washes her soiled garments, Iustitia grieves that her beauty has been spoiled by her human partners in the great collaboration. In these effeminate times her crown has been darkened by schism, her robe spattered by fornicating priests, and all her orders overshadowed like the sun behind a cloud. Every man wants to be a law unto himself, she complains, and those who should still be under the rod of their masters set up as masters themselves. Because priests will neither hearken to the Scriptures nor teach them, the faithful wander joylessly, like a people

---

111. *Scivias* II.1, p. 112.
112. DOD III.10.11, PL 197: 1014bc.

without a king. Although they ought to submit to God's commandments "like a woman to a man," they rebel because there is no man to rule them. But God is not mocked, and Justice will have her revenge. In this context she represents the Church persecuted from within by her ostensible leaders. On the one hand, Iustitia remains a divine, celestial queen more exalted than any mortal. On the other, she has condescended to live as a lonely virgin on earth, entrusted to male guardians for protection while she awaits her bridegroom. Men—especially prelates—are but her servants, yet her honor and her welfare depend on them. As a beleaguered bride, still resplendent despite the marks of her disgrace, she has an air of shabby gentility writ large, inspiring pity as well as awe.

Hildegard's epistle to Werner of Kirchheim—a powerful tract for the times, which the Bollandists read as a prophecy of the Reformation[113]—lets Ecclesia herself take up the lament. The seer wrote in her most exalted style:

> In the year of the Lord 1170, when I had long been lying in sickbed, awake in body and spirit, I saw a most beautiful image in the form of a woman, of such exquisite sweetness and of such rare and delightful beauty that the human mind could by no means comprehend it. Her stature reached from the earth to the sky, and her face shone with a great brightness, and her eyes gazed into heaven. She was dressed in a shining robe of white silk and wrapped in a mantle trimmed with the most precious gems—emerald, sapphire, and pearls; and on her feet she had shoes of onyx. Yet her face was spattered with dust and her robe torn on the right side, her mantle had lost its elegance, and her shoes were blackened with mud. And she cried out to the height of heaven in a loud, plaintive voice, saying:
> "Hear, O heaven, for my face is soiled, and mourn, O earth,

113. "So clearly does she predict the future heretics that no doubt seems to remain about that matter. Yet she intermingles a few good things, and declares well enough that the heretics shall not altogether prevail. St. Hildegard seems here to have predicted the times of Luther, and anyone who wishes to examine all that she accurately predicted, not only in Cologne but also in Trier and to Werner of Kirchheim, perceives this even more clearly." AASS September 17, vol. 5; rpt. PL 197: 43cd.

for my robe is torn. Tremble, O abyss, for my shoes are blackened with mud! Foxes have holes and the birds of heaven have nests, but I have no helper or comforter or staff to uphold me."
And again she spoke:
"I lay hidden in the Father's heart until the Son of man, who was conceived and born in virginity, shed his blood with which he married and endowed me, that by pure and simple regeneration, through water and the Spirit, I might renew those who were crippled and contaminated by the serpent's spume. But my foster fathers, the priests—they who should make my face glow like the dawn, my robe sparkle like lightning, my mantle flash like precious gems, and my shoes gleam like a brilliant light—they have spattered my face with dust, torn my robe, darkened my mantle, and blackened my shoes with mud. They who should have made me beautiful in every part have despoiled me in all! For they soil my face by handling and receiving my bridegroom's body and blood in the great impurity of their lecherous ways, in the great filth of fornication and adultery, and in the wicked plunder of avarice, buying and selling what is not for sale; and they wallow in filth like a babe in a pigsty."[114]

Hildegard's specific charges against the clergy—fornication, adultery, simony, pluralism, soft living, greed, negligence, insubordination—place her squarely in the Gregorian reform tradition. And her imagery again recalls the abbot of Clairvaux. Prelates, in Bernard's view, were "friends of the bridegroom," charged, like John the Baptist, with care of the bride only until Christ returns to claim her.[115] Instead of guarding Christ's virgin, Hildegard charged, the treacherous friends have defiled and disgraced her. For this betrayal they will receive their just but tragic deserts. Princes will take counsel against them, they will be stripped of their wealth and banished, an angry populace will turn against them in the name of God, reckoning their consecration and priesthood as trifles, and monasteries will be dissolved at swordpoint. But, as in the time of Elijah (I Kings 19:18), a remnant "who have not bowed the knee to Baal" will remain. Even in these latter days, history will take its usual fluctuating course: periods of

114. Ep. 51, PL 197: 269–70.
115. Bernard of Clairvaux, Ep. 191.2, *Opera* 8: 43.

peace and justice will alternate with the wicked ages, which are symbolized by a succession of five beasts (Fig. 13, top left).

These prophecies of doom culminate in an apocalyptic vision of Ecclesia assaulted by the Antichrist. Early medieval apocalyptic, including Hildegard's, was strongly influenced by the tenth-century monk Adso's *Treatise on the Antichrist*, which maintains that this final enemy of the Church would be born of an "Antivirgin" in a lurid parody of the birth of Christ.[116] Hildegard took up this notion in *Scivias* III.11, prophesying that Satan would disguise himself as a holy angel to deceive the Antichrist's mother, a harlot versed in magical arts. She would call her fornication holy and pretend not to know the father of her child, so that a foolish and misguided public would reckon her a saint.[117] The same prophecy recurs in the *Activity of God*: "And in that time an impure woman will conceive an impure son; for the ancient serpent who devoured Adam will puff him up together with all his followers, so that nothing good . . . will be able to exist in him."[118] It is not surprising that the impurity of the Antichrist's birth and sexual mores looms large in Hildegard's view. The son of perdition, she said, would seduce many by rejecting the precept of continence under the "scientific" rationale that it runs counter to man's warm and fiery nature. Finally, he would try to assault Ecclesia herself, finishing the job that the wicked prelates had begun. Hence the monstrous vision of Fig. 13 (bottom half):

116. "And just as the Holy Ghost came into the womb of the Mother of our Lord Jesus Christ and covered her with His strength and filled her with divinity, so that she conceived from the Holy Ghost and what was born was divine and holy: so also the devil will go down into the womb of Antichrist's mother and fill her completely, possess her completely inside and out, so that she will conceive by man with the devil's assistance, and what is born will be completely foul, completely evil, completely ruined." Adso, *De ortu et tempore Antichristi*, CCCM 45; trans. Wright, *Play of Antichrist* 103.

117. *Scivias* III.11.25, pp. 589–90.

118. DOD III.10.28, PL 197: 1028b. On the Antichrist see Wilhelm Kamlah, *Apokalypse und Geschichtstheologie. Die mittelalterliche Auslegung der Apokalypse vor Joachim von Fiore* (Berlin, 1935); Richard Emmerson, *Antichrist in the Middle Ages: A Study of Medieval Apocalypticism, Art, and Literature* (Seattle, 1981); and the works cited in ch. 1, n. 58.

Fig. 13. *Virgin Ecclesia assaulted by Antichrist.* Top left: five apocalyptic beasts representing times to come. Top right: Christ, the cornerstone of the celestial City. Bottom: Antichrist, represented as a monstrous head, exalts himself on a heap of excrement and attacks the bloodied Ecclesia. The faithful are torn by uncertainty. *Scivias* III.11, Eibingen ms.

That feminine figure [Ecclesia] which I had formerly seen before the altar in the sight of God now appeared to me again, so that this time I could see her below the navel as well. For from her navel down to the place where a woman's sex is recognized, she had variegated scaly blotches, and in place of her privy parts there appeared a monstrous black head with fiery eyes, asses' ears, and the nose and mouth of a lion gaping wide, horribly gnashing and sharpening its terrible iron teeth.[119]

The head, of course, designates the Antichrist, with his vicious deeds, doctrines, and persecutions. He appears where Ecclesia's genitals should be because his aim is to seduce the Church just as the devil corrupted Eve. So, in lieu of Mater Ecclesia supported by the virile strength of the Holy Spirit (Fig. 11), the miniaturist now painted the Church in the guise of a grotesque hermaphrodite, depicting the Antichrist's ears in the shape of an erect phallus to suggest his attempted rape of Christ's virgin. But Hildegard also perceived the Son of man in her vision (top right), and in place of his genitals she saw the rosy dawn of justice and a lyre with taut strings. These two symbols indicate that the faithful will pass through torments to reach the joy of the heavenly marriage.[120] In these two opposed figures of sexual union, Hildegard expressed the paradox of her own divine and virginal eros at its keenest: the son of Satan assaults the new Eve in an image of gross, repellent perversion, while the symbols of virginity—music and the blushing dawn—evoke the true union of bridegroom and bride. The Antichrist—son of a harlot, apostle of "natural" sexuality, foe of continence—embodies the last and greatest threat to the virgin Church. But, after her final vindication, the ancient serpent will be banished at last and the gates of Paradise will reopen for the new and incorruptible Eve with all her children, there to enjoy an ever-virginal union with the new, eternal Adam "as it was decreed before the foundation of the world."

119. *Scivias* III.11, pp. 576–77.
120. *Scivias* III.11.9, pp. 581–82.

In her many guises Ecclesia, paradoxically, emerges as a more concrete and in a sense more personal figure than the Virgin Mary. She not only conceives and bears but also grieves, rejoices, teaches, nurses, and castigates. Her womanhood is both more varied in its expressions and more compelling to Hildegard's visual imagination. And the purely figural Ecclesia can provide a role model for living women, whereas the historical Mary cannot. One reason for this unexpected finding may be that Mary, maid of Galilee though she was, in Hildegard's writing embodies a supratemporal perfection. While her epiphany on earth gives history its center, it is not itself determined by the conditions of history, nor does it at once draw history into its own realm. Although Paradise is regained in the Virgin, it remains sequestered from ordinary mortal experience. Ecclesia, in contrast, can be said to personify history itself. Like Synagoga's, her image can be "read" from the top downward with reference to successive ages of the world. Her head may be crowned with the eternal counsel, but her lower parts are bloody and lacerated, in token of the trials that the Church must undergo before and during the reign of Antichrist. Because she is vulnerable and subject to historical flux, she can be perceived as acting and suffering in every situation, and her manifestations vary with the crisis of the hour. Thus the symbolic content of the persona remains open to creative adaptation. Again, because Ecclesia is not only a metaphysical reality but also a social construct, her state fluctuates with the condition of her members. While the Virgin's garden is perpetually sealed, inviolate and changeless, the City that is Ecclesia teems with workers and wasters who tear down as often as they build.

Nevertheless, Hildegard's sapiential concept of the Church gives Ecclesia a massive grandeur, which pervades all her appearances. She has a solid, unmistakable "personality" more distinct than any of the shadowy character portraits one could abstract from Hildegard's letters or memoirs. It is hard to escape the conclusion that symbolic representations of this kind constituted the heart of the "real world" as the seer perceived it. Visionary forms like Caritas, Sapientia, and Ecclesia do not

strike the reader as reified abstractions or allegorical con-
structs. On the contrary, they have far more solidity than any
historical individuals described by the abbess. Ursula, the one
female saint with whom she seems to have identified, merges
quickly with the more substantial figure of Ecclesia. Even Richardis, the nun with whom she was most closely bound in
love and conflict, is elegized in an impersonal paean spoken
by the figure of Castitas. And, as we have already seen, Mary
and Eve captured Hildegard's imagination not as individuals
but as symbolic forms, types of the unique *feminea forma*. For
all her work in medicine, administration, and counseling, she
seems genuinely to have endowed the Forms or Ideas that she
saw in her visions with more depth, substance, and detail
than she was prepared to see in individuals. She was a Pla-
tonist not only by virtue of this or that opinion, but in her
most fundamental habits of thought and perception.

This characteristic of Hildegard's may help to account for a
fact that is bound to trouble contemporary readers. In spite
of her extensive feminine imagery for the Church and the
priesthood, she not only assented to but actively supported
the exclusion of women from the clergy and other forms of
female subordination. This is not surprising in light of her
historical circumstances, but neither is it inevitable. There
have been movements to empower women in the Church,
from the third-century Montanists to the thirteenth-century
Guglielmites, under circumstances that seemed no more
promising than Hildegard's. And the mere fact that she raised
the issue at all, and spoke as strongly as she did, indicates
that she was aware of a possible alternative. Her self-valida-
tion as a female prophet for an effeminate age only makes her
an exception to prove the rule: women may continue to
prophesy as long as the times remain womanish, but when
they return to normal such exceptions will presumably be
needless. It is significant that the sequence of apocalyptic ages
prophesied in the *Scivias* and the *Activity of God* gives no hint
of a coming era in which gender roles would be reversed or
altered.

Some readers may be inclined to dismiss Hildegard's elaborate feminine symbolism as a kind of veil to disguise female powerlessness—at best a compensation, at worst a collusion with the oppressor. But Hildegard did not define her world in the categories of modern feminism. In medieval religion generally, "powerlessness" in certain forms was upheld as a value for both genders; Hildegard personified it in such Virtues as Humility, Poverty of Spirit, Obedience, and Patience. We have already observed that she and Elisabeth of Schönau understood weakness as a form of strength.[121] A contemporary critic might still take issue with this position, but the brunt of the criticism would not fall on medieval misogyny. Hildegard's defense of power through frailty is only one application of a much broader principle that is not specifically medieval or misogynist, but merely Christian.

In addition to her Platonism and her understanding of feminine weakness, Hildegard's unusual sensibility is at issue. I have had to speak, for convenience, of her "thought" and her "imagination," but it is essential to remember that, when she took stylus and wax tablets in hand, she did not understand herself to be thinking, imagining, inventing, or composing at all. Unversed in the subtleties of modern psychology and hermeneutics, she was simply "writing the words and visions that [were] revealed" to her.[122] And in those visions she saw Ecclesia, Christ's bride, a living and substantial person. The visionary form of Ecclesia was not, for her, a figure of speech, the verbal adornment of an abstract concept. She was a real, eternal being in heaven, and only by helping to realize her on earth did the assemblage of bishops, priests, monks, nuns, and laypeople of Hildegard's acquaintance constitute themselves as "the Church." What is more, the Church in her understanding was not confined to the select body of prelates and religious who formed its elite; it embraced the whole of

121. See the section on illness, visions, and virginity in Elizabeth Petroff, *Medieval Women's Visionary Literature* (Oxford, 1986): 37–44, which appeared as this book was in press. For a contemporary application see Dorothee Soelle, *The Strength of the Weak: Toward a Christian Feminist Identity*, trans. Robert Kimber and Rita Kimber (Philadelphia, 1984).

122. Ep. 2, Pitra 333.

humanity. Ecclesia comprised everyone Hildegard knew and everyone she was likely to meet, with the exception of the Jews—and even they were to be converted in the end. So when she envisaged the Church as woman, developing ancient typological motifs into a portrait of unprecedented liveliness and complexity, she was testifying that humankind in its totality—women and men in history, in community, in relation with God—had a feminine face. Knowing therefore that her womanhood signified the divine humanity, the saving weakness and the flesh of God, and knowing this with all the force that her Platonic and visionary soul ascribed to the fact of signification, she could overcome her resentment and endure the misogyny of her culture with a serenity that is barely credible in our demythologized world.

7

Sister of Wisdom

In recent years St. Hildegard has found great favor with the gurus of "creation-centered spirituality," who have tried to popularize her as a kind of New Age mystic by stressing the more optimistic, holistic, and naturalistic sides of her thought.[1] There are, indeed, passages in her work that could have been uttered by Dame Nature in *The Romance of the Rose*, and my chapter on the feminine divine highlights precisely those passages. For in a sapiential theology of creation, such as Hildegard's, the feminine is the immanent divine principle that mediates between the transcendent God and his creatures. She is Wisdom and Love, energy, synergy, and beauty. As consort of the masculine Creator, she is the divine Mother of all living. But, properly speaking, Hildegard's teaching is not creation centered at all; it centers on the Incarnation, in which the feminine divine like all else finds its deepest meaning. Sapientia in this context represents the eternal counsel, the absolute predestination of the God-man, which is symbolized in feminine form by the predestination of Mary and Ecclesia. So at every level the feminine is that in God which binds itself most intimately with the human race, and through it with the cosmos.

Conversely, the feminine aspect of humanity is that which enters into union with God: Mary, the Church, the Virtues, the virginal soul, and even the humanity of Christ are or are seen as female. In the analogous words of Louis Bouyer, a contemporary Catholic theologian, "the mystery of woman

---

1. Gabrielle Uhlein, ed., *Meditations with Hildegard of Bingen* (Santa Fe, 1983); Matthew Fox, *Illuminations of Hildegard of Bingen* (Santa Fe, 1985). The so-called translations in these volumes are not to be trusted.

. . . is the mystery of creation redeemed, completed and espoused by God himself." For this reason, woman is joined to man in marriage

> within the archetypal union of the eternal Word with divine Wisdom, accomplished through the marriage of Christ and the Church. This wisdom, in fact, is none other than the plan of God for his creature, and for the union of the creature with him—for which it was created. This is why it is in creation itself that this wisdom is truly realized, from beginning to end: first in the Virgin Mary, lastly in the entire Church.[2]

It is in the nature of sapiential theology, whether viewed from the angle of creation or of redemption, to foster an optimistic attitude toward the world. Wisdom offers herself freely to those who love her; her theophanies render the knowledge of God both possible and actual. The celestial Virtues collaborate with men and women to build the Church, thus fulfilling human moral effort in grace without prejudice to freedom. God is accessible and ever-present in the world, and the cosmos is suffused with healing, life-giving energies. Although sin is acknowledged, it is not understood as the sole cause of the Incarnation; God is not responsible for its inheritance; and the Atonement itself is seen from a sacramental rather than sacrificial point of view. Even the doctrine of predestination, which in Augustinian and Reformation theology wears such a somber hue, is here a cause for assurance and hope. All creatures, and preeminently the Mother of God, exist from before time and forever in the embrace of Love, whatever their vicissitudes in this sublunary sphere.

Yet this reassuring, "life-affirming" vision, nuanced by the thousand subtle harmonies of macrocosm and microcosm, is but half of Hildegard's worldview. The other half, less appreciated by her modern admirers, tends toward renunciation of the world, ascetic transcendence, and a stark moral dualism. This too is linked with the feminine, but in a different fashion. Eve, the first epiphany of woman on earth, is celebrated for

---

2. Louis Bouyer, *Woman in the Church*, trans. Marilyn Teichert (San Francisco, 1979): 29, 35.

the boundless potential of her fertility. But a closer reading indicates that, after the violation of Eve's virginity by Satan, motherhood lost its luster, which it would never regain except in the unique Mother of God. With all her contemporaries, Hildegard delighted in the Virgin's maternity, but, when she turned to actual women, it was only the virginal and not the maternal element that retained its sacred character. The cult of virginity, even in its sublimest praise for the "form of Woman, sister of Wisdom," carries the all but inevitable converse: rejection of sexuality. Hildegard, contrary to the received opinion of her age, did not reserve her revulsion primarily for female sexuality; but the revulsion itself is not to be denied. At best, she could retreat from this traditional disdain for the flesh into the relatively neutral realm of medical writing, where sexual life and maternity could be discussed with insight and some degree of appreciation. Only virgins, however, truly represent the feminine divine on earth. Hildegard saw the maiden beauty of Wisdom revealed in the elite world of the nunnery, while her maternal, nurturing aspect is scarcely embodied in women at all but rather in priests, bishops, and abbots. It is not the least of Hildegard's paradoxes that, while the male humanity of Christ is symbolized by woman, the maternity of the Church is chiefly incarnate in men.

As we have observed before, the richness of Hildegard's visionary world is such that no single motif does more than hint at the whole. Future studies of her cosmology, poetry, spirituality, and political thought will enhance our appreciation of her. Nonetheless, this exploration of the feminine as a theological symbol points clearly enough to her central strengths and weaknesses as a teacher of the Christian faith. Living in the full flower of what M.-M. Davy called "la symbolique romane,"[3] she invited or rather commanded the reader to experience the world as she saw it: meticulously ordered, overwhelmingly alive, dazzling in its sheer architectonic beauty. Her writings represent the culmination of sapi-

---

3. M.-M. Davy, *Initiation à la symbolique romane, XIIe siècle* (Paris, 1964): 163–71 on Hildegard.

ential theology to date, gathering and synthesizing all its elements: christological, liturgical, Marian, cosmological, ecclesial, humanistic. There is no imbalance between divine immanence and transcendence, eternity and historicity, masculine and feminine naming of God. Anthropology is no less richly developed, with particular emphasis on the divine image, the microcosm, free will and virtue, and sexual differentiation. But, in the moral sphere, opposites coincide less happily; the ethics of affirmation and of renunciation make strange bedfellows. As in medieval theology generally, it is renunciation that prevails, although Hildegard's aesthetic notion of virginity gives her ascesis a measure of joyful exuberance.

Her chief weakness stems from that which, to modern eyes, characterizes the medieval Church as a whole: overemphasis on the link between sexuality and sin, with far-reaching consequences that include the devaluation of marriage and hence of the Christian laity, and excessive regard for the clerical and monastic elite on the ground of their celibacy. This clericalism is buttressed by a typically medieval insistence on the value of hierarchy at the expense of its Biblical complement, equality. To be sure, Hildegard's own status as a prophet writing for prelates, and still more as a woman writing for men, introduces the possibility of conflict between charismatic and institutional authority. But unlike later mystics and prophets, from Joachim of Fiore to Martin Luther— or from Guglielma of Milan to Marguerite Porete[4]—Hildegard

---

4. Guglielma of Milan (d. 1279) founded a heretical movement which claimed that she was the Holy Spirit incarnate and established a new Church ruled by a feminine pope, Mayfreda de Pirovano, and female cardinals. A Cistercian monastery at Chiaravalle venerated Guglielma as an orthodox saint until her cult was eradicated by inquisitors in 1300. See Stephen Wessley, "The Thirteenth-Century Guglielmites: Salvation through Women," in Derek Baker, ed., *Medieval Women* (Oxford, 1978): 289–303. Marguerite, who believed in an invisible church of "free souls" with power to judge the established Church, was burned in Paris in 1310. But her long-anonymous book, *The Mirror of Simple Souls*, was nevertheless widely read. See Romana Guarnieri, ed., "Il 'Miroir des simples ames' di Margherita Porete," *Archivio italiano per la storia della pietà* 4 (1965): 501–635, and Peter Dronke, *Women Writers of the Middle Ages* (Cambridge, 1984): 217–28.

attacked only the abuse and not the very form and source of hierarchical power. With her unshakable faith in the divine ordering of society, and especially of the Church, she saw no conflict in principle between the prophetic and the priestly charisms. As to gender, her most radical departure lies in appropriating to herself the Pauline doctrine that divine power is perfected in weakness, and therefore in women. Given the structure of twelfth-century society, such a notion, taken with full seriousness, could have had dangerous implications; just as the claim that woman signifies the humanity of Christ could have shaken the ideology of an all-male priesthood. But, however radical the principles, Hildegard drew no such alarming inferences. She was resourceful enough in defending her own activity and authority, but she certainly did not aim at a full-scale empowerment of women.

THEOLOGY AND GENDER REVISITED

Because the gender issue has become inescapable in any discussion of women's writing, it may be instructive to summarize once more the ways in which Hildegard did and did not address this question. In the first place, she did not express her consciousness of role reversal by "becoming male," a favorite strategy of earlier ascetic women.[5] Nevertheless, her correspondent Richard of Indersdorf praised God for infusing masculine vigor in her feminine breast,[6] and Johannes Braun, writing in 1918, contrasted the "serious, almost masculine Hildegard" with the "soft, feminine" Elisabeth.[7] The twelfth-century almoner of Lutherum found Hildegard to be en-

---

5. Rosemary Ruether, "Misogynism and Virginal Feminism in the Fathers of the Church," in Rosemary Ruether, ed., *Religion and Sexism: Images of Woman in the Jewish and Christian Traditions* (New York, 1974): 159–61. A *locus classicus* is the dream of Perpetua, who in a vision on the eve of her martyrdom "was stripped naked and became a man" in order to vanquish Satan in a wrestling match. Dronke, *Women Writers* 4.

6. Ep. 84, PL 197: 305cd.

7. Johannes Braun, *Die heilige Hildegard, Äbtissin vom Rupertsberg* (Regensburg, 1918): 103.

dowed with a "virile mind" in her frail female body,[8] and Joseph Bernhart in 1929 found her "sickly nature" surprising in
the extent of its "manly activity."[9] Second, if the abbess herself
did not adopt the perennial topos of the virile woman, neither
did she particularly seek out women of the past as role
models. In this respect she differed from Elisabeth of Schönau
and from another of her male correspondents, who justified
her by appealing to Biblical precedents like Deborah, Hannah,
and Elisabeth the cousin of Mary.[10] Insofar as she did identify
with feminine models, she preferred symbolic figures like Ecclesia, Caritas, and Scientia Dei. In the third place, Hildegard
did not resolve the gender problem by significantly revising
or blurring traditional concepts of "male" and "female." She
is thus a marked exception to Bynum's conclusion, based
largely on the study of thirteenth- through fifteenth-century
writers, that "it is men who develop conceptions of gender,
whereas women develop conceptions of humanity."[11] However, she did compensate for the notion of female inferiority,
which she accepted, by accentuating the positive symbolic
connotations of femaleness; by using the symbol of maleness
in a negative as well as a positive sense; and, above all, by
stressing sexual complementarity both in God and in humanity, even as she reasserted the principle of sexual hierarchy.

Hildegard's primary solution to the problem was her claim
that God had inspired a weak woman to shame powerful

8. Ep. 136, PL 197: 363d.
9. Joseph Bernhart, "Hildegard von Bingen," *Archiv für Kulturgeschichte* 20
(1929–30): 254. For further examples see Elisabeth Gössmann, "Das Menschenbild der Hildegard und Elisabeth von Schönau vor dem
Hintergrund der frühscholastischen Anthropologie," in Peter Dinzelbacher
and Dieter Bauer, eds., *Frauenmystik im Mittelalter* (Ostfildern, 1985): 46–47,
n. 48.
10. Ep. 75, PL 197: 297c. The comparisons were intended not to flatter
Hildegard but to assert God's omnipotence in conferring the gift of prophecy
on unlikely subjects. With the same intention two other correspondents compared the abbess to Balaam's ass: see Epp. 6, 157bc, and 92, 313a.
11. Caroline Bynum, "'. . . And Woman His Humanity': Female Imagery
in the Religious Writing of the Later Middle Ages," in Caroline Bynum, Steven Harrell, and Paula Richman, eds., *Gender and Religion: On the Complexity
of Symbols* (Boston, 1986).

men. This rationale was to enjoy a long history in hagiographic writing. It is significant, however, that the topos was taken up not so much by women as by male writers eager to justify their female protégées or spiritual mothers. We find it again in the thirteenth-century biography of Juliana of Cornillon.[12] Fra Arnaldo, an admirer of Angela of Foligno (d. 1309), prefaced a book of her visions with the observation that "this is contrary to the order of God's Providence, and for the shaming of carnal men, to make a woman a doctor."[13] John Marienwerder wrote in his life of Dorothy of Montau (d. 1394), "Let no one despise in her the frailty of her sex: for the Lord of all has chosen the weak to confound the strong. Let not the worldly wise underestimate the depth of her mind, for the Lord is accustomed to choose the foolish to confound the wise."[14] Catherine of Siena, according to her confessor, Raymond of Capua, was told that she need not wear male garb because God could use her, precisely as a woman, in order to shame unworthy men.[15] In the fifteenth century, Pius II tried to vindicate Joan of Arc with the claim that God entrusted the task of saving France "to the weaker sex that the French with their accustomed pride might not be over-confident of their own powers."[16] The topos may have remained in wide usage because it allowed male writers to acknowledge the presence of heroic sanctity in women and to confess the general failings of their own sex, while at the same time affirming that men were naturally meant to be "the strong" and

12. Caroline Bynum, "Women's Stories, Women's Symbols: A Critique of Victor Turner's Theory of Liminality," in R. L. Moore and F. E. Reynolds, eds., *Anthropology and the Study of Religion* (Chicago, 1984): 111. See AASS April, vol. 1: 442.

13. *The Book of the Visions and Instructions of Blessed Angela of Foligno* (London, 1871): 3. Fra Arnaldo cited Jerome's *Dialogus contra Pelagianos* II.22, in which the prophetess Olda's calling (II Chron. 34:22–28) is described as "a secret reproof of the king, and priests, and all men." *St. Jerome: Dogmatic and Polemical Works*, trans. John Hritzu (Washington, 1965): 332.

14. AASS October, vol. 13: 500.

15. AASS April, vol. 3: 884.

16. "The Commentaries of Pius II, Book VI," trans. Florence Gragg, *Smith College Studies in History* 35 (1951): 437–38.

"the wise"; after all, it took special grace to elevate a woman. Although Hildegard did not invent this topos (which had already been used by Hrotsvitha of Gandersheim in the tenth century),[17] it would be interesting to know how far her writings contributed to its later popularity.

Finally, we come to the problematic relation between Hildegard's gender and her predilection for a theology of the feminine. We may begin with a few incontrovertible assertions. It seems obvious that Hildegard's interest in the feminine per se exceeded that of her male predecessors and contemporaries; that she felt a strong affinity for the traits she perceived as essentially feminine (such as virginity, fruitfulness, natural and artistic beauty, and loving-kindness); and that she had a visionary and poetic gift which makes her images of the feminine, inter alia, particularly memorable. But to go further, to argue that her symbolic thinking took the shape that it did *because* she was a woman, would be to go too far. The elements of her sapiential thought, as we have seen, are extremely ancient, and most of its doctrines can be paralleled in twelfth-century male writers like Honorius, Rupert of Deutz, Bernard of Clairvaux, Godfrey of Admont, and Alan of Lille. If we examine the later history of sapiential thought, or theology of the feminine, we find that it was adopted at various periods by both female and male writers; and whether it is perceived at any given moment as "favorable to women" depends very much on the notions of femininity, and of feminism, currently prevailing. A brief sketch of that subsequent history may, in fact, clarify some of the larger issues raised by this study.

17. In the preface to her book of plays, Hrotsvitha wrote that "the more seductive the caresses [of the pagan seducers] . . . the more glorious the victory of those shown triumphing, especially when womanly frailty emerges victorious and virile force, confounded, is laid low." Helene Homeyer, ed., *Hrotsvithae opera* (Paderborn, 1970): 233–34; trans. Dronke, *Women Writers* 69. According to the *Speculum virginum*, the victories of heroines like Jael and Judith show that "the stronger very often falls vanquished by the weaker, and inflated pride yields to holy humility." London BL Arundel 44, fol. 36^v.

SAPIENTIAL THOUGHT THROUGH
THE TWENTIETH CENTURY

In the later Middle Ages, the number of female saints, visionaries, and devotional writers steadily increased. But the records of high medieval *Frauenmystik* differ substantially from
the writings of Hildegard. Despite the richly varied imagery
of their works, women like the two Mechtildes, Marguerite of
Oingt, and Hadewijch were primarily interested in mystical
union, concentrating on God and the soul rather than cosmology and history.[18] Sapiential theology, in the sense I have
defined it, did not flourish in this era. Essentially Platonic in
its assumptions and poetic in its expressions, it lost ground
before the onslaught of Aristotelian logic, which began in the
twelfth century and held triumphant sway in the thirteenth.
For a time, at least, the great scholastics were able to maintain
the balance between immanence and transcendence that had
characterized sapiential theology at its best. But as the gap
between scholastic and devotional literature widened, along
with the rift between professional theologians and the pious
laity, anomalous works like the *Scivias* lost favor because they
fit into neither mold, being too learned and diffuse for the
devout lay reader yet not technical or systematic enough for
the schoolman.

At the same time, speculative mystics in the tradition of
Eckhart pressed increasingly toward the apophatic way.
Many abandoned the sapiential theologians' interest in the
epiphanies of God in nature, turning instead to a quest for
union with the Unknowable in the depths of the spirit. Still
more decisive for the decline of sapiential theology was the
general darkening of fourteenth-century piety, which focused

---

18. On later medieval women see Elizabeth Petroff, *Consolation of the
Blessed: Women Saints in Medieval Tuscany* (New York, 1979), and *Medieval Wom-
en's Visionary Literature* (Oxford, 1986); Caroline Bynum, "Women Mystics in
the Thirteenth Century: The Case of the Nuns of Helfta," in her *Jesus as
Mother: Studies in the Spirituality of the High Middle Ages* (Berkeley, 1982): 170–
262; E. W. MacDonnell, *The Beguines and Beghards in Medieval Culture* (New
Brunswick, N.J., 1954).

almost obsessively on the Passion rather than the Incarnation, patient endurance rather than active collaboration with God, and renunciation rather than celebration of creatures.[19] Certain late medieval writers did take an interest in sapiential themes; for example, Henry Suso designated himself the "Servitor of Eternal Wisdom," and Julian of Norwich wrote that "the high might of the Trinity is our Father, and the deep wisdom of the Trinity is our Mother, and the great love of the Trinity is our Lord."[20] But the context of these motifs was fundamentally altered by devotion to the suffering Christ.

With the advent of a new humanism, the fifteenth century provided a more favorable milieu for sapiential theology. Once again, as in the twelfth century, a flourishing Platonism was cross-fertilized by a renewed interest in classical monastic spirituality. St. Augustine and the Greek fathers, as well as twelfth-century spiritual writers like Bernard of Clairvaux, William of St. Thierry, Guigo II the Carthusian, and Hugh and Richard of St. Victor, enjoyed a surprising surge of popularity in the early Renaissance.[21] Fifteenth-century humanists— Nicholas of Cusa, Ficino, Pico della Mirandola—recall twelfth-century monastics like Hugh of St. Victor, Hildegard, and Alan of Lille in their thirst for a composite wisdom that could reconcile divine contemplation with a zest to know all that is knowable on earth.[22] One of the most interesting figures of this age is Johannes Trithemius (1462–1516), abbot of Sponheim, the monastic humanist who rekindled Hildegard's

19. Richard Kieckhefer, *Unquiet Souls: Fourteenth-Century Saints and Their Religious Milieu* (Chicago, 1984).

20. Julian of Norwich, *Revelations of Divine Love*, longer version, ch. 58, trans. James Walsh (St. Meinrad, Ind., 1975): 159.

21. Giles Constable, "The Popularity of Twelfth-Century Spiritual Writers in the Late Middle Ages," in Anthony Molho and John Tedeschi, eds., *Renaissance Studies in Honor of Hans Baron* (Florence, 1971): 3–28.

22. Eugene Rice has stressed the metaphysical and contemplative character of wisdom in Florentine Platonism. Of Renaissance wisdom generally, he has observed that "it embraces both the divine and human, and culminates in a natural and poetic theology based on Neo-Platonic love theory. There remains, therefore, no opposition between a natural, classical *scientia* and a revealed Christian *sapientia*." *The Renaissance Idea of Wisdom* (Cambridge, Mass., 1958): 104.

fame and in some ways resembled her. He even composed a sequence in her honor, praising her arcane knowledge as well as her virtues.[23] Like the abbess of Bingen, Trithemius devoted his life to the cause of monastic reform. Yet he also had a consuming passion for books and a wide, somewhat embarrassing renown for magic; among his pupils he numbered the famed magician and feminist Cornelius Agrippa von Nettesheim.[24] And it was the mystically inclined French humanist Jacques Lefèvre d'Étaples, author of a treatise *On Natural Magic* (1493), who published the first edition of the *Scivias* in 1513. These devout but intellectually free-ranging souls stood closer to Hildegard, in their way, than the more single-minded faithful of a century before.

A historian of sapiential theology might turn next to the Christian Cabalists of the Renaissance, who combined an androgynous understanding of the Trinity (adapted from medieval Jewish theosophy) with a keen interest in the cosmological process and complex speculations on the original Adam.[25] But the seminal figure for subsequent developments is Jakob Boehme (1575–1624), a Lutheran mystic whose mercurial, immensely influential system of theosophy gives a large place to the "noble Virgin Sophia." She is conceived as (among other things) the mirror of the Godhead, the eternal Idea, the uncreated Heaven or Glory of God, the bride of unfallen Adam, the celestial Virgin who united herself with Mary, and the seer's personal guide and Muse.[26] In the Prot-

---

23. Cujus mentem illustrasti, / Cui mira revelasti, / Quam archanis interesse / Tribuisti superum. // Mundum verbis et exemplis / Illustravit Hildegardis, / Sponsa tua Iesu Christe, / Te docente ab intus. The complete sequence can be found in *Festschrift* 407–8.

24. Noel Brann, *The Abbot Trithemius (1462–1516): The Renaissance of Monastic Humanism* (Leiden, 1981).

25. Joseph Blau, *The Christian Interpretation of the Cabala in the Renaissance* (New York, 1944). In John Reuchlin's cabalistic dialogue *De verbo mirifico* II.17, one of the speakers correlates the first three divine names, or persons of the Trinity, with Zeus, Athena, and Aphrodite. *Artis cabalisticae*, ed. Johannes Pistorius (Basel, 1587):929–30.

26. Two of the more readable works on Boehme are Hans Martensen, *Jacob Boehme: Studies in His Life and Teaching*, trans. T. R. Evans and rev. Stephen

estant world generally, where the divine Father and Son were no longer counterbalanced by the figures of Mary the Mother and Ecclesia the Bride, sapiential theology took on more esoteric and heterodox forms, becoming bolder in its statements of divine androgyny. As its connection with the age-old liturgical tradition was severed, it also tended to express itself in highly imaginative, idiosyncratic, and often ecstatic modes. Boehme's writings inspired theosophists of every sort, notably the English Philadelphians of the late seventeenth century—a circle of visionaries led by John Pordage and the prophetess Jane Leade, who concerned themselves with the mysteries of the divine Sophia and proclaimed that "Eve will now come forth as a mighty, strong, terrible Eagle."[27]

In the eighteenth century the tradition manifested itself in figures as diverse as William Blake, the visionary poet who prophesied of Albion and Jerusalem (and was himself deeply influenced by Boehme), and the blacksmith's daughter Ann Lee, founder of the sect of Shakers. These unorthodox Christian communists, transplanted from England to America, continued to flourish throughout the nineteenth century. During one phase of their history, they venerated their Mother Ann as the Second Coming of Christ in glory, that is, in the form of a woman (I Cor. 11:7). They aimed at a full equality between women and men in the angelic life of celibacy, where there is "neither male nor female," and in their worship they danced the praise of an androgynous God.

> The Father's high eternal throne
> Was never fill'd by one alone:
> There Wisdom holds the Mother's seat,
> And is the Father's helper-meet.[28]

Hobhouse (London, 1949); and John Stoudt, *Sunrise to Eternity: A Study in Jacob Boehme's Life and Thought* (Philadelphia, 1957).

27. Jane Leade, *Fountains of Gardens* (London, 1700), II: 100. On this tradition see Desirée Hirst, *Hidden Riches: Traditional Symbolism from the Renaissance to Blake* (London, 1964); and Nils Thune, *The Behmenists and the Philadelphians* (Uppsala, 1948).

28. *Millennial Praises*, comp. Seth Y. Wells (Hancock, Mass., 1813). See Flo Morse, *The Shakers and the World's People* (New York, 1980); and Robley Whit-

Aside from many lesser theosophical sects, which represent the sapiential tradition in a debased and impoverished form, Boehme's influence led eventually, via German romanticism, to a major revival of that tradition. The resurgence of full-scale theologies of the feminine in the nineteenth and early twentieth centuries can be linked to many cultural factors, such as the bourgeois exaltation of motherhood, the rise of romantic medievalism with its interest in the more rarefied forms of courtly love, and the equally romantic veneration of Nature. Goethe spoke for more than one generation when he introduced *das Ewig-Weibliche* into the mystic chorus at the end of his *Faust*:

> All that is transient
> But as symbol is sent;
> The insufficient
> Becomes here event;
> The indescribable,
> Here is it done;
> Woman eternal
> Leads upward and on.[29]

But it was a Russian, Vladimir Soloviev (1853–1900), who united the currents of romanticism, German idealism, and Boehmian theosophy to bring the feminine divine into the forefront once more. For him, as for Boehme, the Virgin Sophia was both an indispensable religious concept and a visionary bride at the center of his own spiritual life. In his mystical poetry, his philosophical and ecumenical works, and his treatise on the sexes, he set forth his vision of "the eternal divine femininity" and its implications in every sphere, ranging from ecclesiology to romantic love.[30] Soloviev's thought,

---

son, ed., *The Shakers: Two Centuries of Spiritual Reflection* (New York, 1983), especially ch. 4: "God: Father and Mother."

29. Alles Vergängliche / Ist nur ein Gleichnis; / Das Unzulängliche / Hier wirds Ereignis; / Das Unbeschreibliche, / Hier ist es getan; / Das Ewig-Weibliche / Zieht uns hinan. "Chorus Mysticus," *Faust*, pt. 2.

30. Vladimir Soloviev, "Three Meetings," in Carl and Ellendea Proffer, eds., *The Silver Age of Russian Culture* (Ann Arbor, 1971): 128–34; *Russia and the Universal Church*, trans. Herbert Rees (London, 1948); *Lectures concerning God-manhood*, trans. Peter Zouboff (London, 1948); *The Meaning of Love*, trans. Jane Marshall (London, 1945). See also Samuel Cioran, *Vladimir Solov'ev and the Knighthood of the Divine Sophia* (Waterloo, Ont., 1977).

controversial as it was, inspired a whole school of Russian theologians who set out, with varying success, to purge it of gnostic elements and make it impeccably Orthodox. Among these Russian "sophiologists," still relatively unknown in the West, are Pavel Florensky (*The Pillar and Ground of Truth*), Sergei Bulgakov (*The Wisdom of God*), and Paul Evdokimov (*Woman and the Salvation of the World*).[31]

In the Catholic West, sapiential theology experienced an independent revival, sparked by Pierre Teilhard de Chardin's long philosophical poem "The Eternal Feminine" (1918). This epic of ideas charts the evolution of the feminine from the status of a vague, inchoate force of attraction, through the vitality of instinctual life, to the hallowed lure of virginity and ideal beauty. The personified Feminine speaks finally of her role as mediatrix between God and the world.

> Long before I drew you, I drew God towards me.
> . . . .
> Without the lure of my purity, think you, would God
>   ever
>   have come down, as flesh, to dwell in his creation?
> Only love has the power to move being.
> If God, then, was to be able to emerge from himself,
>   he had first to lay a pathway of desire before his feet,
>   he had to spread before him a sweet savour of beauty.
> . . . .
> Lying between God and the earth, as a zone of mutual
>   attraction,
>   I draw them both together in a passionate union
> —until the meeting takes place in me, in which the
>   generation
>   and plenitude of Christ are consummated throughout
>   the centuries.

31. Pavel Florensky, *La colonne et le fondement de la verité: Essai d'une théodicée orthodoxe en douze lettres*, trans. Constantin Andronikof (Lausanne, 1975); Paul Evdokimov, *La femme et le salut du monde* (Paris, 1958); Sergei Bulgakov, *The Wisdom of God: A Brief Summary of Sophiology* (London, 1937). On the tradition as a whole see Nicholas Berdiaeff, "La doctrine de la Sophia et de l'androgyne: Jacob Boehme et les courants sophiologiques russes," introduction to Boehme, *Mysterium Magnum* (Paris, 1945); and Michael Azkoul, *Solov'ev and His Successors: An Exposition of the Neo-Christian Thought of V. Solov'ev and the Sophiologists* (Astoria, N.Y., 1983).

I am the Church, the bride of Christ.
I am Mary the Virgin, mother of all human kind.[32]

Teilhard's theology of the feminine is as closely bound up with traditional Mariology and ascesis as it is with romanticism and with his own peculiar idea of evolution. Some of its distinctive notes resound elsewhere in French Catholicism: in Henri de Lubac, moving spirit of the patristic revival, who devoted a full volume to explication of Teilhard's poem;[33] in Louis Bouyer, cited at the beginning of this chapter; in the poet and dramatist Paul Claudel, whose heroines epitomize the feminine mystique. Commenting on the Biblical heroine Esther, in a work fittingly titled *The Adventures of Sophia*, Claudel praised woman because she is "capable of restoring to man that creative slumber in which she was herself conceived. She is the pillar of destiny. She is the gift. . . . She is the point of attachment of the kindly tie that unceasingly unites the Creator with his work. She understands him. She is the soul that sees and acts. She shares with him in some way the patience and power of creation."[34]

On German soil, Catholic women took the initiative in formulating theologies of the feminine. Gertrud von le Fort's *Eternal Woman* (1934) was translated into six languages and enjoyed high prestige for two decades. It was followed by the Carmelite philosopher Edith Stein's *Woman: Her Task according to Nature and Grace* (1959).[35] But the most theologically profound and evocative of these works is Maura Böckeler's all but forgotten study, *The Great Portent (Apoc. 12:1): Woman as a*

32. Pierre Teilhard de Chardin, "The Eternal Feminine," in *Writings in Time of War*, trans. René Hague (New York, 1968): 200–201.
33. Henri de Lubac, *The Eternal Feminine: A Study on the Poem by Teilhard de Chardin*, trans. René Hague (London, 1971). Cf. Catherine O'Connor, *Woman and Cosmos: The Feminine in the Thought of Pierre Teilhard de Chardin* (Englewood Cliffs, N.J., 1974).
34. Paul Claudel, *Les aventures de Sophie*, in *Oeuvres complètes* (Paris, 1962), 19: 37.
35. Gertrud von le Fort, *Die ewige Frau, Die Frau in der Zeit, Die zeitlose Frau* (Munich, 1934); Edith Stein, *Die Frau: Ihre Aufgabe nach Natur und Gnade* (Louvain, 1959).

Symbol of Divine Reality (1941).[36] Böckeler took her inspiration from the Greek fathers, the German romantics, and the Russian sophiologists, but above all from St. Hildegard; for she was a nun at Eibingen and the German translator of the *Scivias*. Her sapiential theology is grounded in a novel conception of the Trinity as Silence, Word, and Answer (*Wort* and *Antwort*); if Adam represents the Logos, Eve is an image of the Spirit, the responsive third Person who is the eternal virgin, mother, and bride within the Trinity itself. In discussing the creation and fall of Eve, the birth of Mary and the Incarnation, Böckeler followed the broad outlines of Hildegard's theology as I have sketched it in the last five chapters, transposing it into language that is at once more patristic and more romantic. With her work we have come full circle.

FEMINISM AND THE FUTURE OF SOPHIA

As the foregoing pages suggest, Hildegard of Bingen is centrally located not only within the crosscurrents of twelfth-century culture but also within a theological tradition that stretches from Solomon's days to our own. Sapiential theology is not easily defined: its course through the ages is filled with apparent gaps, dead ends, and discontinuities, and the variety of its formulations is bewildering. Its systematic history has yet to be written.[37] One of the most interesting continuities in that history, however, is the flexible but persistent bond between certain ideas about God and related ideas about gender. There is, of course, no simple or direct correlation between the sex of a writer, the perception of feminine qualities in the divine, and particular beliefs about maleness and femaleness. Yet sapiential theology, precisely because of its concern with the feminine divine, has been linked so closely

36. Maura Böckeler, *Das Grosse Zeichen (Apok. 12,1): Die Frau als Symbol Göttlicher Wirklichkeit* (Salzburg, 1941).

37. I am now at work on a book entitled *Sophia: A History of Wisdom from Solomon to Jung.*

with such beliefs that its vicissitudes provide a sensitive barometer for the psychology and sociology of gender.

Since both men and women have historically been attracted to theologies of the feminine, these systems of thought cannot be explained solely by women's alleged need to identify with powerful feminine symbols, or by men's purported need to project these symbols as images of desire. Such motives may indeed be operative in the cases of individual writers, St. Hildegard included. But whether the symbolism is addressing the psychological needs of women or of men, two factors remain constant. One is the perception of radical, even metaphysical difference between the sexes. In a theology of the feminine, "male" and "female" are understood as not merely biological categories, even if these categories are correlated with strongly marked psychological traits and seemingly changeless socioeconomic roles. A residual Platonism, whether overt or attenuated, must define the genders as ontological categories that are first distinguished within the divine realm and only then embodied in the physical, psychological, and cultural polarity of male and female. In the second place, the feminine rather than the masculine is to be singled out for special attention, as if the meaning of maleness were self-evident whereas the meaning of femaleness were in continual need of discovery. This "meaning," it should be stressed, does not remain constant; the divine femininity for Hildegard may have been pure, virginal and radiant, whereas for C. G. Jung it implied materiality and evil.[38] Nor is the feminine necessarily singled out to prove the inferiority of women; it may just as well be stressed to argue their superiority, as I will demonstrate with some contemporary examples. The common denominator is a sense that the feminine is somehow problematic; being neglected, undervalued, or

38. "The *Assumptio Mariae* paves the way not only for the divinity of the Theotokos (i.e., her ultimate recognition as a goddess), but also for the quaternity. At the same time, matter is included in the metaphysical realm, together with the corrupting principle of the cosmos, evil." C. G. Jung, "A Psychological Approach to the Trinity," in *Psychology and Religion: West and East*, vol. 11 of *Collected Works* (Princeton, 1958): 171.

wrongly understood within a patriarchal culture, it needs to be perpetually redefined, revalued, and relocated in the general worldview.

In recent decades both of these philosophical premises have come under fierce attack. As Rosemary Ruether has pointed out, the spectrum of contemporary feminism still reflects the nineteenth-century split between liberals and romantics.[39] The liberals, who represent the overwhelming majority of American and European feminists, have resoundingly vetoed the notion that gender is a metaphysical category, which they see as a more refined version of the claim that anatomy is destiny. A flood of psychological, sociological, and anthropological writing by feminist scholars has attempted to prove that gender-related differences are culturally conditioned rather than innate.[40] At the same time, the direction of critical scrutiny toward "women" rather than "gender" is denounced as a way of perpetuating patriarchal bias. It is argued that reifying the feminine as such merely reinforces constricting stereotypes; that idealizing the feminine supports male dominance by "sheltering" women from political power; and that ascribing "special" functions to the female implies that the male is still the normative human—or divine—being. The liberal critique further charges that theologies of the feminine define women according to their biological status—virgin, wife, mother—leaving no room for self-determination, and moreover that such doctrines victimize women by teaching them to see their socially conditioned "weakness" as part of some divine scheme of things. The critique is a telling one.[41]

---

39. Rosemary Ruether, *Sexism and God-Talk: Toward a Feminist Theology* (Boston, 1983): 102–9.

40. See for instance Michelle Rosaldo and Louise Lamphere, eds., *Woman, Culture and Society* (Stanford, 1974); Nancy Chodorow, *The Reproduction of Mothering: Psychoanalysis and the Sociology of Gender* (Berkeley, 1978); Carol MacCormack and Marilyn Strathern, eds., *Nature, Culture and Gender* (Cambridge, 1980).

41. It begins with Simone de Beauvoir, *The Second Sex*, trans. H. M. Parshley (New York, 1953); and Betty Friedan, *The Feminine Mystique* (New York, 1963). A concise summary of the specifically theological issues is J.-M. Aubert, *La femme: Antiféminisme et christianisme* (Paris, 1975).

Yet the romantics are still with us, and among them are numbered not only conservatives and antifeminists but also many women who strongly endorse the political agenda of feminism. At the conservative end of the spectrum we find one wing of the evangelical movement, which has lately spawned a wave of literature commending "total woman-hood"—by which is meant by and large a repudiation of feminism, together with a reaffirmation of the Pauline and medieval analogies. Woman is to man as man is to God: complementary, well-beloved, and subservient. In this version of womanhood, there is no room for the feminine in heaven; it is essentially the human vis-à-vis the divine.[42] This understanding is shared, within a different theological context, by most of the Catholic, Anglican, and Orthodox writers who oppose the ordination of women.[43] Much of their writing argues that it is not human law but feminine nature, as ordained by God, which renders women incapable of the priesthood.

At the opposite end of the spectrum, however, many radical feminists accept no less absolute a distinction between male and female modes of being in the world. This kind of romanticism characterizes feminist utopian fantasists, lesbian separatists, Jungians, and literary theorists who argue that women's writing is inscribed in a separate "space" set apart from the patriarchal universe of discourse.[44] In the spiritual realm, one school of romantic feminists rejects the Christian tradition altogether in order to celebrate the feminine divine as Goddess in the various forms of witchcraft and neopagan-

42. For example, Vernard Eller has used Wittgensteinian language games to argue a thesis reminiscent of Hildegard: "scripture presents 'the feminine' as the model and paradigm of the human race in its relation to the 'masculinity' of God. . . . In consequence, then, the feminine is also a model for all humans (both male and female) in their relations to one another." *The Language of Canaan and the Grammar of Feminism* (Grand Rapids, 1982): x.

43. See Peter Moore, ed., *Man, Woman, and Priesthood* (London, 1978); and Thomas Hopko, ed., *Woman and the Priesthood* (Crestwood, N.Y., 1984).

44. Elaine Showalter, ed., *The New Feminist Criticism: Essays on Women, Literature, and Theory* (New York, 1985).

ism.[45] Whether or not the Goddess is given a masculine consort, it is she who predominates in this new religion or "theal-
ogy" as unmistakably as women do in her cult. Hildegard's
compromise—the acceptance of traditional women's roles
side by side with a veneration of the feminine divine—seems
no longer possible. Oddly enough, however, the evangelicals
and the witches prove to be joint heirs of the old theologies
of the feminine. What they share, in contrast to the liberals,
is a predilection for "the feminine" as a valid symbolic construct that conveys certain necessary truths about God and
women.

One might ask why, given the force of the liberal critique,
the romantic alternatives still remain so attractive to so many.
Liberals argue that they represent an all-too-familiar collaboration between victim and oppressor. In contrast, advocates
of romantic feminism insist on the celebration of womanhood
because, they maintain, attempts to suppress sexual difference in the interests of "merely human" values will lead only
to the reassertion of dominant, male-defined cultural norms.
Ann Belford Ulanov, a theologian and Jungian analyst, has
argued that "every effort to annihilate the images of sexual
polarity amounts to little more than repressing them into the
unconscious."[46] Perceptions of masculine and feminine difference, she has asserted, are so deeply grounded in human experience that to deny them can only result in massive confu-
sion within the psyche. Although the specific content of the
symbols "male" and "female" varies, the polarity itself is basic
and need not lead to rigid polarization. That destructive process occurs only when the archetypes are flattened into pre-
scriptive stereotypes so that the feminine is reified in a static
and inflexible way, projected like a straitjacket onto women,

45. Starhawk, *The Spiral Dance: A Rebirth of the Ancient Religion of the Great
Goddess* (San Francisco, 1979); Charlene Spretnak, ed., *The Politics of Women's
Spirituality: Essays on the Rise of Spiritual Power within the Feminist Movement*
(New York, 1982).

46. Ann Belford Ulanov, *Receiving Woman: Studies in the Psychology and
Theology of the Feminine* (Philadelphia, 1981): 40.

and rejected as part of the psychic potential of men. Once defined in such a constricting manner, it will be rejected by women themselves in favor of a nondifferentiated, merely human mode of being. But since the male has long been and still remains the dominant sex, "merely human" usually translates into an affirmation of overtly or covertly masculine values. Thus, the literal repression of women gives way to a superficially more just but no less psychically harmful repression of the feminine. To counteract such repression, Jungian feminists have been actively reviving the symbol of Sophia and, along with it, modified theologies of the feminine.[47]

Hildegard, with her frequent use of cross-sexual imagery and inversion, instinctively avoided the peril of associating the feminine exclusively with women. At the same time, she recognized that both masculine and feminine traits, as her culture taught her to define them, were equally though differently symbolic of Christ. In this respect she saw more deeply than modern neoconservative theologians, who tend to see in the feminine only an image of the creature set over against the Creator, rather than united with him and subsumed into the divine. Thus in effect they deny that women are fully created in God's image, while many Goddess religionists pay an inverse compliment to men. But if reified stereotypes prove damaging even to human wholeness, it must be a still greater folly to apply them literally to God, to understand the Transcendent One as "merely" masculine or feminine, or even masculine *and* feminine. Here again, in our current struggles with spirituality and gender, Hildegard can be a guide. For what mystics of the *via negativa* achieve by the systematic denial of images, she accomplished by their sheer profusion. Her visionary forms fade into one another with dazzling and dizzying speed, but within them all, and behind all, shines neither woman nor man but the living Light.

Within that light, we have fixed our gaze for a time on one

47. Ann Belford Ulanov, *The Feminine in Jungian Psychology and in Christian Theology* (Evanston, 1971); Joan C. Engelsman, *The Feminine Dimension of the Divine* (Philadelphia, 1979).

single but complex figure, the figure of woman. In the end she will merge again into the light, not lost in but overshadowed by it. But in the meantime, St. Hildegard stands before us as one who saw her, heard her voice, and, hearing, echoed to all who would heed her: "Say to Wisdom, you are my sister, and call insight your intimate friend."

APPENDIX A

A Hildegard Discography

A feather on the breath of God: Sequences and hymns by Abbess Hildegard of Bingen. Gothic Voices, dir. Christopher Page, with Emma Kirkby, Margaret Philpot, and Emily Van Evera. Hyperion A66039, recorded in London, September 1981. Musical Heritage Society selection for 1984. Contains "Columba aspexit," "Ave generosa," "O ignis Spiritus Paracliti," "O Ierusalem," "O Euchari in leta via," "O viridissima virga," "O presul vere civitatis," and "O Ecclesia." Also available on CD.

Geistliche Musik des Mittelalters und der Renaissance. Instrumentalkreise Helga Weber, dir. Helga Weber, with Almut Teichert-Hailperin. TELDEC 66.22387, recorded in Hamburg, May 1980. Contains "Karitas habundat," "O virtus Sapientie," "O quam mirabilis," "Hodie aperuit," "Alleluia," "O virga mediatrix," "O clarissima mater," and "O frondens virga," with music by Dunstable and Dufay.

Gesänge der hl. Hildegard von Bingen. Schola der Benediktinerinnenabtei St. Hildegard in Eibingen, dir. M.-I. Ritscher, OSB. Psallite 242/040 479 PET, recorded in Eibingen, April 1979. Contains "Cum processit factura," "Cum erubuerint," "O frondens virga," "Ave generosa," "O virga ac diadema," "Karitas habundat," "O pastor animarum," "O quam preciosa," "Kyrie," selections from the *Ordo virtutum,* and music from the Office of St. Hildegard.

Hildegard von Bingen: Ordo virtutum. Sequentia, dir. Barbara Thornton. Harmonia mundi 20395/96, recorded in Germany, June 1982. Two records, containing "O splendidissima gemma" and the complete *Ordo virtutum.*

Hildegard von Bingen: Symphoniae (Geistliche Gesänge). Sequentia, dir. Barbara Thornton. Harmonia mundi 1C 067-19 9976 1, recorded in Germany, June 1983. Contains "O quam mirabilis," "O pulcre facies," O virga ac diadema," "O clarissima mater," "Spiritui sancto," "O virtus Sapientie," "O lucidissima apostolorum turba," "O successores," "O vos felices radices," and "Vos flores rosarum."

Music for the Mass by Nun Composers. University of Arkansas Schola Cantorum, dir. Jack Groh. Leonarda LPI 115, recorded Feb. 1982. Contains the "Kyrie" with a Mass by Isabella Leonarda.

APPENDIX B

Texts of Hildegard's Poetry

The texts that follow are newly edited from the principal manuscript sources of Hildegard's *Symphonia armonie celestium revelationum*.

D = Dendermonde Abbey, Belgium, Cod. 9; Rupertsberg, c. 1175.
R = Riesenkodex (Wiesbaden, Landesbibliothek, Hs. 2); Rupertsberg, 1180–1190.

1. *O virtus Sapientie*

   O virtus Sapientie,
   que circuiens circuisti
   comprehendendo omnia in una via
   que habet vitam,
   5 tres alas habens,
   quarum una in altum volat
   et altera de terra sudat
   et tercia undique volat.
   Laus tibi sit, sicut te decet,
   10 O Sapientia.

2. *O splendidissima gemma*

   O splendidissima gemma
   et serenum decus solis
   qui tibi infusus est,
   fons saliens de corde Patris,
   5 quod est unicum Verbum suum,
   per quod creavit mundi primam materiam,
   quam Eva turbavit.

   Hoc Verbum effabricavit tibi
   Pater hominem,
   10 et ob hoc es tu illa lucida materia
   per quam hoc ipsum Verbum exspiravit

2.6 prima D

275

omnes virtutes,
ut eduxit in prima materia
omnes creaturas.

3.   *O quam preciosa*

O quam preciosa est
virginitas virginis huius
que clausam portam habet,
et cuius viscera sancta divinitas
5   calore suo infudit,
ita quod flos in ea crevit
et Filius Dei per secreta ipsius
quasi aurora exivit.

Unde dulce germen,
10   quod Filius ipsius est,
per clausuram ventris eius
paradisum aperuit.
Et Filius Dei per secreta ipsius
quasi aurora exivit.

4.   *O tu illustrata*

O tu illustrata de divina claritate,
clara Virgo Maria,
Verbo Dei infusa,
unde venter tuus floruit
5   de introitu Spiritus Dei,

qui in te sufflavit
et in te exsuxit
quod Eva abstulit
in abscisione puritatis
10   per contractam contagionem
de suggestione diaboli.

Tu mirabiliter abscondisti in te
inmaculatam carnem
per divinam racionem,
15   cum Filius Dei
in ventre tuo floruit,
sancta divinitate eum educente

3.11   ventris] mentis R
4.7   in te] in te te R

contra carnis iura
que construxit Eva,
20 integritati copulatum
in divinis visceribus.

5. *Cum processit factura*

Cum processit factura digiti Dei
formata ad imaginem Dei
in ortu mixti sanguinis
per peregrinationem casus Ade,
5 elementa susceperunt gaudia in te,
o laudabilis Maria,
celo rutilante
et in laudibus sonante.

6. *O quam magnum miraculum*

O quam magnum miraculum est
quod in subditam femineam formam
rex introivit.
Hoc Deus fecit
5 quia humilitas super omnia ascendit.

Et o quam magna felicitas est
in ista forma,
quia malicia que de femina fluxit,
hanc femina postea detersit,
10 et omnem suavissimum odorem virtutum
edificavit,
ac celum ornavit
plus quam terram prius turbavit.

7. *O virga ac diadema*

1a. O virga ac diadema
purpure regis,
que es in clausura tua
sicut lorica:

1b. Tu frondens floruisti
in alia vicissitudine
quam Adam omne genus humanum
produceret.

4.20 copulatim R
5.5 in te] vite R
5.8 sonante] sonant te R

2a. Ave, ave, de tuo ventre
    alia vita processit
    qua Adam filios suos
    denudaverat.

2b. O flos, tu non germinasti de rore,
    nec de guttis pluvie,
    nec aer desuper te volavit,
    sed divina claritas in nobilissima virga
    te produxit.

3a. O virga, floriditatem tuam
    Deus in prima die creature sue
    previderat.

3b. Et te Verbo suo auream materiam,
    o laudabilis Virgo, fecit.

4a. O quam magnum est in viribus suis latus viri
    de quo Deus formam mulieris produxit,
    quam fecit speculum omnis ornamenti sui
    et amplexionem omnis creature sue.

4b. Inde concinunt celestia organa
    et miratur omnis terra,
    o laudabilis Maria,
    quia Deus te valde amavit.

5a. O quam valde plangendum et lugendum est
    quod tristicia in crimine
    per consilium serpentis
    in mulierem fluxit.

5b. Nam ipsa mulier
    quam Deus matrem omnium posuit
    viscera sua cum vulneribus
    ignorantie decerpsit
    et plenum dolorem generi suo protulit.

2b. claritas in nobilissima virga] the fragmentary text in D
    begins here.

3b. te] de D, R. The reading *te*, which occurs in the *Epilogus
    Vitae S. Ruperti* (R fol. 406ra), is grammatically more dif-
    ficult but gives better sense. Mary is the golden matrix
    prepared *for* the Word, although she could less plau-
    sibly be seen as taken *from* the Word, by analogy with
    Eve and Adam (4a).

5a. O quam] initial missing in R
    plagendum D

6a. Sed, o aurora, de ventre tuo
    novus sol processit,
    qui omnia crimina Eve abstersit
    et maiorem benedictionem per te protulit
    quam Eva hominibus nocuisset.

6b. Unde, o Salvatrix, que novum lumen
    humano generi protulisti:
    collige membra Filii tui
    ad celestem armoniam.

8. *O viridissima virga*

 1. O viridissima virga, ave,
    que in ventoso flabro sciscitationis
    sanctorum prodisti.

 2. Cum venit tempus
    quod tu floruisti in ramis tuis,
    ave, ave sit tibi,
    quia calor solis in te sudavit
    sicut odor balsami.

 3. Nam in te floruit pulcher flos
    qui odorem dedit omnibus aromatibus
    que arida erant.
    Et illa apparuerunt omnia
    in viriditate plena.

 4. Unde celi dederunt rorem super gramen
    et omnis terra leta facta est
    quoniam viscera ipsius frumentum protulerunt
    et quoniam volucres celi nidos
    in ipsa habuerunt.

 5. Deinde facta est esca hominibus
    et gaudium magnum epulantium.
    Unde, o suavis Virgo,
    in te non deficit ullum gaudium.

 6. Hec omnia Eva contempsit.
    Nunc autem laus sit Altissimo.

9. *O orzchis Ecclesia*

    O orzchis Ecclesia,
    armis divinis precincta
    et iacincto ornata,
    tu es caldemia
 5 stigmatum loifolum
    et urbs scientiarum.

> O, o, tu es etiam crizanta
> in alto sono
> et es chorzta gemma.*

10.   *O choruscans lux stellarum*

> O choruscans lux stellarum,
> O splendidissima specialis forma
> regalium nuptiarum,
>
> O fulgens gemma,
> 5   tu es ornata in alta persona
> que non habet maculatam rugam.
>
> Tu es etiam socia angelorum
> et civis sanctorum.
>
> Fuge, fuge speluncam
> 10   antiqui perditoris,
> et veniens veni in palatium regis.

11.   *O Ecclesia*

> 1.   O Ecclesia, oculi tui similes saphiro sunt
> et aures tue monti Bethel
> et nasus tuus est sicut mons mirre et thuris
> et os tuum quasi sonus aquarum multarum.
>
> 2.   In visione vere fidei
> Ursula Filium Dei amavit
> et virum cum hoc seculo reliquit
> et in solem aspexit
> atque pulcherrimum iuvenem vocavit,
> dicens:
>
> 3.   In multo desiderio desideravi
> ad te venire

---

*Latin translations for the words from Hildegard's *Lingua ignota* are supplied in Stuttgart, Landesbibliothek, Cod. Theol. Phil. 4°253 (Rupertsberg and Zwiefalten, 1154–1170).
1   orzchis] immensa
4   caldemia] aroma
5   loifolum] populorum
7   crizanta] uncta
9   chorzta] chorusca

11.1.   saphyro R

et in celestibus nuptiis tecum sedere,
per alienam viam ad te currens velut nubes
que in purissimo aere currit
similis saphiro.

4. Et postquam Ursula sic dixerat,
rumor iste per omnes populos exiit.
Et dixerunt:
Innocentia puellaris ignorantie
nescit quid dicit.

5. Et ceperunt ludere cum illa
in magna symphonia
usque dum ignea sarcina
super eam cecidit.

6. Unde omnes cognoscebant
quia contemptus mundi est sicut mons Bethel.
Et cognoverunt etiam
suavissimum odorem mirre et thuris,
quoniam contemptus mundi
super omnia ascendit.

7. Tunc diabolus membra sua invasit,
que nobilissimos mores in corporibus istis
occiderunt.   (

8. Et hoc in alta voce
omnia elementa audierunt
et ante thronum Dei dixerunt:

9. Wach! rubicundus sanguis innocentis agni
in desponsatione sua
effusus est.

10. Hoc audiant omnes celi
et in summa symphonia laudent Agnum Dei,
quia guttur serpentis antiqui
in istis margaritis materie Verbi Dei
suffocatum est.

12. *Nunc gaudeant*

Nunc gaudeant materna viscera Ecclesie,

---

5.   simphonia D
8.   trhonum D
10. simphonia D
     matherie D

quia in superna simphonia
filii eius in sinum suum
collocati sunt.

5 Unde, o turpissime serpens,
confusus es,
quoniam quos tua estimatio
in visceribus suis habuit
nunc fulgent in sanguine Filii Dei,
10   et ideo laus tibi sit,
rex altissime. Alleluia.

Index

Abelard, Peter, 67–68, 83, 91, 109, 178

Acta S. Hildegardis, 5, 131n, 150–52, 185

Adam, 54, 114; and Christ, 92–93; creation of, 94, 125, 128; fall of, 107–10, 116–17, 168, 172, 210; in Paradise, 96–99, 111–12, 179. *See also* Eve; Man

Adam of Perseigne, 73

Adelard of Bath, 125n

Adrian IV, Pope, 237–38

Adso, 243

Aelred of Rievaulx, 73

Agrippa von Nettesheim, Cornelius, 260

Alan of Lille, 20, 79, 102n, 106n, 156, 257, 259; *Anticlaudianus*, 44; *De planctu Naturae*, 74

Alberic of London, 128

Alcuin of York, 44, 85, 92n, 115

Alexander III, Pope, 13–14, 231

Allegory, 25, 69, 198, 236, 246–47; of Adam and Eve, 110; cosmological, 19–21; of Incarnation, 75–76, 103; in Latin classics, 42–44, 74; of Virtues and Vices, 16, 19, 60, 79–87. *See also* Caritas; Ecclesia; Eve; Sapientia; Virgin Mary

Ambrose, Saint, 39n, 57n, 221n, 230; on the Church, 199, 230; *On Paradise*, 110, 115; on the Virgin, 104, 167, 177

Ambrosius Autpertus, 113n, 180

Androgyny, 261

Angela of Foligno, 256

Angelomus of Luxeuil, 92n

Angels, 113, 180, 216; iconography of, 102–3; theology of, 21, 52, 97, 201; visions of, 37

Anima mundi, 51–52, 67–69

Annales Palidenses, 37

Annunciation, 164, 168, 172, 175, 190, 194. *See also* Virgin Mary

Anselm of Canterbury, xvi, 55, 159

Antichrist, 21, 28, 197, 211n, 243–46

Apocalypse, 74, 113, 200, 211, 222, 227, 239, 240

Apocalypse of Moses, 115–16

Apocalyptic prophecy: in *De operatione Dei*, 21, 240–41, 243; in *Scivias*, 17, 243–45; in sermons, 28–29

Aristotle, 128, 136, 138–40, 142n, 258

Arnold of Bonneval, 91, 110, 118n

Arnold of Brescia, 237–38

Ascension of Isaiah, 177

Astrology, 141–42, 153–54

Augustine, Saint, 23, 51, 94n, 123, 227n, 259; on the Church, 73, 189, 204, 224n; on the image of God, 92; on Paradise and original sin, 61, 103n, 107–10, 112, 119, 167

Avicenna, 123, 138, 142n

Baptism, 176, 211–12, 216; as childbearing, 188–90, 197, 228–31; iconography of, 229–31

Bede, Venerable, 119n

Bergson, Henri, 67

Bernard of Clairvaux, 68n, 80, 183n, 237, 257, 259; on the Church, 199, 232–33, 242; and Hildegard, 8–9, 38; letters of, 76–78; on the Song of Songs, 42, 78, 131, 199, 203n, 224, 232; on the Virgin, 159, 161, 171–72, 175n